THE CHRONICLE OF THEOPHANES

THE MIDDLE AGES SERIES

Ruth Mazo Karras, Series Editor
Edward Peters, Founding Editor

A complete list of books in the series is available from the publisher.

THE CHRONICLE OF THEOPHANES

Anni mundi 6095–6305 (A.D. 602–813)

Edited and translated by Harry Turtledove

PENN

University of Pennsylvania Press
Philadelphia

10 9 8 7 6 5 4 3 2 1

Published by
University of Pennsylvania Press
Philadelphia, Pennsylvania 19104-4112

Library of Congress Cataloging-in-Publication Data

Theophanes, the Confessor, d. ca. 818.
 [Chronographia, English]
 The chronicle of Theophanes / Edited and translated by Harry Turtledove
  p. cm. — (Middle Ages series)
 ISBN-13: 978-0-8122-1128-3 (pbk.: alk. paper)
 ISBN-10: 0-8122-1128-6
 Includes index
 1. World history—early works to 1800. I. Turtledove, Harry. II. Title. III. Series
D17.T513 1982
909'.1—dc19   82004861

CONTENTS

INTRODUCTION

THEOPHANES AND HIS PLACE
IN BYZANTINE HISTORIOGRAPHY

There is, it is said, an old Chinese curse: "May you live
in interesting times." This is a malediction most relevant
to the later Roman, or, as it is usually known by this time,
the Byzantine Empire of the seventh and eighth centuries.
In 602, the Empire's eastern heartland had virtually the
same makeup of territories as it had had three centuries
before: the Balkan peninsula, Asia Minor, Syria, Palestine,
and Egypt. In addition, the coast of north Africa, southern
Spain, Sicily, and a large part of Italy were in Byzantine
hands, thanks to the reconquests of Justinian I (527–565).

These reconquests, though, had cost the Empire far
more in men and wealth than it could hope to realize from
the regained land. At the beginning of the seventh century
its overextended frontiers collapsed, and the next 120
years were little more than a desperate struggle for survival. The great imperial capital, Constantinople, was besieged three times: in 626 by the Persians and Avars, and
in 674–678 and 717–718 by the Arabs. The latter, newly
unified by Islam, wrested Syria and Palestine (638), Egypt
(641), and north Africa (698) from the Byzantines; Byzantine Spain had fallen to the Visigoths by 631, but in 711
the Arabs conquered them as well. While the Byzantines
fought grimly and all too often unsuccessfully to hold the
line in the east, great numbers of Slavs established themselves in the Balkans, to be joined near the close of the
seventh century by the Bulgars, a people originally of Turkic descent. For all the Empire's travails, though, the Persians, Byzantium's long-time rivals for dominance in the
Near East, doubtless would have been happy to exchange
fates. The Sassanid state, even more debilitated than the
Byzantines by their mutually destructive war of 602–628,
was entirely under Arab rule by 651.

Had Constantinople and the Byzantine Empire not
survived, the history of the world would have been incalcu-

lably different. In *The Decline and Fall of the Roman Empire,* Edward Gibbon envisions Oxford dons learnedly expatiating on the Koran rather than the Bible had the Arabs won the battle of Tours against the Franks. The destruction of the Byzantine Empire would have made some such picture likelier yet. With Constantinople gone, what could have stopped the Arabs from sweeping into southeastern Europe—and bringing Islam with them? Their faith, rather than Christianity, might well have taken root among the Balkan Slavs and spread north to the people who would become the Russians, leaving Christendom as an isolated, backwards appendage to a Eurasia largely Muslim. Though the medieval west little appreciated it, one of Byzantium's most important historical roles was precisely this, a bulwark against the expansion of Islam.

After the failure of the great Arab assault of 717–718, it became clear that the Byzantine Empire would not fall to outside attack. Nevertheless, the Empire was far from peaceful during the eighth century. It was caught up in a great religious upheaval over the propriety of the use of images in church worship—the iconoclastic controversy—which had social and political implications as profound as the theological. A measure of the iconoclasts' fury may be seen in the paucity of icons from Byzantine territory which predate the struggle. Only in places like St. Catherine's monastery on Mt. Sinai (which in the eighth century was in Muslim territory and hence beyond the reach of the iconoclasts) have pre-iconoclastic icons survived until the present in any numbers.

The monastic chronicler Theophanes was born in the midst of the dispute over images, at some time in the period 752–760. He was the son of high-ranking and wealthy parents, Isaac and Theodote by name. In later years his family would become related to the Macedonian house, the dynasty which ruled Byzantium for almost two hundred splendid years (867–1056). Isaac and Theodote were as pious as they were rich, and favored the use of images within the Byzantine church. Theophanes' father outwardly concealed his iconophilic sentiments well enough to keep the trust of the arch-iconoclast Emperor Constantine V (741–775). After Theophanes was orphaned while still young, the Emperor saw to his education and upbringing.

During the reign of Constantine V's son and successor, Leo IV (775–780), Theophanes acquired the honorific title of spatharios. During his youth he had been betrothed to Megalo, the daughter of a Byzantine patrician. They were briefly married, but their union does not seem to have been more than a polite fiction designed to circumvent the iconoclastic government's opposition to monasticism: monks were among the staunchest backers of the icons. When iconoclasm and anti-monasticism lost momentum with the death of Leo IV, the two pious partners separated to pursue the monastic way of life. Theophanes founded a monastery near Sigriane on the Asian shore of the Sea of Marmora, and dwelt therein, much of the time in poor health, until 815 or 816. At that time, iconoclasm revived under Leo V, the Armenian (813–820). Theophanes, like most monks, refused to sanction the destruction of images; for his opposition, he was imprisoned in Constantinople and then exiled to the island of Samothrake, where he died in 818. To this day, the Greek church recognizes him as a confessor, one who, though not suffering the trials of a martyr, nevertheless lived a life of outstanding holiness under difficult circumstances.

Were it not for the chronicle he left behind, however, Theophanes would be little more than a footnote on the pages of Byzantine history. Throughout the long history of the Byzantine Empire, there were two distinct approaches to historiography, that of the historians *per se* and that of the chroniclers. These differed from each other both intellectually and linguistically. Beginning in the time of Justinian I with Prokopios (if one neglects the largely vanished historians of the fifth century) and extending through the work of Kritoboulos (who recorded the achievements of Mehmet II, the conqueror of Constantinople), Byzantine historians dealt with discrete chunks of time, usually a half-century or less, which they treated in considerable detail.

It was normal Byzantine practice to have only one historian for any given period, each succeeding author taking up his task where his predecessor had laid it down. There are occasional exceptions to this rule. One is the late sixth century, where Menander Protector, Theophanes of Byzantium (not our chronicler), and John of Epiphaneia each wrote an independent continuation of the work of Agathias. Not one of these three has survived intact. Another exception is the troubled mid-eleventh century, where Michael Psellos and Michael Attaleiates produced works of widely differing approach and political persuasion.

Unlike the situation in the medieval West, in Byzantium knowledge of the classical past was not lost, nor did it become the sole preserve of the church. Byzantine historians were highly educated men. They were quite familiar with a wide range of Greek authors, upon whom they drew for concepts, vocabulary, and even, on occasion, for spellings long archaic in the time during which they themselves wrote. The great ancient historians, Herodotus and, especially, Thucydides, served as their models. In many ways this was admirable; it gave Byzantine historians a detachment and a sophistication of analysis almost totally absent from contemporary western European and Islamic historiography.

Byzantine imitation of the classics, though, brought its own problems. The historians of the Empire did their best to imitate their magnificent forerunners not only in approach but also in style, and here they stumbled badly. The Greek language had changed greatly between the "golden age" of Athens and the time of the Byzantine Empire, and it was no more natural for a Constantinopolitan of, say, the tenth century A.D. to write Thucydidean Attic Greek than it would be for a modern historian to try to express himself in the idiom of Thomas North, the sixteenth-century translator of Plutarch whose work Shakespeare used. Worse yet, the influence of rhetoric on Greek literature made an unusual and convoluted style desirable. Striving for ornateness in a language not quite their own, Byzantine historians commonly produced works which, while rich in data, are neither easy nor pleasant to read.

Because of the changes in the Greek language, the historians of the Empire were not much more accessible to most of its own citizens than they are to nonspecialists of today. To meet the interest of the modestly educated Byzantine majority in its past, chroniclers arose. The earliest surviving example is John Malalas, a younger contemporary of Prokopios. Chroniclers' work differed from that of their more learned colleagues in several ways. Most chroniclers treated events from the creation of the world to their own time. Their accounts of times long before their own drew heavily on the Bible, ecclesiastical authors, and the works of earlier chroniclers, usually somewhat less upon historians unless these latter were excerpted in a chronicle. Theophanes is an exception here, for he was sophisticated enough to draw directly upon and simplify such authors as Prokopios and Theophylaktos Simokatta, whose history covers the reign of the Emperor Maurice (582–602). Later Byzantine chroniclers, even such eminent men as George Kedrenos in the eleventh century and John Zonaras in the twelfth, seem to have used Theophanes as their guide rather than the primary sources he himself employed. It would not be amiss to note here that attitudes toward what we today would consider plagiarism were far different throughout ancient and medieval times. It was thought perfectly proper to adopt for one's own use large segments of another author's work without giving any source citation whatsoever.

Theophanes' chronicle is unusual in that it does not commence with the Creation, but rather deals with the period from 284 to 813: from the accession of Diocletian to that of Leo V. The reason for this is that Theophanes' *Chronographia* is a continuation of the work of George the Synkellos, a fellow monk who had brought his own chronicle from Adam up to A.D. 284 at the time of his own death, probably in 810 or 811. A recent stimulating article proposes that Theophanes was no more than the final editor and compiler of a chronicle actually composed by George, who, it argues, lived on for a couple of years after his supposed death date and continued to write during that time. Because the *Chronographia* refers to the Emperor Leo V as "pious" and as a "legal Roman Emperor" (de Boor edition, p. 502; this translation, pp. 180–81), its *terminus ad quem* is taken to be no later than late 814 (the date of the second outbreak of iconoclasm), leaving too short a time, supposedly, for Theophanes to have completed the work from his commencement after George's death.

It is, however, quite doubtful that the *Chronographia* was actually finished by late 814. When fulminating against the iniquities of the arch-iconoclast Constantine V, the author remarks that he is making a list of the Emperor's transgressions, "so that it may be a clear aid for men in the future *and for those wretched, arrogant manikins who are now stumbling into the loathsome and evil doctrine of the supreme lawbreaker*" (de Boor edition, p. 413; this translation, p. 104—italics added). This can only refer to the second period of iconoclasm initiated by Leo V and his backers, and clearly shows the author of the chronicle was writing at least into 815, well past any proposed death date for George the Synkellos. That Leo V is termed "pious" and a "legal Roman Emperor" bespeaks no more than a lack of revision in the text, as is evident in many other places; indeed, Leo III, the initiator of iconoclasm, is himself once termed "pious" (de Boor edition, p. 396; this translation, p. 88).

There is a second telling argument against George the Synkellos' authorship of the *Chronographia*. Whoever its author may be, he is entirely ignorant of much of the material for the reigns of Herakleios, Constantine III, and Heraklonas which appears in Nikephoros' *Historia Syntomos (Brief History)*, which covers the period 602–769; it is better written and more nearly impartial than the *Chronographia*, but far more obscure in chronology and, especially after 641, much less detailed. The *Historia Syntomos* seems to have been composed sometime between 775 and 797, and probably before 787. Now, George earned his sobriquet by serving as synkellos under the patriarch Tarasios (784–806). Nikephoros, the author of the *Historia Syntomos*, was also Tarasios' protégé, and in fact succeeded him as patriarch, serving from 806 until his ouster by Leo V in 815. He and George must have known each other well. If George the Synkellos was the author of the chronicle usually ascribed to Theophanes, why did he not make use of Nikephoros' already existing chronicle in his own composition? The fact that Theophanes was isolated at Sigriane strongly serves to increase the likelihood of his authorship of the *Chronographia*.

Chroniclers were less sophisticated than historians. Where historians, following their classical exemplars, made a genuine effort to capture the underlying causes of events, chroniclers were content with more simplistic explanations. Thus Theophanes ascribes the explosive expansion of the Arabs and the successes of the Bulgars to divine chastisement of the Byzantines because of the multitude of their sins, and for Constans II's abandonment of Constantinople for Italy and Sicily entirely blames the hostility of the people of the capital, ignoring the desperate position of the Byzantine West at the time.

Both because they were intended for a broad, relatively little-educated audience and because their authors were themselves less learned than historians, Byzantine chronicles do not partake of the pseudo-classical stylistic convolutions and archaizing vocabulary in which the historians so delighted. In these matters, Theophanes' work is typical of the genre; indeed, if measured by classical standards, many of his constructions are not even grammatically correct. He frequently uses genitive absolutes having the same subject as the main verb of his sentence, a construction irregular and abnormal in the classical tongue. He is careless with his prepositions, recognizing no distinction in meaning between $\epsilon i \varsigma$ with the accusative case (properly, "into") and $\epsilon \nu$ with the dative (properly, "in"), and occasionally employing with his prepositions cases which would have made a classical writer cringe, such as $\sigma \nu \nu$ followed by the genitive. Mirroring contemporary speech patterns, he sometimes uses a periphrastic future, creating this tense with $\epsilon \chi \omega$ and the infinitive of the verb instead of a single conjugated verb form. In his writing, as in his time generally, the optative mood is all but extinct, surviving only in such stereotyped expressions as "$\mu \eta$ $\gamma \epsilon \nu o \iota \tau o$" (literally, "May it not come to pass," i.e., "Heaven forbid!"). Most Byzantine historians felt they knew enough to use the optative correctly; some of them were right.

Theophanes' vocabulary is far from classical and, interestingly, becomes steadily less so as his chronicle approaches his own time. In the early part of his work, derived from authors of the fourth and fifth centuries, there are few words not found in Liddell and Scott's *A Greek-English Lexicon,* while scores of such words appear in that part of the *Chronographia* treating the seventh and eighth centuries. Many of these, especially terms dealing with the government and the military, are derived from Latin; in their own eyes, of course, the Byzantines *were* Romans, and called themselves such. The church and its institutions borrowed from Hebrew and Aramaic, while Arabic, Persian, and the speeches of the Empire's Turkic and Slavic northern neighbors also left their marks on the language Theophanes wrote.

Our chronicler is not stylistically impressive. His is for the most part what might best be described as an efficient prose, with the occasional purple passage, especially where his theology is touched (e.g., his vitriolic denunciations of Constantine V). His sentences consist, for the most part, of a simple basic unit accompanied by one or more participial phrases or genitive absolutes. This un-complicated structure is no doubt deliberate, and de-signed to make his chronicle more broadly comprehensi-ble. Theophanes can, and on occasion does, abandon it in favor of a more complex phraseology. As his simplification of such difficult authors as Prokopios and Simokatta shows, he himself was reasonably at home with the difficult Byzantine high style, and purposely avoided it in his own writing.

To carry this point a step further, it must be empha-sized that it would be altogether unfair to expect Theo-phanes to conform totally to linguistic standards obsolete for a millennium and more. If languages do not die, they change. That Theophanes' work bears even limited com-parison to classical Greek is a mark of the tenacious con-servatism of the written, as opposed to the spoken, tongue —a problem which still applies to modern Greek. The spoken tongue in Theophanes' time was much closer to modern spoken Greek than to the ancient language, and only a relatively small part of this shift shows itself, even in popular works like that of the monk.

From the preceding discussion, the question must inevitably arise: if Theophanes' chronicle is unexciting to read and largely derived from previous sources, why should it be bothered with at all? For the first three centu-ries and more of this work (i.e., for the period 284–602), the chronicle is of very limited independent historical value, as we have in the original most of the authors from whom the monk borrowed. There are occasional snippets of information unknown elsewhere, but on the whole this early part of the work is no more than a minor supplement to more nearly contemporary sources.

For the period 602–813, however, just the opposite is true. Almost all of Theophanes' sources have themselves perished, leaving his chronicle as the indispensable guide to a time crucial in the evolution of the Byzantine Empire. The seventh and eighth centuries are so barren of surviv-ing historical literature (or, in fact, literature of any sort) that they have been termed, with justice, "the dark age of Byzantium." The reasons for this scarcity of sources are not hard to understand. As we have seen, the seventh century was for Byzantium a time of almost continuous dire warfare. While great deeds aplenty were done, there was scant leisure to record them. The iconoclastic controversy which followed was, if anything, more damaging to literary survival than the previous strife had been. While in power (726–780), the iconoclasts did their best to destroy the writings of their opponents, and when those who favored images returned to a position of authority, it was the turn of iconoclastic literature to see the torch.

After Simokatta brought his history to an end with the overthrow and murder of Maurice in 602, no historian whose work survives would labor for more than two hundred years, and with the Byzantine historical tradition thus running dry, Theophanes was compelled to make do with such other materials as were available to him. He used George of Pisidia's epic poetry on Herakleios' defense of the Empire against the Persians as a source for the reign of that Emperor; his long excursus on monotheletism is drawn from the *vita* of St. Maximus the Confessor. For the history of the later seventh century and first half of the eighth, Theophanes used a chronicle probably written by the patrician Trajan (a work now lost) and an equally perished anonymous monastic work written after the death of Constantine V, both of which are also recognized as sources for the historical works of the patriarch Nikephoros. A newly-published monograph on the reign of the Emperor Constantine VI (780–797) has referred to the existence of a biography of that Emperor and a separate chronicle as sources for Theophanes' treatment of him, unfortunately without documenting the suggestion.

In addition to using these surviving, lost, and hypothetical Greek works, Theophanes' chronicle is uniquely valuable because it also employs a Greek translation of a late eighth-century chronicle originally written in Syriac. This is the source from which Theophanes obtained his surprisingly accurate information on events in Muslim-held territory. Passages paralleling this chronicle's contributions to Theophanes occur in the works of the much later Syriac writers, Michael the Syrian and Bar Hebraeus; the original, once more, has not survived. The most likely means of transmission of this chronicle to Theophanes was by the monks who, fleeing Muslim persecution, arrived in Constantinople via Cyprus from the Holy Land in 813. Another possibility, raised by Mango in the same article in which authorship of the *Chronographia* is ascribed to George the Synkellos, is that George, who was himself at one time a resident of Palestine, brought a copy of this chronicle with him to Constantinople and either translated it into Greek or had it translated.

Where Nikephoros' chronology in the *Historia Syntomos* is casual, that of Theophanes is far and away the most elaborately developed of any Byzantine chronicler's. In this he emulated George the Synkellos' careful chronological schema, and for the seventh and eighth centuries provides much of our chronological framework for Byzantine affairs. His work is in the form of annals, the events of each year being listed separately. As his work continues that of George the Synkellos, he employs the same world-era as did that monk: the Alexandrian era, which dates the creation of the universe to September 1, 5493 B.C. Most earlier authors who used the Alexandrian era dated the Creation at the vernal equinox rather than on September 1, but the Byzantine year began on the latter date, and Theophanes uses it as the first day of his year (there is a minority opinion, headed by Vénance Grumel, which feels that Theophanes sometimes begins his years on March 25, but the evidence does not seem to favor this hypothesis).

Each year's events, then, in Theophanes' chronicle, are headed by an *annus mundi,* a year [since the Creation] of the world to which they are assigned. To convert an *annus mundi* of Theophanes to a date A.D., subtract 5492 if it is between January 1 and August 31, or 5493 if between September 1 and December 31. From time to time Theophanes provides his own dates A.D.. This method was not a usual Byzantine practice; we should not be surprised to learn that his conversion factor from *annus mundi* to A.D. differs from ours. His years A.D. begin, like any Byzantine years, on September 1, and differ from the *annus mundi* by exactly 5,500. In this translation, Theophanes' *annus mundi* is converted into modern reckoning in parentheses beside it; where Theophanes lists them, his dates "A.D." are retained, but should be ignored, e.g.:

ANNUS MUNDI 6095 (SEPTEMBER 1, 602–AUGUST 31, 603)—*correct date by modern reckoning*
AD. 595—*Theophanes' own—incorrect*—A.D.

Along with the *annus mundi,* Theophanes also always reports the regnal year of the reigning Byzantine Emperor, that of the ruler of Byzantium's eastern neighbor (first the

Sassanid king of Persia, then the Arab caliph), and that of the patriarch of Constantinople. These three dates are almost always quite accurate, especially, of course, the first and third. Theophanes also reports as much information as he can on the reigns of the other four patriarchs—the patriarchs of Rome (that is, the Popes), Alexandria, Antioch, and Jerusalem. Through the end of the sixth century, he has fairly thorough data on all these sees, but the Slavic penetration into the Balkans and the Arab conquests in the Near East progressively disrupt his knowledge of the various patriarchal successions, and for the seventh and eighth centuries his information on the patriarchates no longer under Byzantine control is sketchy and not always accurate. Still, it can be seen that he is, to the best of his ability, constructing a thorough and most elaborate chronological skeleton on which to place his chronicle's flesh.

There is yet another method Theophanes uses throughout the *Chronographia* to keep track of time: the indiction. This was originally a fifteen-year cycle for the reassessment of taxes. Though obsolete in that sense long before Theophanes' time, the fifteen-year cycle itself survived to become a Byzantine means of reckoning time: it was common practice to date an event by saying that it took place in, for example, the sixth year of the indiction cycle, which was usually shortened to simply the "sixth indiction."

It is in reconciling dates as expressed by the *annus mundi* and as expressed by the indiction that we encounter the knottiest problems in clarifying Theophanes' chronology. The principal reason, indeed, for believing that Theophanes may have done such a curious thing as to use two different dates for the beginning of his year is that this would clear up some of the chronological difficulties his work poses. Besides being inherently illogical for anyone as vitally concerned with clear chronology as was the monk, however, the dual-date hypothesis by no means explains all the dilemmas in the chronicle.

George Ostrogorsky offers a more satisfactory solution to the riddle. The Russian Byzantinist made a painstaking comparison of the dates of accession and death of the Byzantine Emperors of the seventh and eighth centuries as listed in Theophanes and as given by other sources. He also performed a similar task for the accessions of the Arab caliphs, comparing those dates given in Theophanes with their counterparts in Muslim historiography. Ostrogorsky's conclusion is that Theophanes always correctly reports the number of the year in the indiction cycle, but that for most of the seventh and eighth centuries the *annus mundi* is a year behind the stated number of the indiction. The discrepancy begins with *annus mundi* 6102 (which should be A.D. 609/610, but is in fact 610/611) and continues through *annus mundi* 6265 (which should be A.D. 772/773 but is in fact 773/774), except for the period *annus mundi* 6207–7218 (A.D. 714/715–725/726), where the monk's errors apparently cancel out each other. It should be noted that Ostrogorsky's scheme is probably not perfect. An eclipse Theophanes dates to 5 Hyperbataios (i.e., October), *annus mundi* 6186, which by Ostrogorsky's chronology would be A.D. 694, actually took place in the previous year. On balance, though, Ostrogorsky does give the best and most consistent solution to the problems Theophanes presents, and the dates in the modern calendar given in this translation follow Ostrogorsky's reckoning.

The profound influence Theophanes' work had on later Byzantine chroniclers has already been mentioned. They used the *Chronographia* not only as a source of information but also as a model of what a chronicle should be; it is a pity more of them did not emulate the monk's meticulous establishment of chronology. Theophanes' chronicle was also of great importance to western medieval historical writing. A papal librarian, Anastasius, translated Theophanes from Greek into Latin in the second half of the ninth century, perhaps half a century after the death of the author. Anastasius' translation was widely read and used in its own time, and has not lost its importance to scholars to this day. The papal librarian's work was translated from a manuscript of Theophanes older than any which is yet extant, and is therefore an important aid in establishing the proper text of the chronicle.

Theophanes has never before been rendered into English, even in part. There is a German translation of the period 717–813, published as *Bilderstreit und Arabersturm* in volume six of the series *Byzantinische Geschichtsschreiber* (Graz, 1957). The present translation of the period 602–813 (that is, the period for which Theophanes is of chief independent historical value) is based on the standard edition of the work, edited and with commentary by C. de

Boor (Leipzig, 2 volumes, 1883, 1885). The numbers in the left margin of the translation indicate the pagination in volume I of de Boor's edition; volume II consists of an edition of Anastasius' translation of Theophanes, as well as a most valuable and thorough commentary and indices.

Translating a language whose genius is as different from that of English as is Greek's is fraught with a multitude of dangers. If one sticks to the letter, the spirit disappears, but straying too far from literality inevitably introduces distortions of its own. My goal is to present as clear an English version of Theophanes as is possible. The division of the work into paragraphs is, for the most part, my own. I have rearranged the clauses of Theophanes' sentences when this was needed to make his meaning clear in a tongue that cannot have the complex structure permitted by Greek's inflections. On one or two occasions, when Theophanes makes a brief digression before returning to his original topic, I have shifted the digression to a place where it does not break the flow of the narrative. I have rendered his unending stream of participial phrases and genitive absolutes in a variety of ways, each as seemed appropriate in its own context, and have, though much less frequently, reversed active and passive voices. A good many *aforementioned*s, *so-called*s, *the same*s, and *himself*s, good Greek but dreadful English, have fallen by the wayside, and a fair number of superlative adverbs and adjectives such as "most terrible" have been toned down in accordance with conventional English practice. The distribution of nouns and pronouns also follows the demands of English, not Greek.

A final perplexity facing the translator of Byzantine Greek lies in his method of transliterating proper names and toponyms. Where a person or place has a well-known English version (e.g., John, Jerusalem), I have used it. Most other names have been transliterated from Greek into English without a detour through Latin (Herakleios, not Heraclius). Exceptions are those names and titles of Latin origin (e.g., Valentinus, cubicularius), which are rendered in latinized form. Also excepted are most names of Arabic origin, which are given in their native form rather than disguised by hellenized spellings and nominal endings, as is Theophanes' usual practice.

One of the pleasures of translating is being able to acknowledge one's debts. I first learned of the existence of

Byzantium from the works of the scholar and novelist L. Sprague de Camp. Theophanes and I made our first acquaintance in Speros Vryonis, Jr.'s seminar in 1972. Professor Vryonis has given me invaluable aid on the more obscure portions of the text. The first draft of this translation came into being in 1973, in Milton V. Anastos' seminar on Byzantine Greek. Professor Anastos, too, gave me a great deal of essential help.

Finally, I would like to thank John Langdon, Steve Reinert, and my wife, Laura, whose encouragement kept this project, which has advanced only by fits and starts, from halting altogether. Without the assistance and friendship of all these people this translation would be much poorer; any remaining defects are, of course, only my own.

BYZANTINE EMPERORS 602–813

Maurice	582–602
Phokas	602–610
Herakleios*	610–641
Constantine III*	641
Heraklonas*	641
Constans II*	641–668
Constantine IV*	668–685
Justinian II*	685–695
Leontios	695–698
Apsimaros (Tiberius III)	698–705
Justinian II (again)*	705–711
Bardanes Philippikos	711–713
Artemios (Anastasios II)	713–715
Theodosios III	715–717
Leo III**	717–741
Constantine V**	741–775
Leo IV**	775–780
Constantine VI**	780–797
Irene**	797–802
Nikephoros I	802–811
Staurakios	811
Michael I Rhangabe	811–813
Leo V	813–820

*Dynasty of Herakleios
**Isaurian dynasty

PERSIAN KINGS 602–651

Khosroes II	591–628
Kavad II (known to Theophanes as Siroes)	628
Ardaser III	628–629
Sarbaros (also called Sarbarazas)	629
Borane	629–630
Hormisdas V	630–632 (?)
Yazdagird III	632–651

ARAB RULERS 622-813

Muhammad   622–632

The "rightly-guided" caliphs

Abu Bakr	632–634
Umar I	634–644
Uthman	644–656
Ali	656–661

The Umayyads

Muawiyah I	661–680
Yezid I	680–683
Muawiyah II	683–684 (?)
Marwan I	684–685
Abd al-Malik	685–705
Walid I	705–715
Suleiman	715–717
Umar II	717–720
Yezid II	720–724
Hisham	724–743
Walid II	743–744
Yezid III	744
Ibrahim	744
Marwan II	744–750

The Abbasids

Abu-l-Abbas as-Saffah (known to Theophanes as Muhammad)	750–754
Al-Mansur (known to Theophanes as Abd Allah)	754–775
Mahdi	775–785
Al-Hadi (known to Theophanes as Musa)	785–786
Harun ar-Rashid	786–809
Al-Amin (known to Theophanes as Muhammad)	809–813
Al-Mamun	813–833

PATRIARCHS OF CONSTANTINOPLE 602–813

Kyriakos	595–606
Thomas I	607–610
Sergios	610–638
Pyrrhos I	638–641
Paul II	641–654
Pyrrhos I (again)	655
Peter	655–666
Thomas II	667–669
John V	669–675
Constantine I	675–677
Theodore I	677–679
George I	679–686
Theodore I (again)	686–687
Paul III	688–694
Kallinikos I	694–705
Cyrus	705–712 (?)
John VI	712 (?)–715
Germanos I	715–730
Anastasios	730–754
Constantine II	754–766
Niketas I	766–780
Paul IV	780–784
Tarasios	784–806
Nikephoros	806–815

POPES 602–813

Gregory I ("the Great")	590–604
Sabinianus	604–606
Boniface III	607
Boniface IV	608–615
Deodatus I	615–618
Boniface V	619–625
Honorius I	625–638
Severinus	640
John IV	640–642
Theodore I	642–649
Martin I	649–655
Eugenius I	654–657
Vitalianus	657–672
Deodatus II	672–676

xxiii

ANTIPOPES 602–813

290 ANNUS MUNDI[1] 6095 (SEPTEMBER 1, 602—AUGUST 31, 603)

A.D. 595
Roman Emperor Phokas: 7 years: year 1
Persian King Khosroes: 39 years: year 15
Bishop of Constantinople Kyriakos: 11 years: year 9
Bishop of Jerusalem Isaac: 8 years: year 3
Bishop of Alexandria Eulogios: 27 years: year 24
Bishop of Antioch Anastasios: 9 years: year 3

291 In this year—the sixth indiction[2]—in November Phokas became Emperor. As was said before, the rebel killed Maurice[3] and his five sons. He ordered their heads placed in the Camp of the Tribunal for a number of days. The inhabitants of the city went out to look at them until they began to stink. Maurice's brother Peter and many others were also killed, but there was a strong rumor that Maurice's son Theodosios had got away and still survived.

The Persian king Khosroes strengthened this rumor: he lied now one way, now another, saying he had Theodosios with him and intended to restore him to rule over the Romans. He hoped to conquer the Roman Empire by deception, as was proved in many ways, most of all by his inciting unforeseen enemies and devastating Roman territory. When Phokas sent Bilios as an ambassador to him, he seized the man and imprisoned him so he could not return to Roman land, answering Phokas with dishonorable letters.

The tyrant put the Empress Constantina[4] and her three daughters in a private house called that of Leo.

1. Theophanes, as noted in the introduction, reckons the Creation to have taken place in 5493 B.C., and reckons his *annus mundi*—"year [since the creation] of the world"—accordingly.
2. The indiction was a levy in kind introduced by Diocletian in the late third century. It was collected uniformly throughout the Empire, and was based on units of land roughly equivalent in productive capacity. As the system was originally designed, these were subject to reassessment every fifteen years. Many of these payments in kind had been commuted to cash payments by the end of the fifth century, but the fifteen-year cycle remained as a means of dating events: as here, 602/603 being the sixth [year of the] indiction [cycle].
3. A most able man, Maurice was Emperor from 582 to 602. In 591, thanks to civil war among the Persians, he brought to a successful conclusion the Byzantine-Persian war which had begun in 572. He then turned against the Avars, who had been raiding the Balkans with virtual impunity while the bulk of the Roman forces were in the east. But the weak financial condition of the Empire forced him to scant his troops (not for the first time), and in 602, angered at being ordered to winter in Avar territory, they rebelled, named Phokas Emperor, and marched on Constantinople, where Maurice and his sons met their fate.
4. The widow of Maurice.

1

In Alexandria a pious copyist who during the middle of the night was traveling home from a vigil saw statues[5] being dragged down from their pedestals while they were loudly saying Maurice and his sons had been killed and were relating all the mishaps which had occurred at Byzantium. At dawn the man went to the Augustal prefect[6] and told him about this. He told the man not to reveal it to anyone, made note of the day, and eagerly awaited the arrival of a messenger. Nine days later the messenger arrived, saying Maurice had been killed. Then the Augustal prefect triumphantly told the people of the divinities' prediction.

The Roman general Narses rose up against the tyrant and took Edessa. Phokas wrote to the general Germanos to besiege that town. Narses wrote to the Persian king Khosroes, asking him to assemble his 292 forces and attack the Romans. Phokas appointed his own brother Domentziolos magistros[7] and Priskos count of the excubitores.[8]

ANNUS MUNDI 6096 (SEPTEMBER 1, 603—AUGUST 31, 604)

2. 16. 10. 4. 25. 4.[9]

In this year—the seventh indiction—in December, Phokas, continuing his celebrations, distributed much consular largess.[10] The Persian king Khosroes mustered a large force and sent it out against the Romans. When Germanos heard this he was terrified but, having no choice, joined battle. Although he was wounded in the fighting, his guardsmen got him safely to Constantina. The Romans were defeated, and on the eleventh day Germanos died.

5. Of the gods.
6. The head of the diocese of Egypt. Most leaders of dioceses were known as vicars; Egypt's governor kept the older title, which had existed since Octavian annexed Egypt to the Empire in 30 B.C. The province, which would become in later years the breadbasket of Constantinople, was virtually the private domain of the Emperors during the early Empire, and was ruled by a special imperial appointee.
7. Chief officer of the palace.
8. The excubitores were a unit of palace guards established by Leo I in 466 or 467. Their commander, the count, was a powerful officer; two counts of the excubitores ultimately became Emperors: Tiberius II Constantine in 578, and Maurice in 582.
9. These are the regnal years of, respectively, the Emperor, the Persian king (whose place will later be taken by the Arab caliph), and the patriarchs of Constantinople, Jerusalem, Alexandria, and Antioch. When Theophanes has data on the patriarch of Rome, his dates precede those of the patriarch of Constantinople.
10. During the reign of Justinian I (527–565) the consulship became too expensive for any private citizen to hold; the last to do so was Basilius in 541. After Justinian's reign, each Emperor assumed the consulship in the first year of his reign.

Thinking to keep the Avars quiet, Phokas strengthened his treaties with the Khagan[11] and transferred his forces from Europe to Asia. He divided his forces, sending some against the Persians and the rest to besiege Narses at Edessa. The eunuch Leontios was Phokas' leading officer. Narses left Edessa and fled to Hierapolis.

Khosroes arrived at Arxamoun at the same time as the Romans; he began the battle by assaulting the fortress with elephants, and won a great victory. He took many Romans alive and then put them to death. After doing this Khosroes returned to his own country, leaving behind a force under Zonggoes. When Phokas learned this he became insanely angry at Leontios and brought him in disgrace to Byzantium in irons. He appointed his brother Domentziolos general, and also made him curopalates.[12]

ANNUS MUNDI 6097 (SEPTEMBER 1, 604—AUGUST 31, 605)

3. 17. 11. 5. 26. 5.

In this year Khosroes sent out Kardarigas and Rousmiazas, who plundered manyRoman cities. Domentziolos gave Narses a pledge and persuaded him with many oaths that he would not suffer a single unjust act from Phokas, then sent him off free to Phokas. But Phokas did not keep his word; he burned Narses alive. Since Narses had caused the Persians such great fear that Persian children shivered when they heard his name, the Romans were greatly distressed at his death, but the Persians joyfully exulted.

ANNUS MUNDI 6098 (SEPTEMBER 1, 605—AUGUST 31, 606)

Bishop of Constantinople Thomas: 3 years
4. 18. 1. 6. 27. 6.

In this year a scholastic[13] eunuch, a man of high repute in the palace, took the Empress Constantina and her three daughters in the middle of the night and fled to the great church.[14] He did so at the advice of the patrician[15] Germanos, who was grasping at imperial power. A great deal of factional strife ensued in the city because of

11. The ruler of the Avars.
12. A high title first borne by Justin II (Emperor 565–578), the office of curopalates ranked below that of Caesar. It carried some presumption of heirship, especially if the reigning Emperor had no sons.
13. That is to say, a eunuch with legal training.
14. The church of Hagia Sophia.
15. In the Roman Republic, the patricians made up an hereditary aristocracy. Under Constantine I (306–337) the largely moribund title was revived and given to individuals as an honorific.

3

this action. The Greens[16] banded together at the Kokhlias[17] to revile Constantina. Germanos sent a talent of gold to the leader of the Greens to gain their cooperation, but the deme's leadership did not accept it.

The tyrant sent men to the church to drag away the women. But the patriarch Kyriakos opposed him and would not permit the women lawlessly to be dragged from the church. When Phokas had assured him he would not treat them unjustly, they were led from the holy precinct and shut up in a monastery. Phokas tonsured Germanos, made him a priest, and put him under house arrest. At that time Philippikos was also deprived of his hair; he took holy orders and lived in the monastery he had built at Chrysopolis.

In this year the Persians captured Daras and all Mesopotamia and Syria, taking innumerable prisoners.

After the patriarch Kyriakos died, Thomas, who was deacon and sakellarios[18] of the great church, was chosen in his place on October 11.

294   ANNUS MUNDI 6099 (SEPTEMBER 1, 606—AUGUST 31, 607)

A.D. **599**
Roman Emperor Phokas: 7 years: year 5
Persian King Khosroes: 39 years: year 19
Bishop of Constantinople Thomas: 3 years: year 2
Bishop of Jerusalem Isaac: 8 years: year 7

16. Much ingenuity has been expended on the Byzantine Empire's circus factions, the Greens and Blues and their less prominent rivals the Whites and Reds. As Alan Cameron has shown in an important new study, *Circus Factions: Blues and Greens at Rome and Byzantium* (Oxford, 1976), much of this has been wasted effort. Their apparent rise to importance in the fifth century resulted from an amalgamation of public entertainments, joining the previously mild racing fans with the boisterous followers of the theater, but under the names of the former's identifying colors. This caused formerly anonymous acts of rowdyism to become the hallmark of the "new" Greens and Blues. Moreover, the hippodrome now saw introduced the systematic applause and ceremonial responses formerly used only in the theater. This made the public element of the factions (as opposed to the government-sponsored groups which actually put on the races) an important ceremonial part of the court; as they became more responsible they rioted less, though they remained influential because of their part in the imperial coronation ceremonies and—by extension—their ability to proclaim usurpers. Their political and military roles (as well as their influence on imperial policy) appear to have been greatly exaggerated; Cameron compares them to the riotous fans at British soccer matches.

17. The Kokhlias is the spiral staircase through which the Emperor entered the hippodrome.

18. Keeper of the purse.

4

Bishop of Alexandria Theodore: 2 years: year 1
Bishop of Antioch Anastasios: 9 years: year 7

In this year the tyrant Phokas married his daughter Domentzia to Priskos the patrician, who was also count of the excubitores; the wedding was held in the palace of the descendants of Marine.

Phokas ordered horse-races held.[19] The leaders of the two factions erected images of Priskos and Domentzia with the imperial portraits on a four-columned monument. When he saw this, the Emperor became angry. He sent out men who brought back Theophanes and Pamphilos (the leaders of the factions). He stood them naked on the stama[20] and ordered them executed. First, though, he sent his chief courier to ask them what had prompted them to do this. They said that the artists had followed custom in doing it. The members of the factions were shouting, "Many years for the merciful Emperor!" The artists were asked why they had done it. They said, "Everyone called them children of the Emperor; we did it for their sake." Since the masses were crying for him to have mercy on the leaders of the demes, the Emperor acquiesced. Priskos was terrified by the Emperor's anger; later he became angry himself, and from then on was not in agreement with Phokas.

The Empress Constantina had a serving-wench named Petronia, who, instead of being a body-servant, brought messages from Constantina to Germanos. When the rumor spread that Maurice's son Theodosios was alive, both Constantina and Germanos had high hopes because of it. But the impious Petronia revealed this to the tyrant. He gave Constantina to the prefect Theopemptos for torture. As a result of the torture, she confessed that the patrician Romanos knew of what had been said between herself and Germanos. He was seized and interrogated, and agreed there were others cooperating with him in a plot against the tyrant. The praetorian prefect of the east[21] Theodore was also arrested; the tyrant beat him to death with rawhide straps. He cut off Elpidios' hands and feet and burned him alive, and decapitated Romanos. He put Constantina and her three daughters to the sword at the mole of Eutropios, where Maurice had also been killed. He also put to the sword Germanos and his daughter

295

19. In celebration.
20. The station of the imperial guards in the hippodrome, just below the Emperor's seat.
21. In the administrative system evolved by Diocletian and Constantine, the praetorian prefect of the east was the chief administrative officer for Egypt, Syria, Palestine, Asia Minor, and Thrace: the highest-ranking official in the Byzantine Empire's early years. The office (along with much of the territory) would disappear in the chaotic seventh century, though surviving as a sinecure at least until 680.

on the Prince's Island,[22] and executed in the same way John, Tzitas, Patrikios, Theodosios (who held the rank of soubadioubas[23]), Andrew Skombros, and David the chartophylax[24] of the monastery of Hormisdas.

In the same year the Persians crossed the Euphrates, took prisoners throughout Syria, Palestine, and Phoenicia, and did great damage to the Romans.

ANNUS MUNDI 6100 (SEPTEMBER 1, 607—AUGUST 31, 608)

A.D. 600
Roman Emperor Phokas: 7 years: year 6
Persian King Khosroes: 39 years: year 20
Bishop of Constantinople Thomas: 3 years: year 3
Bishop of Jerusalem Isaac: 8 years: year 8
Bishop of Alexandria Theodore: 2 years: year 2
Bishop of Antioch Anastasios: 9 years: year 8

In this year Priskos, no longer able to stand seeing the unjust murders and evils worked by Phokas, wrote to the patrician and master of soldiers of Africa Herakleios that he should send his son Herakleios and Niketas (the son of his lieutenant-general, the patrician Gregoras) to oppose the tyrant. For Priskos had heard that rebellion against Phokas was being planned in Africa. For this reason, ships sailed from Africa at that time. Phokas mercilessly killed all the relatives of Maurice, Komentiolos the master of soldiers of Thrace, and many others. At this time there was a plague and misfortunes of every sort.

The Persians under Kardarigas sallied forth and took Armenia and Kappadokia; they routed the Roman armies they attacked. They took Galatia and Paphlagonia and advanced all the way to Chalcedon, ravaging every age group. The Persians outside the city[25] tyrannized the Romans, but Phokas, murdering and making arrests within it, did worse things than they.

ANNUS MUNDI 6101 (SEPTEMBER 1, 608—AUGUST 31, 609)

Bishop of Constantinople Sergios: 29 years
Bishop of Jerusalem Zachariah: 22 years

22. One of several small islands in the Sea of Marmora, off the Asian coast southeast of Constantinople.
23. An assistant or bodyguard.
24. Archivist.
25. Constantinople is very often referred to by Byzantine authors as *"the city."*

296

Bishop of Alexandria John: 10 years
6101. 601. 7. 21. 1. 1. 1. 9.[26]

In this year the Antiochene Hebrews went out of control and revolted against the Christians. They slaughtered Anastasios, the great patriarch of Antioch: they hurled his genitals into his face, then dragged him into the Mese and murdered him and many landowners. Then they burned their bodies. Phokas appointed Bonosos count of the east and Kottanas general and sent them against the Hebrews, but they were unable to quell their rebellion. The Hebrews gathered together an army, attacked them, killed and mutilated many of their men, and drove them away from the city.

Phokas held horse-races, and the Greens reviled him: "You are drunk again, and long ago lost your mind." Phokas relied on the city prefect[27] Kosmas. The prefect mutilated many people and hung their members in the Sphendone.[28] He decapitated others, and still others he shut up in sacks, flung into the sea, and drowned. The Greens gathered together and set fire to the Praitorion.[29] They burned its offices, archives, and jail, whose inmates got out and fled. Phokas was enraged and ordered the Greens no longer to meddle in politics.

Since the senate had begged him to do so, Herakleios the master of soldiers of Africa armed his son and loosed him against the tyrant Phokas. Likewise, his lieutenant-general Gregoras sent out his son Niketas by dry land;[30] whichever one of them got to Constantinople first and conquered the tyrant would become Emperor.

In the same year the winter was very harsh, so that the sea froze. Also, a great fish was cast forth at that time.

When he learned that Makrobios the commander of his bodyguard had been part of a plot against him, Phokas ordered him shot to death in the marketplace. His body was hung on a spear at the castle

297

26. Although Theophanes shows a regnal year for the patriarch of Antioch here, after the death of Anastasios it will be many years before he knows the name of that city's bishop.
27. The city prefect was the officer who administered Constantinople; he was responsible for maintaining law and order, the courts, keeping the city supplied with food, and controlling its trade and industry. The importance of the position is shown by the fact that the Byzantines themselves termed the prefect "the city's father," and said that his office was imperial in dignity, except that it did not entitle him to wear the purple.
28. The semicircular southern portion of the hippodrome.
29. Located not far west of the imperial palaces, the Praitorion was the main government office building in Constantinople. It housed the office of the praetor (or minister of justice), was the repository for government records, and also contained a prison.
30. Not all the way to Constantinople by land, but to Egypt to gather troops to aid the rebellion.

of the Theodosianoi in Hebdomon.[31] Theodore the governor of Kappadokia and Elpidios the commander of the arsenal had formed this plot to kill Phokas during the games. Theodore the praetorian prefect held a breakfast and began to reveal his plan to the others. Now it happened that Anastasios the count of the sacred largess[32] was there. After the breakfast was done and Theodore was explaining how the plot would work, Anastasios regretted his presence. He did not speak from his heart, but kept silent.

Elpidios promised to give them arms, then went right on, "Do you not want me to seize him while he is sitting on his throne during the games, blind him, and kill him?" After Anastasios betrayed the plot to Phokas, the Emperor ordered the governor, Elpidios, and the nobles who knew of the plot examined most thoroughly. On examination, 298 they deposed the details of the plot, and also their desire to make Theodore Emperor. Phokas ordered Theodore, Elpidios, Anastasios, and everyone who had known of their plot decapitated.

ANNUS MUNDI 6102 (SEPTEMBER 1, 610—AUGUST 31, 611)[33]

A.D. 602
Roman Emperor Herakleios: 31 years: year 1
Persian King Khosroes: 39 years: year 22
Bishop of Constantinople Sergios: 29 years: year 2
Bishop of Jerusalem Zachariah: 22 years: year 2
Bishop of Alexandria John: 10 years: year 2

In this year—the fourteenth indiction—on October 4, a Monday, Herakleios arrived from Africa with his towered ships. As George of Pisidia[34] says, they had reliquaries and icons of the Mother of God on their masts and carried a large army from Africa and Mauretania. At the same time Niketas the son of the patrician Gregoras arrived from Alexandria and Pentapolis with a large infantry force.

Now at this time Herakleios was engaged to Eudokia (the daughter of Rhogas son of Aphros), who was in Constantinople with Herakleios'

31. Hebdomon is a European suburb of Constantinople, a little more than two miles southwest of the city on the shore of the Propontis.
32. The chief official of the treasury; the office would soon be replaced by an imperial sakellarios.
33. See the discussion of chronology in the introduction, p. xviii.
34. A Byzantine poet who composed epics celebrating the triumphs of Herakleios, and a contemporary of that Emperor. His work, which is still extant, was an important source for Theophanes. The Byzantines esteemed George of Pisidia highly, ranking him with Euripides; modern taste does not raise him to such prominence.

mother Epiphaneia. When Phokas heard that Herakleios' mother and his fiancée Eudokia were in the city, he seized them and kept them under guard in the imperial monastery, which is called the New Repentance.

When he came to Abydos, Herakleios met its count Theodore and learned from him what was afoot in Constantinople. Phokas had sent his brother Domentziolosto guard the Long Walls.[35] When he learned Herakleios had reached Abydos, he abandoned the Walls and fled into Constantinople. In Abydos Herakleios received all the nobles Phokas had exiled, and went up to Herakleia with them. Stephen the metropolitan of Kyzikos took a diadem from the church of the holy Mother of God of Artake and brought it to Herakleios.

When Herakleios reached Constantinople he attacked the harbor of Sophia. By the grace of God, when battle was joined he defeated the tyrant Phokas. The people seized Phokas and killed him, burning him to death in the Forum of the Ox.[36] Herakleios entered the palaces and was crowned by Sergios in the oratory of St. Stephen there. On the same day his fiancée Eudokia was crowned Augusta, and they both received the crowns of marriage[37] from patriarch Sergios. Herakleios was revealed as autokrator and bridegroom on the same day.

In May the Persians campaigned against Syria, took Apamea and Edessa, and advanced as far as Antioch. The Romans met them, fought, and were beaten. The whole Roman army was destroyed, so that very few men got away.

On July 7 of the same indiction Epiphaneia the daughter of Eudokia was born to the Emperor, and was baptized on August 15 at Blakhernai[38] by patriarch Sergios.

ANNUS MUNDI 6103 (SEPTEMBER 1, 611—AUGUST 31, 612)

A.D. **603**
Roman Emperor Herakleios: 31 years: year 2
Persian King Khosroes: 39 years: year 23

35. Erected by Anastasios I (491–518), these outwalls ran from the Sea of Marmora to the Black Sea about forty miles west of Constantinople. They consisted of an unditched stone wall about eleven feet thick, with round towers at intervals projecting about thirty feet in front.
36. A square located on Constantinople's main street, about halfway between Hagia Sophia and the Golden Gate.
37. The "crowns of marriage" are actually wreaths placed on the heads of the bride and groom in an Orthodox wedding. During the most solemn part of the ceremony, the couple's godparents hold the wreaths.
38. The extreme northwestern district of Constantinople, in which there was a secondary imperial palace.

Bishop of Constantinople Sergios: 29 years: year 3
Bishop of Jerusalem Zachariah: 22 years: year 3
Bishop of Alexandria John: 10 years: year 3

300   In this year the Persians captured Kappadokian Caesarea, taking tens of thousands of prisoners. The Emperor Herakleios found the Roman state had become exhausted. The Avars were devastating Europe and the Persians had trampled on Asia, captured its cities, and destroyed the Roman army in their battles. As he examined these problems, Herakleios was at a loss as to what he could do. For when he investigated the army to see if there were any survivors from among those who had campaigned with Phokas during his rebellion against Maurice, he found only two among all the detachments.[39]

In the same year—the fifteenth indiction—on May 3, a son, little Herakleios (also called young Constantine) was born to the Emperor of Eudokia. On August 14 of the same fifteenth indiction the Augusta Eudokia died.

ANNUS MUNDI 6104 (SEPTEMBER 1, 612–AUGUST 31, 613)

3. 24. 4. 4. 4.

In this year—the first indiction—on October 4 Herakleios' daughter Epiphaneia was crowned Augusta by the patriarch Sergios in the oratory of St. Stephen in the palace. On December 25 in the same first indiction Herakleios' son the young Herakleios (also called Constantine) was crowned by the patriarch Sergios.

39. This is the earliest recorded use of the important Byzantine technical term "theme," here translated as "detachment." Theophanes uses the term several times during Herakleios' reign, but it is anachronistic when applied to such early times. The army units of the four original themes of Asia Minor—the Anatolics, Armeniacs, Thrakesians, and Opsikion—came into being long before the Persian and Arab crises of the first half of the seventh century, whose vicissitudes pushed them back into the locations they occupied thereafter. In the course of the seventh and eighth centuries the army commanders of the themes gradually took over the functions of the civilian provincial administrations in their districts, so that the word "theme" came to mean a province as well as the army corps quartered in it. Moreover, the thematic troops settled on the countryside of Asia Minor, and they and their descendants made most of their livings from these lands rather than from wages paid by the central government. The freeholding peasantry—both that part liable to military service in exchange for land tenure and the portion that was not—formed the basis of Byzantine social, economic, and military strength from the late seventh through the eleventh centuries. The Empire would be badly weakened when large landowners eventually succeeded in subverting the system and gaining dominance over the peasantry from the central government, though it must be admitted that, when faced with the harsh demands of the imperial tax collectors, many peasants actively sought protection from them at the hands of their more affluent neighbors.

In the same year the Saracens campaigned against Syria; they withdrew after they had plundered a number of villages.

ANNUS MUNDI 6105 (SEPTEMBER 1, 613—AUGUST 31, 614)
4. 25. 5. 5. 5.

In this year the Persians captured Damascus, taking many prisoners. The Emperor Herakleios sent envoys to Khosroes to stop the merciless bloodshed, set the payment of tribute, and obtain treaties. But Khosroes sent the ambassadors away unsuccessful. He held no discussions with them, since he hoped totally to conquer the Roman Empire.

In the same year Herakleios married Martina[40] and proclaimed her Augusta, crowning her in the Augusteion[41] (she was crowned by patriarch Sergios).

ANNUS MUNDI 6106 (SEPTEMBER 1, 614—AUGUST 31, 615)
5. 26. 6. 6. 6.

301   In this year the Persians took Jordan, Palestine, and its holy city in battle. At the hands of the Jews they killed many people in it: as some say, 90,000. The Jews, according to their means, bought the Christians and then killed them. The Persians captured and led off to Persia Zachariah the patriarch of Jerusalem, the precious and lifegiving wood,[42] and many prisoners.

In the same year another Constantine was born to the Emperor of Martina; the patriarch Sergios baptized him at Blakhernai.

ANNUS MUNDI 6107 (SEPTEMBER 1, 615—AUGUST 31, 616)
6. 27. 7. 7. 7.

In this year the Persians captured all Egypt, up to Ethiopia, Alexandria, and Libya. They took many prisoners and a great amount of booty, then withdrew. They were not able to take Carthage,[43] but withdrew after leaving behind a garrison to besiege it.

---

40. Martina was also Herakleios' niece; their union was perceived in many circles as incestuous.
41. A reception hall in the square which had been the civic center of Byzantium before it became Constantinople. The Augusteion was now surrounded by Hagia Sophia, the senate house, and the imperial palace.
42. I.e., a fragment of the True Cross on which Christ was crucified.
43. There is no evidence of this whatever; it appears to be a copyist's error for Chalcedon. In Greek the two are quite similar (Καρχηδών vs. Καλχηδών).

ANNUS MUNDI 6108 (SEPTEMBER 1, 616—AUGUST 31, 617)

7. 28. 8. 8. 8.

In this year the Persians attacked Carthage[43] and took it in battle.

In the same year—the fifth indiction—on January 1 young Constantine (also called Herakleios) the son of Herakleios became consul. He appointed his brother little Constantine (who had been born of Herakleios and Martina) Caesar.[44]

ANNUS MUNDI 6109 (SEPTEMBER 1, 617—AUGUST 31, 618)

8. 29. 9. 9. 9.

In this year Herakleios again sent ambassadors requesting peace to Khosroes in Persia. But Khosroes sent them away once more, saying, "I will have no mercy on you until you renounce him who was crucified and worship the sun."

ANNUS MUNDI 6110 (SEPTEMBER 1, 618—AUGUST 31, 619)

9. 30. 10. 10. 10.

In this year the Avars attacked Thrace. Herakleios sent envoys to them to ask for peace, and when the Khagan agreed to this, the Emperor went outside the Long Walls with the entire imperial bodyguard. He promised the Khagan many great gifts, and got pledges from him that they would make peace with each other. But the barbarian set aside his agreements and oaths, suddenly and treacherously advancing against the Emperor. Herakleios was thunderstruck at this unexpected 302 affair, and fled to the city. The barbarian captured the imperial gear and bodyguard and whatever else he could reach, then withdrew, plundering many villages in Thrace thanks to his having unexpectedly cheated the hopes of peace.

ANNUS MUNDI 6111 (SEPTEMBER 1, 619—AUGUST 31, 620)

A.D. 611
Roman Emperor Herakleios: 31 years: year 10
Persian King Khosroes: 39 years: year 31
Bishop of Constantinople Sergios: 29 years: year 11
Bishop of Jerusalem Zachariah: 22 years: year 11
Bishop of Alexandria George: 14 years: year 1

In this year Herakleios sent envoys to the Avar Khagan. He condemned him for his lawless actions and urged him toward peace. For,

44. This title is restricted to the imperial family, and designates potential heirs to the throne.

as he planned to campaign against Persia, Herakleios wanted to make peace with the Khagan. The Khagan was impressed by the Emperor's benevolence; he alleged that he had reformed and promised to make peace. The envoys arranged the terms and returned in peace.

In the same year the Persians took Galatian Ankyra in battle.

ANNUS MUNDI 6112 (SEPTEMBER 1, 620—AUGUST 31, 621)

11. 32. 12. 12. 2.

In this year Khosroes, thirsty for blood and tribute, hardened his heart and put his yoke over every man. He was exalted by his victories and could no longer remain calm. Therefore Herakleios, who had assumed divine zeal and made peace with the Avars (as he thought), transferred his European armies to Asia and, with God's help, planned to march on Persia.

ANNUS MUNDI 6113 (SEPTEMBER 1, 621—AUGUST 31, 622)

12. 33. 13. 13. 3.

In this year—the tenth indiction—on April 4 the Emperor Herakleios finished celebrating Easter and at once moved against Persia: he did so on Monday evening. He took the money of the pious houses as a loan; because poverty compelled him, he even took the candelabra and other suitable equipment from the great church, and minted a great number of nomismata and miliaresia.[45] To manage affairs in Constantinople, he left behind his own son, the patriarch Sergios, and the patrician Bonosos (a prudent, intelligent, and ready man). Herakleios also wrote to the Avar Khagan, calling on him to be an ally since they had made peace and naming him the guardian of his son.

After he left the imperial city, he sailed to the "Gates."[46] When he had reached the lands of the themes, he assembled his troops and added new forces to them. He began to train them and thoroughly instruct them in the art of war. He divided his army into two battle-lines and ordered them to engage each other without bloodshed. He taught them to maintain warlike cries, shouts, and paeans so that in

45. The nomisma (plural, nomismata) is the standard Byzantine gold-piece, coined at the rate of seventy-two to the pound. Its purity is, with rare exceptions, maintained from its introduction during the reign of Constantine I to the early eleventh century. The miliaresion, the Byzantine silver coin, has a value of one twelfth of a nomisma.

46. These are the Kilikian Gates, the passes through the Taurus mountains in southeastern Asia Minor, the mountains which separate Asia Minor and Syria.

battle they would not be caught by surprise, but would take courage and march against their foes as into a game.

The Emperor took into his hand an image of the God-man (which hands did not paint, but which, just as He was conceived without semen, the Word which formed and shaped everything created without painting). Putting his faith in the God-limned image, he began his struggles. He promised the army that he would struggle along with them until death and treat them like his own children. For he did not want his power to be that of fear, but of love.

He found that the army was lazy, cowardly, disorderly, and undisciplined, and also that it had been widely dispersed. He immediately collected it all into one place. As with one voice, everyone hymned the Emperor's might and courage. He addressed them with words designed to stir their bravery: "Brothers and children, you see that God's enemies have overrun our land, laid waste our cities, burned our

304 altars, and filled the tables of bloodless sacrifice with bloody murders. They take great pleasure in defiling our churches, which should not suffer."

Once more he armed the army for training, forming two armed lines of battle. The men stood in their armor; there were trumpet-calls and phalanxes of shields. After the regiments were well organized, he ordered them to engage each other: there were violent struggles and conflicts between them, and the appearance of warfare. It was like seeing the horrible, fearful spectacle without its danger, or men converging for murder without bloodshed, or the methods of force before force itself. Thus each man got a start from this danger-less slaughter and was more secure thereafter. After Herakleios had armed everyone, he ordered them to abstain from injustice and cleave to piety.

When he came to the districts of Armenia he ordered some select men to scout ahead. A host of Saracen cavalry who were tributary to the Persians intended to ambush the Emperor. His scouts met them and brought their general back in bonds to Herakleios; they had routed the Saracens and killed many of them. When winter came, the Emperor moved to the vicinity of the Black Sea, and the barbarians thought it a good idea to besiege him while he was wintering there. But he escaped the Persians, turned round, and invaded their land. This surprise invasion startled the barbarians when they learned of it.

The Persian general Sarbaros took his forces to Kilikia in order to enter Roman territory and overthrow the Emperor. He was afraid lest the Emperor, who had invaded Persia through Armenia, should throw it into chaos, but he did not have any definite idea of what to do. He

305 was compelled to follow the Roman army; he was thinking about stealing a victory by taking the Romans during the lightless night. But since

the night was that of the full moon, he was dissuaded from his plan and cursed the moon he had formerly worshiped because it did not set until the night was done. Because of that, Sarbaros was too cowardly to attack the Emperor. Like deer, Sarbaros' army came to the mountains and from their heights saw the Romans' crisp maneuvers and sound strategy.

The Emperor, knowing of Sarbaros' cowardice, was confident and camped restfully in a cramped space. This roused Sarbaros to battle. He stealthily came down from his mountain to make many small-scale attacks, but the Romans won all of them. Their army became more courageous when it saw the Emperor leaping forward everywhere and fighting daringly. Now there was a Persian refugee who a little while before had been enrolled in the Emperor's army. He deserted to the Persians, expecting them to destroy the Roman force. But he saw their cowardice, and after ten days went back to the Emperor and told him in great detail of the barbarians' low morale.

Sarbaros could no longer stand wasting time in the mountains and was forced to move to the attack. Readying his army for battle, he divided it into three parts and suddenly came down just at dawn, before sunrise. The Emperor had anticipated him and arranged his own army into three phalanxes; now he led it into battle. He had the easterly position, and when the sun rose its rays blinded the Persians; they had worshiped it as a god. The Emperor turned his army in a feigned flight, and the Persians broke ranks in their hot pursuit. Then the Romans courageously wheeled round and put them to rout, killing many. They drove them to the cliffs, forced them into badlands, and crushed them. The Persians went about on the crags like wild goats.

306 Many were also taken alive.

The Romans captured their camp and all their gear. They raised their hands on high and thanked God; they also eagerly prayed for the Emperor, who had led them well. For before they had never thought to see Persian dust; now they had found and plundered their still-pitched tents. Who could have expected the invincible Persian race ever to show its back to the Romans? The Emperor left the army in Armenia under a general, while he returned to winter in Byzantium.

ANNUS MUNDI 6114 (SEPTEMBER 1, 622—AUGUST 31, 623)

A.D. 614
Roman Emperor Herakleios: 31 years: year 13
Persian King Khosroes: 39 years: year 35 [sic]
Bishop of Constantinople Sergios: 29 years: year 14

Bishop of Jerusalem Zachariah: 22 years: year 14
Bishop of Alexandria George: 14 years: year 4

In this year—the eleventh indiction—on March 15 the Emperor Herakleios left the imperial city and quickly came to Armenia. The Persian king dispatched Sarbarazas'[47] army into Roman territory. Herakleios wrote to Khosroes that either he should espouse peace or the Emperor would invade Persia with his army. But Khosroes neither espoused peace nor believed the statement that Herakleios would dare approach Persia.

On April 20 the Emperor invaded Persia, and when Khosroes learned this he ordered Sarbarazas to withdraw. He assembled his own forces from all over Persia and gave them to Saïn, ordering these forces to join Sarbarazas quickly and, thus united, move against the Emperor.

307

Herakleios summoned his army and roused it with this oration: "Brothers, let us keep in mind the fear of God and struggle to avenge insults to Him. Let us nobly oppose our enemies, who have done many terrible things to Christians. Let us respect the independent Roman state; let us resist our enemies, who are impiously in arms, and let us pledge murder for their murders. Let us consider that we are within Persian territory and that flight bears great danger. Let us avenge the ravishing of our maidens; when we see our soldiers' mutilated members, our hearts must be distressed. Our danger is not without reward, but is the harbinger of eternal life. Let us bravely take our stand—the Lord God will work with us, and will destroy our foes."

After the Emperor had exhorted the army with these and many other ideas, one man who spoke for all answered him: "You have opened our hearts, master, by opening your mouth in exhortation. Your words have stirred us. We blush when we see you going to the fore during battle, and will follow you in all you command."

The Emperor took up his army and at once advanced into the Persian heartland, burning its cities and villages. Then a miracle occurred: the air became humid in summer, refreshing the Romans and raising their spirits. When Herakleios heard that Khosroes was in the city of Gazakon with 40,000 warlike men, he hastened against him, sending some of his Saracens ahead to scout. They met Khosroes' guard-force, slew some, and bound the rest (including their general) and brought them to the Emperor. Khosroes fled when he learned of this, abandoning the city and his army. Herakleios, who was in pursuit, slew some as he arrived; the rest dis-

47. Sarbarazas is the same person as the Persian general Sarbaros referred to earlier.

308   persed and fled. When he reached the city of the Gazacenes, he rested his army in its suburbs.

    The fugitive Persians told him Khosroes had burned all the crops in the area and gone to the city of Thebarmaïs in the east. In it were a fire-temple[48] and the treasures of the Lydian king Kroisos,[49] and also the deceit of the coals. Khosroes took them and marched to Dastigerd. The Emperor left Gazakon and reached Thebarmaïs. He entered it, burned the fire-temple and the whole city, then followed Khosroes through the passes of the land of the Medes: Khosroes was moving from place to place in the rugged territory. Herakleios pursued him, sacking many cities and villages.

    Since winter was coming, he held a council with his army as to where to spend it. Some said in Albania, others said in the same place Khosroes did. The Emperor ordered the army purified for three days. Then he opened God's gospels and found on referring to them that he should winter in Albania.[50] In the midst of his journey Persian armies attacked him even though he had not a few Persian prisoners; with God's help he beat them all. Although winter and icy cold assailed him on the journey, he arrived in Albania with 50,000 prisoners. Out of the goodness of his heart he took pity on them and freed them from their bonds, cared for them, and let them rest. They all acclaimed him in tears as the savior of Persia, who would kill Khosroes, the universal destroyer.

ANNUS MUNDI 6115 (SEPTEMBER 1, 623—AUGUST 31, 624)

14. 36. 15. 15. 5.

    In this year the Persian king Khosroes appointed as general Sara-blangas, a vigorous man, but arrogant and conceited. As an army he
309   gave him the so-called Khosroegetai and Perozitai,[51] then sent him to oppose Herakleios in Albania. He penetrated the Albanian highlands but did not have the courage to meet the Emperor face to face in battle. Instead, he held the passes leading to Persia, thinking to waylay him.

    48. The Persian Zoroastrians venerated fire as well as the sun. They deemed it a symbol of the good god Ahura Mazda, the deity who in their dualistic system was opposed by Ahriman.
    49. Kroisos the king of Lydia (in western Asia Minor) was conquered by the Achaemenid Persian king Cyrus in 546 B.C.; his wealth was proverbial. It is, to say the least, highly unlikely that this treasure was once his.
    50. The *sortes biblicae*, a method of divination where a question was asked and the Bible then opened at random to find the answer. The Albania in question is in the Caucasus, not the Balkans.
    51. As these units are named for Persian kings, they are presumably crack regiments of the Persian forces.

But at the start of spring Herakleios left Albania by taking a side-road into Persia through thriving plains full of victuals, even if it was a great deal out of his way. Sarablangas drove through the passes (as this was the short way) to get ahead of him on Persian territory.

Herakleios addressed his army: "Brothers, we know that the Persians' army has been wandering in rugged land; they have exhausted their horses, and hamstrung them, too. We should try to hurry against Khosroes, so as to confuse him by falling upon him unexpectedly." But the army (especially the Lazikan, Abasgian, and Iberian allies) advised him not to do this.

This had an unfortunate result. Sarbarazas was also arriving with his army, which Khosroes had powerfully equipped and sent against Herakleios by way of Armenia. Sarablangas had followed Herakleios but would not engage him; he was expecting to join Sarbarazas and then start battle. When they learned Sarbarazas had arrived, the Romans became afraid and fell in tears at the feet of the Emperor, repenting of the evils which had occurred because of their disobedience. They realized how wicked it was for a servant not to yield to his master's plans. They said, "Your hand, master, before you destroy us wretches: for we will follow you in whatever you order."

Then the Emperor hurried to engage Sarablangas before he could join Sarbarazas. He attacked him repeatedly, by night and day, and made him afraid. After getting ahead of both Persian generals, he eagerly moved against Khosroes.

Two Romans who deserted to the Persians persuaded them the Romans were fleeing out of cowardice. Another rumor also reached the Persians: that their general Saïn had arrived with another army to help them. When Sarablangas and Sarbarazas heard this, they both struggled to bring Herakleios to battle before Saïn could arrive and take the credit for the victory for himself. Also, they believed the deserters. They marched against Herakleios and camped near him, wanting to attack at dawn. But Herakleios left at nightfall and traveled all night long. When he was a good way away from them, he camped in a verdant plain. The barbarians thought he had fled from cowardice and drove on in a disorderly fashion to overtake him. But he met them and joined battle with them, mustering his army at a wooded hill. With God's help, he routed the barbarians. He chased them through gullies and killed a large number; even Sarablangas fell, struck in the back with a sword.

In the middle of these struggles Saïn and his army arrived. The Emperor routed him too, killed many of his troops, and captured their baggage-train. Sarbarazas joined Saïn and assembled the surviving barbarians; they planned to move against Herakleios once more.

The Emperor marched through country rough and difficult to

310

18

traverse to the country of the Huns and their badlands; the barbarians followed him. The Lazikans and Abasgians became afraid, detached themselves from their Roman alliance, and returned to their own country. Pleased at this, Saïn and Sarbaros angrily marched after Herakleios.

The Emperor assembled his army and encouraged and exhorted them. He readied them by saying, "Brothers, do not be troubled by your enemies' numbers for, God willing, one will chase thousands.[52] Let us sacrifice ourselves to God for the salvation of our brothers. Let us take the martyrs' crown so the future will applaud us and God will give us our reward." He encouraged his army with these and many other notions, then, his face shining, arranged the battle-line.

311

The armies stood a little way apart from each other from dawn to dusk but did not engage one another. When evening came the Emperor shifted his position and the barbarians followed him. They wanted to get ahead of him, and so shifted their route, but they fell into marshes, got lost, and came into great danger. The Emperor crossed and recrossed the regions of Persarmenia. But as this land belonged to the Persians, many Persarmenians joined Sarbarazas, and he enlarged his army.

But after winter came, the members of Sarbarazas' host dispersed to their own districts so they could rest in their homes. When Herakleios learned this he planned a surprise night engagement. Sarbaros had no suspicion of what was going on. When it was deep winter, Herakleios selected stout horses and the army's braver troops. He divided them into two bands and armed them, ordering one group to lead the way against Sarbaros, while he followed behind with the other. They sped through the night, reaching the village of the Salbanoi around its ninth hour.[53] When the Persians in the village realized the Romans had come, they sprang up and rushed against them. But the Romans killed all of them save one, who informed Sarbaros. He got up, climbed aboard his horse naked and barefoot, and got away safely.

312

The Romans overtook his wives and the whole flower of the Persian officers, satraps, and select troops while they were going back into their families' tents. They attacked and burned them to death, though some were killed in battle and others bound in legirons. Except for Sarbaros, almost no-one was saved. The Romans even took Sarbaros' arms: his gold shield, sword, and spear, and his belt and sandals, which were incrusted with precious stones. Once they had seized all these

---

52. Cf. Deuteronomy 32:20.
53. Day and night were considered to begin at sunrise and sunset, respectively; each was divided into twelve hours. Thus, the ninth hour of the night would be about three A.M.

things, they marched on the men who were dispersed to their villages. When these troops learned of Sarbaros' flight they ran away without offering resistance. Herakleios pursued them; he killed some and captured others, while the rest returned to Persia in disgrace. The Emperor reassembled his army and joyfully wintered in that area.

ANNUS MUNDI 6116 (SEPTEMBER 1, 624—AUGUST 31, 625)

A.D. 616
Roman Emperor Herakleios: 31 years: year 15
Persian King Khosroes: 39 years: year 37
Bishop of Constantinople Sergios: 29 years: year 16
Bishop of Jerusalem Zachariah: 22 years: year 16
Bishop of Alexandria George: 14 years: year 6

In this year on March 1 the Emperor Herakleios assembled his army to hold a council on which road to travel. For two roads, narrow and difficult to travel, lay ahead, one leading to Taranton, the other to the land of the Syrians. The one leading to Taranton was more profitable, but lacked supplies. The other went over the Taurus mountains to Syria and had plenty of food on it. Everyone preferred the latter, even if it was more precipitate and under a lot of snow. With much labor they traversed it in seven days, reached and crossed the Tigris river, and came to Martyropolis and Amida. The army and its prisoners rested. From that area the Emperor was able to send letters 313 to Byzantium which told of everything that had happened to him; they caused great joy in the city.

Sarbaros assembled his scattered army and attacked him. The Emperor selected a squadron of soldiers and sent them to guard the passes leading to his position. He himself went off to the eastward passes to confront Sarbaros. He crossed the Nymphios river and reached the Euphrates, in which there was a bridge made of woven ropes and boats. But Sarbaros loosed the ropes from one bank and moved the whole bridge to the other. When the Emperor arrived he found he could not cross at the bridge, but went further and discovered a ford. Incredibly, he crossed it with no danger in March, and came to Samosata. He then recrossed the Taurus mountains, reaching Germanikeia; he bypassed Adana and came to the Saros river. Sarbaros stretched out the bridge once more, crossed the Euphrates without embarrassment, and followed Herakleios.

The Emperor crossed the Saros' bridge, found a resting place for his army and animals, and camped there to give them a breather. Sarbaros came to the opposite bank, and encamped there when he found the Romans held the bridge and its guardtowers. Many Romans ran across the bridge in a disorderly way to attack the Persians, slaughtering many of them. The Emperor tried to stop his men from crossing in disorder, lest the enemy find a way to get to the bridge and come back across it with them. The army, however, did not obey Herakleios. Sarbaros laid an ambush: by showing himself as if in flight, he drew many Romans across the bridge in pursuit, contrary to the Emperor's will. They were punished for the disobedience: Sarbaros wheeled round and routed them, killing as many as had gone beyond the bridge. After the Emperor saw that the barbarians had broken ranks in their pursuit and that the Romans stationed in the guardtower were killing many, he marched against them.

314

A giant of a man met and attacked him in the middle of the bridge. The Emperor struck him and hurled him into the river. When he fell the barbarians turned in flight and threw themselves into the river like frogs near the far end of the bridge, though some were put to the sword. But the barbarian host massed at the riverbank shot at the Romans and did not let them cross. Fighting in superhuman fashion, the Emperor nobly crossed and attacked the barbarians with only a few companions, amazing even Sarbaros. He said to Kosmas (a fugitive apostate from the Romans who was standing near him), "Look at the Caesar, Kosmas: how boldly he stands in battle, struggling alone against such a multitude: like an anvil he spurns their blows." For the Emperor was recognizable because of his true boots[54] and received many blows, though none was fatal in this battle.

Both sides fought all day in this battle, separating from each other when evening came. Sarbaros grew afraid and retreated. The Emperor assembled his army and hastened to Sebasteia. He crossed the Halys river and spent the whole winter in that country.

. Khosroes, that madman, sent messengers to take the treasures from all the churches under Persian control. He even forced the Christians to become Nestorians[55] in order to confound the Emperor.

315 ANNUS MUNDI 6117 (SEPTEMBER 1, 625–AUGUST 31, 626)

16. 38. 17. 17. 7.

In this year the Persian king Khosroes created a new army, recruiting foreigners, citizens, and house-slaves, and making a levy from

54. As part of his regalia, the Emperor wore scarlet boots, a privilege denied his subjects.

55. Nestorian Christianity was the only form of that religion the Persians tolerated; they did so precisely because the Nestorians (who emphasized Christ's humanity at the expense of His divinity) were persecuted within the Byzantine Empire, and thus unlikely to be pro-Roman.

every people. He gave this levy to the general Saïn, along with 50,000 men he took from Sarbaros' phalanx. Khosroes named them the "golden spears" and sent them out against the Emperor. He dispatched Sarbaros and the remainder of his army against Constantinople so that, with the Huns of the west (whom they call Avars), Bulgars, Sklavinians, and Gepids (with all of whom he had conspired), he could march on and besiege the city.

When the Emperor learned this he split his army into three divisions. He sent some to guard the city and gave others to his brother Theodore, whom he ordered to make war on Saïn. The third part he himself took to Lazika. In that country he parleyed with the Turks of the east (whom they call Khazars), and called on them for an alliance.

Together with his newly-assembled army, Saïn overtook the Emperor's brother Theodore and armed for battle. When it was joined, God worked with Theodore at the intercession of His all-exalted Mother: incredibly, hail fell on and struck many of the barbarians, but the Romans' formation remained undisturbed. The Romans routed the Persians, killing a large number of them. When Khosroes learned this, he became furious at Saïn. His general's spirit was utterly broken; he fell ill and died. Khosroes ordered his body preserved in salt and carried home to him, and subjected the corpse to many indignities.

316   The Khazars broke through the Caspian Gates and invaded Persia, entering the land of Adraiga under their general Ziebel, who was second in rank to their Khagan. In the places they traversed, they took Persian prisoners and burned their cities and villages. The Emperor left Lazika to meet them. When Ziebel saw him he ran toward him, bowed his neck, and prostrated himself before him: the Persians saw this from the city of Tiflis. All the Turkish people fell face down to the ground. While stretched out on their faces they acclaimed the Emperor, an honor unusual from their tribe. Their leaders climbed onto stones, then prostrated themselves in the same way. Ziebel presented his firstborn son to the Emperor; the Khazar took pleasure in Herakleios' words and was amazed at his appearance and wisdom. Ziebel collected 40,000 noble men, whom he gave to the Emperor in alliance; he himself returned to his own country. Once the Emperor had received the Khazars, he marched against Khosroes.

Sarbaros attacked Chalcedon while the Avars approached Constantinople from Thrace. They wanted to take it, and set many engines in motion against it. A host of dug-out boats arrived from the Danube; there was a countless number of them, and they filled the Golden Horn.[56] For ten days they besieged the city by land and sea, but were defeated by God's power and cooperation and the intercession of His

56. The inlet which washed Constantinople to the north and held its principal harbor.

immaculate virgin Mother. In great disgrace, the Avars withdrew to their own country. But Sarbaros, who was stationed by Chalcedon, did not retreat, but wintered there, denuding the opposite shore and its cities.[57]

317 ANNUS MUNDI 6118 (SEPTEMBER 1, 626—AUGUST 31, 627)

A.D. 618
Roman Emperor Herakleios: 31 years: year 17
Persian King Khosroes: 39 years: year 39
Bishop of Constantinople Sergios: 29 years: year 18
Bishop of Jerusalem Zachariah: 22 years: year 18
Bishop of Alexandria George: 14 years: year 8

In this year, beginning in September, Herakleios and the Turks invaded Persia. Because of winter this was unexpected; Khosroes was astonished to learn of it. When the Turks saw the winter and the continuous Persian attacks, they could not stand toiling with the Emperor; they gave him up for lost and turned back, beginning to drift away a few at a time. The Emperor talked this over with his army. He said, "Brothers, you know that no-one wants to ally with us except God and she who bore Him without semen. This is so He can reveal His power, since salvation does not lie in masses of men or arms. Rather He sends down His aid to those who believe in His mercy."

Khosroes assembled all his forces, appointing Rhazates (a brave and warlike man) as their general. He dispatched them against Herakleios. The Emperor was burning the cities and towns of Persia, and put to the sword the Persians he overtook. On October 9 of the fifteenth indiction he entered the land of Khamantha, where he rested the army for a week. Rhazates went to Gazakon, while the Romans used up the supplies ahead. Because he was behind he was like a hungry dog, barely nourished from Herakleios' crumbs. Many of his horses were lost because he could not find supplies.

318   On December 1 the Emperor reached the Greater Zab river; he crossed it and camped near Nineveh. Rhazates followed him to the ford; he went down the river, found another three miles away, and crossed. The Emperor sent out his general Baanes with a few chosen soldiers, who encountered a Persian battalion. They slew its count and brought back his head and solid-gold sword. They killed many men and brought back two alive, one of whom was Rhazates' spatharios.[58] He told the Emperor that Rhazates wanted to make war on him; he had

57. I.e., the Asian shore of the Bosporos and the Sea of Marmora.
58. A title of honor with the literal meaning of *swordbearer* or "bodyguard," the word often means little more than "aide."

been so ordered by Khosroes, who had also sent him 3,000 armed
men, though these had not yet arrived.

The Emperor sent his baggage train ahead when he learned of
this. He followed, looking for a place where he could give battle before
the 3,000 could join his enemies. He found a plain quite suitable for
battle, harangued his army, and arranged it in battle formation. When
he arrived, Rhazates arranged his own army in three wedges and
marched on the Emperor. On December 12 (the sabbath day) battle
was joined. The Emperor sprang out ahead of everyone to meet a
Persian officer: by the power of God and His Mother he overthrew him.
He met another and overthrew him too. A third man, who struck him
with a spear and wounded his lip, attacked him, but the Emperor killed
him as well.

With echoing trumpets the two sides engaged each other. Once
the battle was well under way, infantrymen wounded the Emperor's
roan horse (which was called Antelope): it took a spear in its thigh.
There were also many sword-strokes at its face but, as it was wearing
319 leather armor, it was not harmed, nor were the blows effective. In the
battle Rhazates, the three Persian division commanders, almost all
their officers, and most of their army fell. Fifty Romans were slain, not
counting ten more who were wounded but did not die. The battle
lasted from dawn until the eleventh hour. The Romans set up twenty-
eight Persian standards, not counting those that were broken.[59]

They plundered the corpses, taking their corselets, helmets, and
all their arms. The Romans took many solid-gold swords, gold-
encrusted belts, pearls, Rhazates' solid-gold shield (which had a hundred twenty golden leaves), and his solid-gold corselet. They brought
back his robe, his bracelets, his solid-gold saddle, and his head. Bar-
samouses, the commander of the Persians' Iberian subjects, was taken
alive.

The armies remained two bowshots apart from each other, for
there was no rout. During the night the Roman soldiers watered their
horses, holding them out as bait. The Persian cavalrymen stood guard
over the corpses of their dead until the seventh hour of the night; at
the eighth hour of the night they retreated and withdrew behind their
trench. From there they went off to camp in the rugged foothills of the
mountains, for they had been intimidated. No-one remembers such a
battle taking place between Persians and Romans: the fighting did not
stop through the whole day. The Romans won, but by God's help
alone.

The Emperor encouraged his army to march on Khosroes to terrify him. Khosroes sent messengers summoning Sarbaros from

59. As a victory monument.

320   Byzantium and Chalcedon. On December 21 the Emperor learned that Rhazates' army, which had disengaged from combat, had been joined by the 3,000 men Khosroes had sent. It followed him to Nineveh. The Emperor crossed the Greater Zab, then sent out the turmarch[60] George with 1,000 soldiers to drive on to seize control of the bridges over the Lesser Zab before Khosroes learned about it. George marched forty-eight miles during the night and seized the four bridges of the Lesser Zab. He took alive the Persians he found in the bridges' watch-towers. On December 23 the Emperor arrived at the bridges, crossed, and camped in the buildings of Iesdem. The army and its beasts rested there, celebrating the festival of the birth of Christ.

When Khosroes learned the Romans had captured the Lesser Zab's bridges, he sent messages to the Persian army under Rhazates that they should make haste, get ahead of the Emperor, and attack him. Inspired, they crossed the Lesser Zab elsewhere before the Emperor had crossed and moved ahead of him. The Emperor reached a place called Dezerida, which he took and burned. The Persians crossed the Torna River's bridge and camped there. The Emperor came to and took another palace of Khosroes', which was called Rhousa. He suspected that the enemy intended to attack him at the bridge over the Torna River, but when they saw him they abandoned the bridge and fled. He crossed it without hindrance and came to a place called Beklal; once he had taken it, he held horse-races there.

Some Armenians who were with the Persians came to the Emperor by night, saying, "Khosroes is camped with his elephants and his army
321   at a place called Barasroth, which is five miles from the palace of Dastagerd. He ordered his army gathered there to attack you. For in that spot there is a river which is hard to cross; it has a narrow bridge, narrow streets among the village's houses, and rushing torrents." The Emperor stayed at the palace Beklal while he took counsel with his officers and the army. In one palace enclosure he found three hundred fattened antelope, and in another around a hundred fattened wild asses. He gave them all to the army. He spent January 1 there, as he had also found innumerable sheep, pigs, and cattle. The whole army rested, extolling God and enjoying His benefits.

They seized some herders and learned from them that on December 23 Khosroes had heard the Emperor had crossed the bridge of the Torna. He immediately evacuated the palace at Dastagerd and went to Ctesiphon[61] in great haste, throwing all the money he had in the palace onto his retinue's elephants, camels, and mules. He also wrote Rha-

60. A rank approximately equivalent to brigadier-general.
61. The capital of the Persian Empire.

zates' army that it could enter the same palace and his officers' houses and carry away whatever it found in them.[62]

The Emperor sent half his army to Dastagerd; he went to another palace called Bebdark by another road. He took and burned it, thanking God for working such marvels at the intercession of His Mother. For who would have expected Khosroes to flee from the face of the Roman Emperor, going out of his palace and into Ctesiphon? He had not deigned to see Ctesiphon for twenty-four years, as even his palaces were at Dastagerd.

322

In the palace at Dastagerd the Roman soldiers found three hundred Roman standards which had been taken at various times. They also found goods which had been left behind: aloes and logs of aloes of seventy or eighty pounds, silk, so many linen shirts as to be beyond counting, sugar, ginger, and many other goods. Some also found silver, pure-silk cloaks, and a great number of beautiful fleecy carpets and woven rugs: they burned all these because of their weight. After they were done camping among the pavilions and arcades Khosroes had built, they burned them all, and his many statues as well. In these palaces they also found countless numbers of ostriches, antelope, wild asses, peacocks, and pheasants; huge lions and tigers lived in Khosroes' hunting grounds. A great number of prisoners from Edessa, Alexandria, and other cities fled to the Emperor. He made a celebration of lights, which gladdened the army, and rested it and its horses. Once he had taken Khosroes' palaces, which were very valuable, marvelous, and amazing buildings, he razed them to the ground so Khosroes would learn how much suffering he had caused the Romans by laying waste and burning their cities.

Many of the palace overseers were captured. When they were asked when Khosroes had left Dastagerd, they said, "He heard you were near nine days before you arrived, and secretly bored through the city wall near his palace. Thus he left through the orchards in a great hurry, as did his wife and children. They did this so there would be no confusion in the city." Neither Khosroes' soldiers nor his officers had learned of this until he was five miles away. Then he let them know so they could follow him to Ctestiphon. He had not been able to make five miles a day, but made twenty-five while fleeing. His wives and children fled in utter confusion, losing sight and touch with each other. When night came Khosroes entered the house of a lowly farmer to stay there, though he could barely get through the door; Herakleios was amazed when he heard this.

323

On the third day Khosroes reached Ctesiphon. Twenty-four years

---

62. His reasoning presumably being that it was better for his own subjects to plunder his possessions than for the Romans to do so.

before, when he was besieging Daras during the reign of the Roman Emperor Phokas, sorcerers and astrologers had predicted he would be destroyed when he entered Ctesiphon. He had not been willing to go so much as a fraction of a mile from Dastagerd, but then went off to Ctesiphon in flight. He did not have the courage to stay there, but crossed the bridge over the Tigris to the city which is called Seleukeia by us, but Goudeser by the Persians. He stored up all his treasure in it, and stayed there with his wife Seirem and three of his daughters. He sent the rest of his wives and most of his children to a strongpoint forty miles further east.

Some Persians slandered Sarbaros to Khosroes: they said he was pro-Roman and had spoken slightingly of the king. Khosroes dispatched a spatharios of his with an order he had written to Kardarigas, Sarbaros' second-in-command: that he should execute Sarbaros, take his army, and hurry to Persia to help Khosroes. But in Galatia the Romans captured the man carrying the letters. His captors escaped the Persians, bringing him to Byzantium to present him to the Emperor's son. When the Emperor[63] learned the truth from the messenger, he immediately summoned Sarbaros. He came in and presented himself to the Emperor, who gave him the letter to Kardarigas and showed him the messenger. Reading the letter, he was fully satisfied as to its truth, and at once turned round to make agreements with the Emperor's son and the patriarch. He falsified Khosroes' letter by inserting into it another four hundred satraps, officers, commanders of a thousand, and commanders of a hundred who were to be killed along with himself. Then he put the seal back on the letter in the proper way and convened a meeting with his high officers and Kardarigas. He read the letter, then asked Kardarigas, "What do you plan to do about this?" Filled with rage, the officers renounced Khosroes and made peace-agreements with the Emperor, who, after they held a common council, thought it good that they should withdraw from Chalcedon and return to their own country without doing any damage.

Herakleios wrote to Khosroes: "I am pursuing and chasing peace. For I do not willingly burn Persia; rather, you force me to do so. Let us now, therefore, throw down our arms and welcome peace. Let us quench this fire, before it consumes everything." When Khosroes would not agree, the Persian army's hatred of him increased.

Khosroes enlisted all his officers' men, his entire retinue, and that of his wives; he armed them and sent them to join Rhazates' army at the Narbas River twelve miles from Ctesiphon. He ordered them to cut the bridge and the boat-bridge when the Emperor crossed the river. On January 7, the Emperor moved out from Dastagerd. After traveling

---

63. Herakleios' son Constantine III, in Constantinople.

325   for three days, he camped twelve miles from the Persian encampment on the Narbas River, in which the Persians even had two hundred elephants. The Emperor sent George, the turmarch of the Armeniacs,[64] to advance up to the Narbas and find out if it had a ford. He found that the Persians had cut the bridges and that the Narbas had no ford, and then returned to the Emperor. Herakleios went to Siazouros; he spent the whole month of February moving here and there and burning villages and towns. In March he came to a village called Barzan. He spent seven days there, then sent out his general Mezezios on a raid.

Goundabousan, one of the commanders of a thousand of Sarbaros' army, went over to Mezezios along with five other men: three were counts, the other two officers. Mezezios brought them to the Emperor, to whom Goundabousan gave important news. He said, "When Khosroes fled from Dastagerd to Ctesiphon and Seleukeia, he contracted dysentery and wanted to crown his son Merdasas, who was his child by Seirem. He recrossed the river with Merdasas, Seirem, and her other son Saliar. But he left his firstborn son Siroes and his brothers and wives on the other side of the river. When Siroes learned Khosroes wanted to crown Merdasas, he was dismayed, and sent a man who had had the same wet nurse as himself to me, saying, 'Come across the river so I can meet you.' I was afraid to cross because of Khosroes, and told Siroes, 'Write me through your close comrade if you want anything.' Siroes wrote to me, 'You know the wicked Khosroes has destroyed the Persian state. He wants to crown Merdasas, and has contempt for me, his firstborn. If you speak to the army and make it

326   accept me, I promise to increase its wages and to make peace with the Roman Emperor and the Turks; we will live well. Hurry with your army, so I can become king. I promise to unite and exalt you all, especially you yourself.' Through his close friend I told him that if I could I would talk to the army and work on it. I talked to twenty-two counts and other officers and to many soldiers, and won them over. When I revealed this to Siroes, he told me that on March 23 I should take some of the younger members of the garrison and meet him at the Tigris' boat-bridge so we could take him to the army and move against Khosroes. With Siroes are the two sons of Sarbarazas, the son of Iesdem, and many other officers' sons, as well as the son of Aram: all of them select men. If they can kill Khosroes, well and good. If they fail, they will all go over to you, Siroes included. He sent me to you, my lord, because he respects the Roman Empire which once saved

64. The Armeniacs were garrisoned in northeastern Asia Minor once the moves of the seventh century were completed.

Khosroes.[65] From Khosroes Roman soil has suffered many evils, and because of the king's ingratitude you may not believe me."[66]

Herakleios sent a messenger back to Siroes, telling him to open the prisons, release the Romans held in them, arm them, and move against Khosroes in that way. Siroes obeyed the Emperor. He released the men who had been imprisoned and attacked his parricidal father Khosroes, who thought fit to flee but, unable to do so, was caught. The Persians fettered him with his elbows behind him; they put heavy irons on his feet and his neck, then put him in the "house of darkness," which he himself had fortified. He had built it at first in order to store his money there. They gave him poor bread and water and starved him, for Siroes said, "Let him eat the gold which he accumulated in vain, for which he starved many and devastated the world." He sent satraps to revile Khosroes and spit on him, then slew his son Merdasas (whom he had wished to crown) and all the rest of his sons in his sight. He sent every one of Khosroes' enemies to curse him, beat him, and spit on him. After five days of this, Siroes ordered them to kill him by archery. Thus, in these terrible conditions, Khosroes gave up his wicked life.

Then Siroes wrote to Herakleios, sending him the good news of bloody Khosroes' end. He made a perpetual peace with the Emperor and restored to him all the imprisoned Christians, the captives from all over Persia (including the patriarch Zachariah), and the precious and lifegiving wood which Sarbarazas took from Jerusalem when he seized that city.

ANNUS MUNDI 6119 (SEPTEMBER 1, 627—AUGUST 31, 628)

Persian King Siroes: 1 year
6119. 619. 18. 1. 19. 19. 9.

In this year there was peace between Persians and Romans. The Emperor sent his brother Theodore with the Persian king's letters and men so that the Persians in Edessa, Palestine, Jerusalem, and the rest of the Roman cities could traverse Roman territory without harm while peacefully withdrawing to Persia. In six years the Emperor had overthrown Persia; in the seventh he returned to Constantinople with great joy, and in that year performed a mystic celebration. God, Who had made every created thing in six days, named the seventh day that of

65. In 591 Maurice had restored Khosroes II to his throne, helping him overthrow the rebel Bahram. Khosroes justified his attacks to the Empire after the accession of Phokas by claiming to be Maurice's avenger.
66. Me: i.e., Siroes.

328 rest. Similarly, Herakleios, who had completed many labors in six years, returned with peace and joy in the seventh year and rested.

When the people of the city learned of his arrival, they were all filled with irresistible love and went to Hiereia[67] to meet him, as did the patriarch and Constantine, his son the co-Emperor. They carried upraised olive branches and torches, and acclaimed Herakleios with joy and tears. His son came forward, fell at his feet, and embraced him. They both moistened the ground with their tears; when the people saw this, they all sent up hymns of thanksgiving to God. They caught up the Emperor and, leaping for joy, entered the city.

ANNUS MUNDI 6120 (SEPTEMBER 1, 628—AUGUST 31, 629)

Persian king Ardaser: 7 months
6120. 620. 19. 1. 20. 20. 10.

In this year at spring the Emperor left the imperial city to travel to Jerusalem, bringing back the precious and lifegiving wood to restore it as a thanksgiving to God. When he came to Tiberias, the Christians denounced a man named Benjamin on the grounds that he had mistreated them. He was very rich, and received the Emperor and his army. The Emperor condemned him, and asked, "For what reason did you mistreat the Christians?"

He said, "Because they are enemies of my faith," for he was a Jew. Then the Emperor warned him, persuaded him to convert, and baptized him in the house of Eustathios the Neapolitan, a Christian who had received the Emperor.

Herakleios entered Jerusalem. He restored Zachariah the patriarch and the precious and lifegiving wood to their own place and gave thanks to God. He expelled the Hebrews from the holy city, ordering that they should not be allowed to come within three miles of it. When

329 he reached Edessa he restored to the orthodox the church the Nestorians had held since Khosroes' time.

When he came to Hierapolis, Herakleios heard that the Persian king Siroes had died and his son Ardaser succeeded to rule over the Persians. After he had held power for seven months Sarbarazas rebelled against him, smote him down, and ruled the Persians for two months. The Persians killed him and set up Khosroes' daughter Borane as ruler; she ruled the Persian Empire for seven months. Hormisdas succeeded her but was run out by the Saracens, and the Persian Empire has been subject to the Arabs until the present day.

67. A suburb of Constantinople on the Asian side of the Bosporos, south and east of Chalcedon.

ANNUS MUNDI 6121 (SEPTEMBER 1, 629—AUGUST 31, 630)

A.D. 621
Roman Emperor Herakleios: 31 years: year 20
Persian King Hormisdas: 11 years: year 1
Bishop of Constantinople Sergios: 29 years: year 21
Bishop of Jerusalem Zachariah: 22 years: year 21
Bishop of Alexandria George: 14 years: year 11

In this year Athanasios the patriarch of the Jacobites[68] came to the Emperor Herakleios while he was in Hierapolis. He was a tricky man, and an evildoer because of his innate Syrian knavery. When he began talks on the faith with the Emperor, Herakleios promised to make him patriarch of Antioch if he would accept the council of Chalcedon.[69] He hypocritically accepted the synod, agreeing there were two conjoint natures in Christ. But then he asked the Emperor how he should refer to Christ's energies and wills: were they dual or single? The Emperor was confused; he wrote to Sergios the bishop of Constantinople and also called on Cyrus the bishop of Phasis, who agreed with Sergios that there was one will and one energy. For Sergios maintained there was one natural will and energy in Christ and so wrote, as he was Syrian-born and had Jacobite ancestors. The Emperor took their joint advice, and also found Athanasios agreeing with them. For Athanasios knew

330

68. Jacob Baradaios was chosen as the monophysite (see note 69) bishop of Edessa in 541, an office he held until his death in 578. He strengthened and reorganized the monophysite church of Syria, which thereafter often bore his name.

69. Held in 451, the fourth ecumenical council, that of Chalcedon, dealt with the relation of the human and divine natures of Christ. Eutykhes, following the Alexandrian school of theology (which always stressed Christ's divinity), declared that after the incarnation Christ had but one nature, and that divine. This view, the very opposite of Nestorianism, was popular in Egypt and Syria, but not in the rest of the Empire. The council of Chalcedon anathematized Eutykhes and declared Christ had two natures, human and divine, without "confusion, change, separation, or division." However, despite the decision of the council, Egypt and much of Syria remained monophysite: that is, believed Christ had but one nature. This religious disaffection caused the Empire great difficulty. If the Emperor tried to conciliate Egypt and Syria theologically, he would antagonize many of his own subjects, as well as the staunchly orthodox west. If he persecuted the monophysites, they would not remain loyal. Like many of his predecessors, and with equal lack of success, Herakleios sought a formula to satisfy everyone, and especially to rally the disaffected provinces of Syria and Egypt against the incursions of the Muslims. This would prove futile, and once it was recognized that Syria and Egypt were permanently lost to the Arabs, the Empire no longer had to cater to the theological views of their inhabitants. The expression of the rejection of the Syrian and Egyptian view was the third council of Constantinople, of 680–681.

that where one energy is found, there also one nature is recognized.

Once he was sure of his course, the Emperor communicated the opinion of Sergios and Cyrus to John, the pope of Rome.[70] He would not agree with their heresy.

After George the bishop of Alexandria died, Cyrus was dispatched as bishop of Alexandria. He joined with Theodore the bishop of Pharas to celebrate this union, though it was not durable. They both wrote that Christ had one natural energy. After these events came one right after the other, the council of Chalcedon and the Catholic church encountered great censure. For the Jacobites and the Theodosianoi[71] were boasting, "Not we to Chalcedon, but rather Chalcedon has accomodated itself to us. Through His one energy it agrees Christ has one nature."

At this time Sophronios was elected bishop of Jerusalem. Assembling the bishops under him, he anathematized the monothelite[72] doctrine and sent confessions of faith to Sergios of Constantinople and John of Rome. When he heard this, Herakleios was ashamed. He did not want to dissolve his own creations, but could not stand censure either. Thinking he was doing something great, he then promulgated the Edict, which said one should not confess either one or two energies in Christ.[73] When the party of Severus[74] read it, they dragged the reputation of the Catholic church through the taverns and bathhouses, saying, "The Chalcedonians formerly were pro-Nestorian; then they sobered and turned toward the truth, joining us in the one nature of Christ through His one energy. But now they have decided against that which they rightly believed, and have destroyed both sides, as they confess neither one nor two energies in Christ."

70. Theophanes' chronology is confused, as is often the case when he discusses events in the west; the pope in question is John IV, pope from 640 to 642.

71. A monophysite sect.

72. This is the attempted compromise doctrine put forward by Herakleios and his grandson Constans II: while accepting Christ's two natures, as decided at Chalcedon, monotheletism said they were guided by a single will (*thelēma*). Most monophysites were willing enough to accept this doctrine, but their acceptance did nothing to restore to the Byzantines their eastern provinces, lost for good to Islam. The papacy, with the exception of pope Honorius (anathematized by the third council of Constantinople), was always hostile to monotheletism and its predecessor monenergism (an early attempt at compromise which said that Christ's two natures shared a single energy rather than a single will).

73. This document was in the tradition of the Henotikon of Zeno (promulgated in 481), which tried to ban argument as to whether Christ had one or two natures. Like that earlier imperial effort, this attempt to paper over a theological problem failed because it was attacked from both sides.

74. That is, the Jacobites. Severus was a monophysite who was bishop of Antioch from 512 to 518.

331 After the death of Sergios, Pyrrhos succeeded to the throne of Constantinople. After Herakleios died and his son Constantine became Emperor, Pyrrhos and Martina poisoned him,[75] and Martina's son Heraklonas became Emperor. Because Pyrrhos was impious, the senate and city ousted him, Martina, and her son; Constantine's son Constans became Emperor. Paul—himself a heretic—was chosen bishop of Constantinople.

The pope of Rome, John, convened a synod of bishops to anathematize the monothelite heresy. In like fashion, various bishops in Africa, Byzakion, Numidia, and Mauretania convened and anathematized the monophysites. After John the bishop of Rome died, Theodore was chosen pope in his place.[76] Pyrrhos came to Africa and had a meeting with the holy abbot Maximus (who was highly respected for his monastic accomplishments) and the inspired prelates there. They confuted and convinced him, then sent him to pope Theodore. He gave the pope a statement of orthodoxy and was favorably received by him. But when he retired from Rome to Ravenna[77] he turned about, as a dog does toward its own vomit.[78]

When he learned this, the pope convened the full numbers of the church and went to the grave of the chief of the apostles.[79] He asked for the holy chalice and, with the blood of Christ falling drop by drop into the ink, drafted a condemnation of Pyrrhos and those in communion with him.

When Pyrrhos reached Constantinople, the bold heretics restored him to its throne, as Paul had died. After pope Theodore died, the most holy Martin was elected at Rome.[80] Maximus came from Africa to kindle Martin's zeal. They convened a synod of a hundred fifty bishops, anathematized Sergios, Pyrrhos, Cyrus, and Paul, and clarified and strengthened the doctrine of Christ our God's two wills and

332 energies. This was in the eighth indiction—the ninth year of the reign of Herakleios' grandson Constans, who was outraged when he learned of it. He brought the holy Martin and Maximus to Constantinople, tortured them, then sent them into exile in the Cherson[81] and its environs. He also took vengeance on many western bishops. After Martin's exile Agathon was chosen pope of Rome.[82] He was moved by

75. This is a slander; his death was almost certainly due to natural causes, and was most probably caused by tuberculosis.
76. Theodore I, pope from 642 to 649.
77. The capital of Byzantine Italy.
78. Cf. Proverbs 26:11, 2 Peter 1:19.
79. That is, St. Peter.
80. Martin I, pope from 649 to 655.
81. The Crimea.
82. Agathon, pope from 678 to 681—Theophanes, poorly informed as to affairs in Rome, has omitted the names of four popes.

holy zeal to convene a holy synod which renounced the monothelite heresy and clarified Christ's two wills and energies.

At the same time as the church was being harassed by the Emperors and their impious priests, the desolate Amalek rose up to smite us, Christ's people. The first fearful fall of the Roman army came to pass: I mean the one at Gabitha, the Yarmuk, and Dathesmos. After this the fall of Palestine, Caesarea, and Jerusalem came one after the other, then the ruin of Egypt, the capture of the Mediterranean, its islands, and all Romania,[83] the final destruction of the Roman expedition and army in Phoenicia, and the devastation of all Christian peoples and places, which did not cease until the tormentor of the church was wickedly killed.[84]

ANNUS MUNDI 6122 (SEPTEMBER 1, 630–AUGUST 31, 631)

A.D. 622
Roman Emperor Herakleios: 31 years: year 21
Arab ruler Muhammad: 9 years: year 9
Bishop of Constantinople Sergios: 29 years: year 22
Bishop of Jerusalem Zachariah: 22 years: year 22
Bishop of Alexandria George: 14 years: year 12

333   In this year[85] died Muhammad, the Saracens' ruler and false prophet. He had previously chosen his relative Abu Bakr as his successor. As soon as rumor of him arrived, everyone became afraid.

When he first appeared, the Hebrews were misled and thought he was the Anointed One[86] they expected, so that some of their leaders came to him, accepted his religion, and gave up of that of Moses, who had looked on God. Those who did this were ten in number, and they stayed with Muhammad until his death. But when they saw him eating of a camel[87] they knew he was not the man they had thought. They were at a loss as to what to do; as they were afraid to give up his religion, they stayed at his side and taught him lawless behavior toward us Christians.

I think it necessary to discuss his ancestry in full. He sprang from a noble tribe descended from Ishmael the son of Abraham, for Ishmael's descendant Nizaros is proclaimed to be the father of all Arabs. He had two sons, Moudaros and Rhabias. Moudaros begat

83. That is, the Roman (or Byzantine) Empire.
84. Constans II was assassinated in Sicily in 668 (see below, under *annus mundi* 6160).
85. Actually, in 632.
86. Or, "the Christ."
87. The camel is an unclean beast under Jewish dietary standards.

Quraysh,[88] Qais, Themime, Asad, and other unknown tribes. They lived in the desert of Madianitin and kept cattle; they dwelt in tents. In the more distant regions the men are not of their tribe, but of that of Iektan: the Yemenites (that is, Homeritai[89]). Some of them made their living from camels.

334 Since Muhammad was a helpless orphan, he thought it good to go to a rich woman named Khadija (who was his relative) to hire on to manage her camels and conduct her business in Egypt and Palestine. Being a bold speaker, a little later he secretly went to the woman, who was a widow, married her, and took control of her camels and property.

When he went to Palestine he lived with both Jews and Christians, and hunted for certain writings among them. He had an epileptic seizure, and when his wife noticed this she became very distressed, for she was noble and had now been joined to a man who was not only helpless but epileptic as well. He turned to conciliating her, saying, "I see a vision of the angel known as Gabriel, and faint and fall because I cannot bear up under the sight of him." She had a friend living there who was a monk exiled for false belief, and she told him everything, even the angel's name.

He wanted to reassure her, and told her, "He has spoken the truth, for this angel is sent to all prophets." She was the first to accept the false abbot's statement; she believed in Muhammad, and told other women of her tribe that he was a prophet. Then from women the report spread to men: the first was Abu Bakr, whom Muhammad left behind as successor. At last his heresy conquered the land of Ethrib[90] by force. It had at first been practiced secretly for ten years, during warfare for another ten, and openly for nine.

Muhammad taught those who harkened to him that he who killed an enemy or was killed by an enemy entered paradise. He said paradise was a place of carnal eating, drinking, and intercourse with women: there were rivers of wine, honey, and milk, and the women there were not like those here, but of another sort, and intercourse was longlasting and its pleasure enduring. He said many other prodigal and foolish things. Also, his followers were to have sympathy for one another and help those treated unjustly.

335 In the same year—the fourth indiction—on November 7 a son, David, was born to Herakleios in the east. On the same day was also born Herakleios, the son of little Herakleios (also known as Constan-

---

88. The eponymous ancestor of Muhammad's tribe.

89. This is the Byzantine name for the Himyarites, a pre-Muslim Arab state in the Yemen.

90. That is, Medina, to which Muhammad emigrated from Mecca in 622.

tine), who was the son of the great Herakleios. He was baptized on November 3 of the fifth indiction by patriarch Sergios at Blakhernai.

ANNUS MUNDI 6123 (SEPTEMBER 1, 631—AUGUST 31, 632)

Arab ruler Abu Bakr: 3 years
Bishop of Jerusalem Modestus: 2 years
6123. 623. 22. 1. 23. 1. 13.

In this year the Persians rose up against each other in civil war.

In the same year the king of the Indians sent Herakleios congratulatory gifts for his victory over the Persians: pearls and a number of precious stones.

Muhammad was already dead, but had appointed four emirs to attack Christians of Arab race. As they wanted to attack the Arabs on the day of their own sacrifice to idols, they came to a country called Moukheon, in which place was the vicar[91] Theodore. When the vicar learned this from his servant Koutabas, who was a man of Quraysh, he assembled all the desert guards. He determined from the Saracen the day and hour on which the emirs intended to attack, and attacked them at a place called Mothous. He killed three of them and most of their army, but one emir, Khalid (whom they call the sword of God[92]), got away.

Some of the nearby Arabs received a small subsidy from the Emperor for guarding the mouths of the desert.[93] At that time a eunuch came to distribute the soldiers' wages. The Arabs came to get their pay, as was customary, but the eunuch drove them away, saying, "The Emperor pays his soldiers with difficulty; with how much more to such 336 dogs as you?" The oppressed Arabs went to their fellow-tribesmen and showed them the route to the land of Gaza, which is the mouth of the desert for Mt. Sinai and is very rich.

91. Under Diocletian's reforms at the end of the third century, the Empire was divided into about a dozen dioceses, each of which was composed of several small provinces and administered by a vicar. These officials, between provincial governors and the great praetorian prefects in authority, were partially removed from the governmental hierarchy by Justinian I in the 530s.

92. Theophanes must have had some source ultimately derived from the Arabs to know this, for it was among them that Khalid ibn al-Walid bore this title, which was given him by Muhammad. Although he fought against the Muslims until 629, Khalid became one of their greatest marshals. He helped defeat the Arabs who tried to apostasize after Muhammad's death, and went on to conquer Syria and Palestine and aid in the attack on Persia.

93. That is, the mouths of the desert wadis or dry riverbeds (my thanks to S. Thomas Parker for this suggestion).

ANNUS MUNDI 6124 (SEPTEMBER 1, 632—AUGUST 31, 633)

A.D. 624
Roman Emperor Herakleios: 31 years: year 23
Arab ruler Abu Bakr: 3 years: year 2
Bishop of Constantinople Sergios: 29 years: year 24
Bishop of Jerusalem Modestus: 2 years: year 2
Bishop of Alexandria George: 14 years: year 14

In this year Abu Bakr sent out four generals who, as I said before, were shown the way by the Arabs—they took Hira and the whole land of Gaza. Sergios had just come from Palestinian Caesarea with a few soldiers; he engaged the Arabs in battle but was the first one killed. So were three hundred of his soldiers. The Arabs withdrew after a decisive victory, having taken many prisoners and much booty.

In the same year there was an earthquake in Palestine. Also, a sign —known as an "apparition"—appeared in the southern sky. It was sword-shaped, and remained for thirty days, stretching from south to north and predicting the Arab conquest.

ANNUS MUNDI 6125 (SEPTEMBER 1, 633–AUGUST 31, 634)

Bishop of Jerusalem Sophronios: 3 years
Bishop of Alexandria Cyrus: 10 years
24. 3. 25. 1. 1.

337

In this year Abu Bakr died; he had been caliph for two and a half years. Umar took over the rule. He dispatched an army against Arabia,[94] which took Bostra, among other cities, and advanced as far as Gabitha. Herakleios' brother Theodore engaged it but was defeated; he went to the Emperor at Edessa. The Emperor appointed another general, Baanes by name, and dispatched the sakellarios Theodore with a Roman force against the Arabs. Theodore met a host of Saracens near Emesa; he killed some of them (including their emir) and drove the rest all the way to Damascus. He camped there, by the Bardanesios River. But Herakleios had despaired and abandoned Syria; he took the precious wood from Jerusalem and went off to Constantinople. He transferred Baanes and the sakellarios Theodore (who had an army of 40,000 men) from Damascus to Emesa; they chased the Arabs from Emesa to Damascus.

94. This refers only to the Byzantine province of Arabia, which is more or less contiguous with modern Jordan and southern Syria.

ANNUS MUNDI 6126 (SEPTEMBER 1, 634—AUGUST 31, 635)

A.D. 626
Roman Emperor Herakleios: 31 years: year 25
Arab ruler Umar: 12 years: year 1
Bishop of Constantinople Sergios: 29 years: year 26
Bishop of Jerusalem Sophronios: 3 years: year 2
Bishop of Alexandria Cyrus: 10 years: year 2

In this year a countless host of Saracens left Arabia behind and campaigned in the vicinity of Damascus. When Baanes learned this he sent a message to the imperial sakellarios Theodore so he and his army could come help Baanes because of the Arabs' numbers. The sakellarios came to Baanes; they departed from Emesa and met the Arabs. On the first day of the engagement (it was the third day of the week, and the twenty-third of Lōos[95]) the sakellarios' troops were defeated.

Baanes' men rebelled and chose him Emperor, renouncing Herakleios. Then the sakellarios' troops withdrew; the Saracens found an opportunity to join battle. Since the south wind was blowing against the Romans, they were unable to face their foes because of the dust, and were defeated. They leaped into the Yarmuk River where it is narrow, and were destroyed there: both generals had had 40,000 men.

Upon their decisive victory, the Saracens went to Damascus; they took it and the land of Phoenicia. They settled there and campaigned against Egypt. When Cyrus the bishop of Alexandria learned this he aided their onslaught. But he was afraid of their greed, and so made treaties which promised that Egypt would provide them 120,000 denarii per year and would send them gold up to that amount. While he furnished this for three years, Egypt had no share in destruction. But because Cyrus was giving the Saracens Egypt's gold, he was denounced to the Emperor. Angry, Herakleios sent a message recalling him, and dispatched Manuel (an Armenian in race) as Augustal prefect.

When a year had gone by, the Saracen tax collectors came to get their gold. Manuel drove them off unsuccessful, saying, "I am not weaponless Cyrus, to give you taxes; rather, I am armed." After the tax collectors were gone, the Saracens assailed Egypt. They attacked Manuel and drove him away, though he and a few men held out at Alexandria. From that time on the Saracens levied tribute on Egypt.

When he heard what had happened, Herakleios sent Cyrus back to Egypt to persuade the Arabs to withdraw on the terms of the first agreement. When Cyrus reached the Saracens' camp he excused his breaking of the agreement on the grounds that it had not been his

338

95. August 23.

339 fault, and said that if they wanted he would confirm the former agreement with oaths. The Saracens were not persuaded by these arguments. They asked the bishop, "Could you gulp down that huge pillar?" He said, "That is impossible." And they said, "Nor is it still possible for us to withdraw from Egypt."

ANNUS MUNDI 6127 (SEPTEMBER 1, 635–AUGUST 31, 636)

A.D. 627
Roman Emperor Herakleios: 31 years: year 26
Arab ruler Umar: 12 years: year 2
Bishop of Constantinople Sergios: 29 years: year 27
Bishop of Jerusalem Sophronios: 3 years: year 3
Bishop of Alexandria Cyrus: 10 years: year 3

In this year Umar campaigned against Palestine; after he had besieged the holy city for two years' time he took it on terms. For Sophronios, the chief prelate of Jerusalem, negotiated a treaty for the security of all Palestine. Umar entered the holy city clad in a filthy camel-hair garment. When Sophronios saw him, he said, "In truth, this is the abomination of the desolation established in the holy place, which Daniel the prophet spoke of."[96] With many tears, the champion of piety bitterly lamented over the Christian people. While Umar was in Jerusalem, the patriarch asked him to accept a muslin garment to wear, but he would not let himself wear it. Sophronios barely persuaded him to do so until his own cloak was washed — then Umar gave it back to him once more and wore his own. In this year Sophronios died; he had been an ornament to the church of Jerusalem by his words and actions, and had struggled against the wicked doctrine of Herakleios and his monothelites Sergios and Pyrrhos.

In this year Umar loosed into Syria Iad, who subjected it all to the Saracens.

340 ## ANNUS MUNDI 6128 (SEPTEMBER 1, 636—AUGUST 31, 637)
27. 3. 28. 4.[97]

In this year John (whose surname was Kataias) the governor of Osrhoene came to Iad at Chalcis. He arranged to give Iad 100,000 nomismata per year not to cross the Euphrates either in peace or war until the Roman had given up as much gold as he could. On these

96. Daniel 9:27, 11:31, 12:11; cf. Matthew 24:15, 1 Maccabees 1:54, 6:7.
97. Theophanes now lacks information concerning the succession of the bishops of Jerusalem.

terms John went back to Edessa, raised the annual tribute, and sent it to Iad. When Herakleios heard this he judged John culpable, as he had done it without imperial authorization. He recalled him and condemned him to exile, in his place dispatching a general, Ptolemaios.

ANNUS MUNDI 6129 (SEPTEMBER 1, 637—AUGUST 31, 638)
28. 4. 29. 5.

In this year the Arabs took Antioch. Umar dispatched Muawiyah as general and emir of all land under the Arabs, from Egypt to the Euphrates.

ANNUS MUNDI 6130 (SEPTEMBER 1, 638—AUGUST 31, 639)

A.D. **630**
Roman Emperor Herakleios: 31 years: year 29
Arab ruler Umar: 12 years: year 5
Bishop of Constantinople Pyrrhos: 3 years: year 1
Bishop of Alexandria Cyrus: 10 years: year 6

In this year Iad crossed the Euphrates with his whole army. When he reached Edessa, the Edessans opened their city and gained a treaty for their land, their general, and the Romans with him. The Arabs went to Constantia; after besieging it, they took it in battle and killed three hundred Romans. From there they went to Daras, which they took in battle, killing many in it. Thus Iad conquered all of Mesopotamia.

341 ANNUS MUNDI 6131 (SEPTEMBER 1, 639—AUGUST 31, 640)
30. 6. 2. 7.

In this year the Arabs attacked Persia and came into conflict with the Persians. By their victory they overpowered and subjected all the Persians. The Persian king Hormisdas fled to the interior, abandoning his palaces. The Saracens captured all the royal gear and Khosroes' daughters, who were brought to Umar.

In the same year Umar ordered his entire domain registered: there was a census of men, flocks, and agricultural products.

ANNUS MUNDI 6132 (SEPTEMBER 1, 640–AUGUST 31, 641)
31. 7. 3. 8.

In this year—the fourteenth indiction—the Emperor Herakleios died of dropsy in March, after ruling for thirty years and ten months.

After him, his son Constantine was Emperor for four months. He died when his stepmother Martina and the patriarch Pyrrhos poisoned him. Then Martina's son Heraklonas ruled along with his mother.

ANNUS MUNDI 6133 (SEPTEMBER 1, 641—AUGUST 31, 642)

Roman Emperor Heraklonas: 6 months
Bishop of Constantinople Paul: 12 years
1. 8. 1. 9.

In this year Muawiyah took Palestinian Caesarea after a seven-year siege; he killed 7,000 Romans there.

In this year the senate ousted Heraklonas, his mother Martina, and Valentinus. They cut out Martina's tongue, slit Heraklonas' nose, and exiled them, elevating to the throne Constantine's son Constans, who ruled for twenty-seven years. After Pyrrhos was expelled from the episcopacy, Paul (a priest and church administrator) was chosen patriarch of Constantinople in October of the fifteenth indiction. He was bishop for twelve years.

ANNUS MUNDI 6134 (SEPTEMBER 1, 642—AUGUST 31, 643)

A.D. 634
Roman Emperor Constans: 27 years: year 1
Arab ruler Umar: 12 years: year 9
Bishop of Constantinople Paul: 12 years: year 2
Bishop of Alexandria Cyrus: 10 years: year 10

In this year Constans, who had become Emperor, spoke to the senate: "After my father Constantine was born, he was Emperor with his own father (my grandfather) Herakleios for a long time during Herakleios' life, but after him for a very short while, for the envy of his stepmother Martina ended his high hopes and his life. She did this for the sake of Heraklonas, who was her illegitimate son by Herakleios.[98] It was mostly your decision which expelled her and her son from the imperial power, and your great dignity knows it well. Therefore I call on you to be advisors and judges for the common welfare of our subjects." After he spoke thus, he dismissed the senate, honoring it with numerous gifts.

98. See note 40 above. If the marriage of Herakleios and Martina was incestuous, it was therefore invalid, and the issue from it illegitimate.

41

ANNUS MUNDI 6135 (SEPTEMBER 1, 643—AUGUST 31, 644)

2. 10. 3. 11 [sic].

In this year Umar began to build a temple in Jerusalem; the building would not stand, but fell down. When he asked why, the Jews told him the reason: "If you do not tear down the cross on top of the church on the Mount of Olives, your building will not stay up." Therefore the cross there was torn down, and thus their building arose. For this reason the Christ-haters tore down many crosses.

343 ## ANNUS MUNDI 6136 (SEPTEMBER 1, 644—AUGUST 31, 645)

Bishop of Alexandria Peter: 10 years
3. 11. 4. 1.

In this year Valentinian the patrician rebelled against Constans. The Emperor dispatched a man who killed him and brought his army back to its allegiance.

There was an eclipse of the sun on Saturday the fifth of Dios at the ninth hour.[99]

ANNUS MUNDI 6137 (SEPTEMBER 1, 645—AUGUST 31, 646)

4. 12. 5. 2.

In this year Umar, the ruler of the Saracens, was assassinated by a Persian convert on the fifth of Dios. He found Umar worshiping and stabbed him in the belly with his sword, taking his life in this way after he had been caliph for twelve years. After Umar his relative Uthman the son of Affan came to power.

ANNUS MUNDI 6138 (SEPTEMBER 1, 646—AUGUST 31, 647)

Arab ruler Uthman: 10 years
5. 1. 6. 3.

In this year the Africans rebelled under their patrician Gregory.

---

99. November 5, 644, at about three P.M.—for Theophanes' reports on eclipses, see especially Robert R. Newton, *Medieval Chronicles and the Rotation of the Earth* (Baltimore, 1972), 531–532, 534–536, 542–547.

ANNUS MUNDI 6139 (SEPTEMBER 1, 647—AUGUST 31, 648)

A.D. **639**
Roman Emperor Constans: 27 years: year 6
Arab ruler Uthman: 10 years: year 2
Bishop of Constantinople Paul: 12 years: year 7
Bishop of Alexandria Peter: 10 years: year 4

In this year there was a violent windstorm, which uprooted many plants and pulled up huge trees by the roots.

In this year the Saracens attacked Africa; they engaged and routed the rebel Gregory, slew his men, and drove him from Africa. After levying tribute on the Africans, they withdrew.

ANNUS MUNDI 6140 (SEPTEMBER 1, 648—AUGUST 31, 649)

7. 3. 8. 5.

In this year Muawiyah attacked Cyprus with 1,700 ships. He took and devastated Constantia and the whole island. When he heard the cubicularius[100] Kakorizos was moving against him with a large Roman force, he sailed across to Arados.[101] He brought his naval expedition to anchor at Castellus, a small town on an island, and tried to take it with all sorts of engines. When he was unable to do so, he sent a bishop named Thomarikhos to the people of Castellus to terrify them into handing over their city and making a treaty with him, and also into leaving the island. When the bishop arrived they seized him as soon as he came in, and did not yield to Muawiyah. Since the siege of Arados was useless, Muawiyah retreated to Damascus when winter came.

344

ANNUS MUNDI 6141 (SEPTEMBER 1, 649—AUGUST 31, 650)

8. 4. 9. 6.

In this year Muawiyah mustered his forces and began a great campaign against Arados. He took it on his agreement to settle its inhabitants wherever they wished. He burned the town, destroyed its walls, and left its island uninhabited up to the present.

In the same year Martin the pope convened a synod at Rome against the monothelites.

100. The cubicularius was the imperial chamberlain, and the holder of the office was almost always a eunuch; eunuchs were trusted to be close to the Emperors and their families because they were themselves ineligible for the throne. Because of the intimate relationship the cubicularii had with their imperial masters, they were often of great influence and power.
101. Arados is a coastal city of Phoenicia.

ANNUS MUNDI 6142 (SEPTEMBER 1, 650—AUGUST 31, 651)

9. 5. 10. 7.

In this year the commander Busr and his Arabs campaigned against Isauria. Besides killing many people, he took prisoners, returning with 5,000 men in bonds. The Emperor sent Prokopios to Muawiyah to ask for peace. There was peace for two years; at Damascus Muawiyah received as a hostage Gregory the son of Theodore.

ANNUS MUNDI 6143 (SEPTEMBER 1, 651—AUGUST 31, 652)

10. 6. 11. 8.

In this year Pasagnathes the patrician of the Armenians rebelled against the Emperor. He made agreements with Muawiyah and even gave him his own son. When the Emperor heard this he advanced as far as Kappadokian Caesarea but, losing hope for Armenia, returned.

ANNUS MUNDI 6144 (SEPTEMBER 1, 652—AUGUST 31, 653)

A.D. 644
Roman Emperor Constans: 27 years: year 11
Arab ruler Uthman: 10 years: year 7
Bishop of Constantinople Paul: 12 years: year 12
Bishop of Alexandria Peter: 10 years: year 9

345 In this year Herakleios' nephew Gregory died at Heliopolis. His body was embalmed in myrrh and brought to Constantinople.

In the same year dust came down from the sky, and terror descended on mankind.

ANNUS MUNDI 6145 (SEPTEMBER 1, 653—AUGUST 31, 654)

Bishop of Constantinople Peter: 12 years (Paul died and Pyrrhos was again restored for four months and twenty-three days)
12. 8. 1. 10.

In this year Muawiyah over ran Rhodes and destroyed the Colossus of Rhodes 1,370 years after its erection.[102] A Jewish merchant from Edessa bought it and carried off its bronze on nine hundred camels.

In the same year the Arab general Habib attacked and ravaged Armenia. Meeting the Roman general Maurianos, he chased him all the way to the Caucasus Mountains.

102. This is incorrect; the Colossus of Rhodes was built in 280 B.C., 934 years before Muawiyah's arrival.

ANNUS MUNDI 6146 (SEPTEMBER 1, 654—AUGUST 31, 655)

13. 9. 2.[103]

In this year Muawiyah ordered a great force of ships readied for an expedition against Constantinople. All this preparation took place in Phoenician Tripolis. Two Christ-loving brothers—the sons of Bucinator—who were staying in Tripolis noticed this. Overcome by divine zeal, they hurried to the city's prison (which held a host of Roman prisoners), broke open its gates, and rushed against the city's emir. They killed him and his men, burned all their gear, and sailed to Romania. However, they did not stop the preparation by their action; Muawiyah was campaigning against Kappadokian Caesarea, but he appointed Abu 'l-Awar commander of the naval expedition.

Abu 'l-Awar came to Phoenix in Lykia, where he fought a sea-battle against the Emperor Constans and his Roman expeditionary force. On the night before the Emperor was going to fight at sea, he saw himself at Thessalonike in a dream. When he awoke he told this to a man who could interpret dreams. He said, "Emperor, would that you had not been asleep and had not seen this dream! For your being in Thessalonike means, 'Give the win to someone else.'[104] That is, victory inclines toward your enemy."

Although he had not made any preparations for the naval engagement, the Emperor ordered the Roman fleet into combat. When the two forces joined battle, the Romans were defeated, and the sea was mixed with Roman blood. The Emperor clothed someone else in his garments. Then one of Bucinator's sons leaped onto the imperial ship; he picked up the Emperor and hurled him onto another vessel, unexpectedly saving him. He himself stayed on the imperial ship; the noble fellow gave up his life for the Emperor. After he had killed many, the enemy slew him and the man wearing the imperial raiment. But the Emperor, who had been put to flight like this, was saved. He abandoned all his men and sailed away to Constantinople.

ANNUS MUNDI 6147 (SEPTEMBER 1, 655—AUGUST 31, 656)

14. 10. 3.

In this year the Arab ruler Uthman was assassinated by the inhabitants of Medina. He had been caliph for ten years. There was civil strife among the Arabs: those in the Arabian desert wanted Ali the nephew

103. Theophanes now loses information about the bishops of Alexandria and their succession.
104. This is a pun in the Greek, unfortunately altogether untranslatable.

of Ali, who was Muhammad's son-in-law, while those in Syria and Egypt favored Muawiyah, who won and ruled for twenty-four years.

ANNUS MUNDI 6148 (SEPTEMBER 1, 656—AUGUST 31, 657)

Arab ruler Muawiyah: 24 years
15. 1. 4.

347   In this year Muawiyah campaigned against Ali. Both assembled in the interior of Barbalissos: at Caesarium near the Euphrates. Muawiyah's men, who were stronger, controlled the water supply, and Ali's men deserted as they grew thirsty. Muawiyah had not wanted to fight, but to gain the victory without effort.

ANNUS MUNDI 6149 (SEPTEMBER 1, 657—AUGUST 31, 658)

16. 2. 5.

In this year the Emperor campaigned against Sklavinia;[105] he took many prisoners and brought many people under his control.

Also in the same year occurred the matter of the holy Maximus and his pupils: they were struggling for the true faith against monotheletism. Constans could not shift them to his evil belief. He cut out the saint's tongue, which was wise in God's ways, and cut off his right hand, since Maximus (along with his pupils the Anastasioi) had written a great deal in opposition to the Emperor's impiety. They wrote the exact truth, as those who love learning know.

ANNUS MUNDI 6150 (SEPTEMBER 1, 658—AUGUST 31, 659)

17. 3. 6.

In this year an arrangement was made between the Romans and Arabs. Because of disorder, Muawiyah sent an embassy so the Arabs could pay the Romans 1,000 nomismata, a horse, and a slave per day.

Also in this year—the second indiction—there was a great earthquake and collapse in Palestine and Syria in the month of Daisios.[106]

In the same year the holy pope of Rome, Martin, was exiled. He had struggled nobly for the truth and became a confessor, dying in eastern regions.

105. Those areas of the Balkans overrun by the Slavs since the death of Maurice in 602, and especially since the failure of the Avar-Persian siege of Constantinople in 626, a failure which fatally weakened the Slavs' Avar overlords.

106. June.

ANNUS MUNDI 6151 (SEPTEMBER 1, 659—AUGUST 31, 660)

18. 4. 7.

In this year Constans killed his brother Theodore.

While the Arabs were at Sapphis Ali the Persian was assassinated. Muawiyah became sole ruler; he lived at Damascus in royal style and stored up his monetary treasures there.

ANNUS MUNDI 6152 (SEPTEMBER 1, 660—AUGUST 31, 661)

19. 5. 8.

In this year an Arab heresy, that of the Kharijites,[107] appeared. Muawiyah overpowered them, humbling the inhabitants of Persia but favoring those of Syria. He called the ones Isamitai and the others Herakitai. He gave the Isamitai a donative of two hundred nomismata, but gave the Herakitai only thirty nomismata.

ANNUS MUNDI 6153 (SEPTEMBER 1, 661—AUGUST 31, 662)

20. 6. 9.

In this year the Emperor abandoned Constantinople and moved to Sicilian Syracuse; he wanted to transfer the capital to Rome. He sent a messenger to fetch his wife and three sons Constantine, Herakleios, and Tiberius, but the Byzantines would not let them go.

ANNUS MUNDI 6154 (SEPTEMBER 1, 662—AUGUST 31, 663)

21. 7. 10.

In this year the Arabs campaigned against Romania, taking many prisoners and devastating many places.

ANNUS MUNDI 6155 (SEPTEMBER 1, 663—AUGUST 31, 664)

22. 8. 11.

In this year part of Sicily was captured and, at their wish, its inhabitants were settled at Damascus.

107. The Kharijites are Muslim extremists. They insisted it was the duty of all Muslims at all times to inspire men to do good and prevent them from doing evil, even at the cost of life itself. They were not prepared under any conditions to let circumstances alter cases. The Kharijites saw those less extreme than themselves as no true Muslims, and physically attacked them. The sect survives to this day, but as a tiny minority in Islam.

ANNUS MUNDI 6156 (SEPTEMBER 1, 664—AUGUST 31, 665)

23. 9. 12.

In this year there was a heresy concerning fasting.

Also, Abd ar-Rahman the son of Khalid attacked Romania; he wintered there after devastating many towns. The Sklavinoi went over to him, and 5,000 went down to Syria with him. They were settled in the village of Seleukobolos near Apamea.

ANNUS MUNDI 6157 (SEPTEMBER 1, 665—AUGUST 31, 666)

Bishop of Constantinople Thomas: 3 years
24. 10. 1.

In this year Busr attacked Romania.

Also, Thomarikhos the bishop of Apamea died, and the bishop of Emesa was burned alive.

ANNUS MUNDI 6158 (SEPTEMBER 1, 666—AUGUST 31, 667)

25. 11. 2.

In this year Busr again attacked Romania, devastating the territory of Hexapolis. Fudhala wintered there.

ANNUS MUNDI 6159 (SEPTEMBER 1, 667—AUGUST 31, 668)

26. 12. 3.

In this year the general of the Armeniacs Saborios (who was of Persian race) rebelled against the Emperor Constans. He sent his general Sergios to Muawiyah, promising to subject Romania to him if he would ally with Saborios against the Emperor. When the Emperor's son Constantine[108] learned of this, he sent Andrew the cubicularius to Muawiyah with gifts so he would not cooperate with the rebel.

When Andrew reached Damascus he found Sergios had got there first, but Muawiyah was pretending to be sympathetic to the Emperor. Sergios was sitting in front of Muawiyah when Andrew came in, and stood up when he saw Andrew.

Muawiyah reproached him: "What are you afraid of?" Sergios answered that he had done this out of force of habit. Muawiyah turned and asked Andrew, "What do you want?"

He answered, "That you give aid against the rebel."

349

108. Constantine IV administered affairs at Constantinople while his father Constans II was in the west.

"You are both enemies," said Muawiyah. "I will help him who gives me most."

Andrew told him, "You should not doubt, Caliph, that it is better for you to get a little from the Emperor than a great deal from a rebel. Do this after all, as you are friendly." Andrew was silent after this.

Muawiyah said, "I will think this over," and ordered both of them to go away. He called Sergios in private and told him, "You should not bow to Andrew any more, or else you will accomplish nothing."

On the next day Sergios got there before Andrew and sat in front of Muawiyah. When Andrew came in, Sergios did not stand as he had the day before. Andrew stared at him, terribly cursing and threatening him. He said, "If I live, I promise to show you who I am!"

Sergios said, "I will not rise for you, for you are neither a man nor a woman."

Muawiyah stopped them both, then said to Andrew, "Do you agree to give as much as Sergios?"

"How much is that?" Andrew asked.

"He will furnish the Arabs the income from the public revenues," Muawiyah said.

Andrew said, "Good heavens, Muawiyah, you advise me to give you the body and keep its shadow. As you please; line up with Sergios, for I will not do this. Besides, for God's sake we will neglect you and take refuge and put our hopes in Him, since He is more able than you to protect the Romans." After he had said this, he told Muawiyah, "Take care!"

He went from Damascus to Melitene because the rebel was in that area; Sergios would also be traveling there. When he came to Arabissos he met the officer who guarded the mountain passes, for that man had not gone over to the rebel. He ordered him to watch carefully for Sergios' return so he could bring Sergios to Andrew. Once he had made sure about Sergios, Andrew went to Amnesia and told the Emperor what had been done.

Sergios had entered into agreements with Muawiyah over what seemed good; as allies for Saborios he had gained the Arab general Fudhala and barbarian aid. Sergios traveled ahead to Fudhala, then happily went off to Saborios. But in the mountain passes he encountered Andrew's troops, who captured him and brought him, bound, to Andrew. When he saw Andrew, Sergios threw himself at his feet and begged him to have mercy.

Said Andrew to him, "You are Sergios, who were so proud of your genitals in front of Muawiyah, and you called me effeminate. Well! Now your genitals are no good to you at all, and will even be your death." He ordered Sergios castrated, then hung him on a stake.

When Constantine heard that Fudhala had come to ally with Sa-

49

borios, he dispatched a Roman force under the patrician Nikephoros to oppose the rebel. Saborios was in Adrianople readying himself for battle, as he had learned Nikephoros was approaching. It happened that one day he left the city on horseback, as was his wont. He whipped his horse while near the gate. Refusing to obey the reins, it dashed his head against the gate and evilly put an end to his life. Thus God gave the Emperor victory.

Fudhala learned everything when he reached Hexapolis, and was at a loss. He sent Muawiyah a message asking for help because the Romans were at peace. Muawiyah sent his son Yezid to him at the head of a host of barbarians. The two men advanced to Chalcedon, taking many prisoners; they captured Phrygian Amorion. Leaving it a garrison of 5,000 armed men, they returned to Syria.

351

After winter came, the Emperor dispatched the same cubicularius Andrew, who arrived on a night of heavy snow. His men used stakes to climb up onto the wall, and got into Amorion. They killed all 5,000 Arabs, and not one of them was left.

In the same winter there was a flood at Edessa, and many perished. Also, a sign appeared in the sky.

ANNUS MUNDI 6160 (SEPTEMBER 1, 668—AUGUST 31, 669)

Bishop of Constantinople John: 6 years.
6160. 660. 27. 13. 1.

In this year the Emperor Constans was assassinated in Sicily at the Syracusan bath-house called Daphne. This was the reason: the Byzantines had hated him after he killed his brother Theodore, and even more after he brought the holy pope of Rome, Martin, to Constantinople and exiled him to the Cherson. He had also cut out the tongue and cut off the hand of the brilliant Maximus the confessor, and had condemned many of the orthodox to torture, exile, and confiscation because they would not follow his heresy. He had also given over to torture and exile the two Anastasioi, who were disciples of Maximus the confessor and martyr. For these reasons, then, he was mightily hated by everyone.

He grew fearful and wanted to transfer the capital to Rome, for which he even wanted the Empress and his three sons to depart from Constantinople. However, Andrew the cubicularius and Theodore of Koloneia foiled his plan. He spent six years in Sicily.[109]

As he entered the aforementioned bath-house, his servant (a certain Andrew son of Troilos) went in with him. As the Emperor began

---

109. He had fought the Lombards in Italy, and was now directing Byzantine operations against the Arabs attacking Carthage and the surviving Roman possessions in North Africa.

352 to wash himself, Andrew picked up the soap dish, hit him over the head, and ran away at once. After the Emperor had been in the bath-house for some time, the men outside rushed in to find him dead. Once they had buried him, they named Mizizios—an Armenian—Emperor, for he was very handsome and in the full bloom of youth.

When Constantine heard of his father's death he overran Sicily with a huge naval expedition. He overcame Mizizios and executed him along with his father's murderers. Once he had stabilized the western lands, he hurried back to Constantinople and became Roman Emperor, with his brothers Tiberius and Herakleios as co-Emperors.[110]

ANNUS MUNDI 6161 (SEPTEMBER 1, 669—AUGUST 31, 670)

Roman Emperor Constantine: 17 years
1. 14. 2.

In this year Constantine became Emperor (with his brothers).

The Saracens attacked Africa and, as they say, took 80,000 prisoners.

The troops of the Anatolic theme[111] came to Chrysopolis, saying, "We believe in a Trinity: let us crown the three."[112] Constantine grew alarmed, for he alone had been crowned: his brothers had no rank at all. He sent out the patrician Theodore of Koloneia, who harangued the men and put them to flight in this way: he took their leaders into the city so they could take counsel with the senate and do what they decided. But the Emperor immediately hanged some of them at Sykai;[113] seeing this, the Anatolic troops were dishonored, and went back to their own land in dismay. The Emperor slit his brothers' noses.

353 ANNUS MUNDI 6162 (SEPTEMBER 1, 670—AUGUST 31, 671)

A.D. **662**
Roman Emperor Constantine: 17 years: year 2
Arab ruler Muawiyah: 24 years: year 15
Bishop of Constantinople John: 6 years: year 3

In this year there was a harsh winter, and many men and beasts were endangered. Fudhala wintered at Kyzikos.

110. All three sons of Constans II had been crowned before he left for the west.
111. The Anatolic theme extended across central Asia Minor from the Aegean coast to the Taurus mountains.
112. Once Constans II was dead, Constantine IV gathered all power into his own hands; his brothers Tiberius and Herakleios had no authority whatever.
113. A suburb of Constantinople on the European shore, just across the Golden Horn from the city; it was also known as Galata.

ANNUS MUNDI 6163 (SEPTEMBER 1, 671—AUGUST 31, 672)

3. 16. 4.

In this year Busr attacked, took many prisoners, and withdrew.

ANNUS MUNDI 6164 (SEPTEMBER 1, 672—AUGUST 31, 673)

4. 17. 5.

In this year in March (or Dystros) a rainbow appeared in the sky, and all mankind shuddered. Everyone said it was the end of the world.

In this year the deniers of Christ readied a great expedition. They sailed to and wintered in Kilikia; Muhammad son of Abd Allah was at Smyrna, and Qais in Kilikia and Lykia. Muawiyah also sent the emir Khalid with yet another expedition to help them. Also, there was a plague in Egypt.

When Constantine learned of the movement of God's enemies against Constantinople, he prepared huge two-storied warships equipped with Greek fire[114] and siphon-carrying warships,[115] ordering them to anchor in the Proklianesian harbor of the Caesarium.[116]

ANNUS MUNDI 6165 (SEPTEMBER 1, 673—AUGUST 31, 674)

5. 18. 6.

In this year the expedition of the enemies of God anchored in Thracian territory from the heights of Hebdomon known as Magnaura on the west to the cape of Kyklobion on the east.[117] All day long from dawn to dusk there was combat from the outworks of the Golden Gate[118] to Kyklobion; both sides were thrusting and counterthrusting. They continued these struggles from April to September.

354

The Arabs retreated to Kyzikos, which they had taken, to winter there. In spring they set out in the same way to meet the Christians in sea-battle. They did the same thing for seven years,[119] but with the aid

114. Invented about this time, Greek fire was so efficiently kept a state secret by the Byzantines that its precise composition still causes scholarly debate. It was definitely a flammable liquid which would burn on the surface of the sea; a modern analog might be napalm.

115. The "siphon" was a metal tube through which Greek fire was discharged.

116. A small harbor located just east of the greatest of Constantinople's harbors, that of Eleutherios (also known as that of Theodosios).

117. Hebdomon and Kyklobion are suburbs on the European shore of the Propontis. Kyklobion is about a mile southwest of the walls of Constantinople; for Hebdomon, see above, note 31.

118. The Golden Gate is the most southerly gate of the land wall of Constantinople, and that gate nearest Kyklobion.

119. This counts from the first preparation of the Arabs' force, *annus mundi* 6164 (A.D. 672/673). The siege of Constantinople proper lasted from 674 to 678.

of God and His Mother they were disgraced, expending a host of warlike men. They retreated in great distress, with severe wounds inflicted on themselves.

As their expedition was going away after God had ruined it, it was overtaken by a tempestuous winter storm near Syllaion. It was shivered to atoms and completely destroyed. A second brother, Sufyan the son of Auf, joined battle with a Roman force under Florus, Petronas, and Kyprianos; 30,000 Arabs were killed.

At that time Kallinikos, an artificer from Heliopolis, fled to the Romans. He had devised a sea fire which ignited the Arab ships and burned them with all hands. Thus it was that the Romans returned with victory and discovered the sea fire.

ANNUS MUNDI 6166 (SEPTEMBER 1, 674—AUGUST 31, 675)

Bishop of Constantinople Constantine: 2 years: year 1
6. 19. 1.

In this year Abd Allah (the son of Qais) and Fudhala wintered in Crete.

ANNUS MUNDI 6167 (SEPTEMBER 1, 675—AUGUST 31, 676)

7. 20. 2.

In this year a sign was seen in the sky on a sabbath day.

ANNUS MUNDI 6168 (SEPTEMBER 1, 676—AUGUST 31, 677)

Bishop of Constantinople Theodore: 2 years
8. 21. 1.

In this year there was a great locust plague in Syria and Mesopotamia.

355 ## ANNUS MUNDI 6169 (SEPTEMBER 1, 677—AUGUST 31, 678)

A.D. 669
Roman Emperor Constantine: 17 years: year 9
Arab ruler Muawiyah: 24 years: year 22
Bishop of Constantinople Theodore: 2 years: year 2

In this year the Mardaites invaded Lebanon and conquered it from Mt. Mauros to the holy city, overpowering its most important centers. Many slaves, prisoners, and natives fled to them, so that in a little while there were many thousands of them. When Muawiyah and his advisers learned this they were quite discomfited, as they reckoned that the Roman Empire was watched over by God.[120] Muawiyah sent ambassadors to the autokrator Constantine asking for peace, and even promised to pay the Emperor a yearly tribute.

When the Emperor had received these envoys and heard their request, he sent the patrician John (surnamed Pitzigaudis) back to Syria with them, as he had spent a long time in government and was highly experienced and prudent. His purpose was to negotiate with the Arabs in a suitable fashion and to agree on peace terms. Muawiyah, who had convened an assembly of his emirs and members of the tribe of Quraysh, received him with great honor when he arrived in Syria.

After long peace talks between them, it was agreed by each of the two that there should be a written peace accord with an oath. The terms were for annual tribute, with the Romans being furnished 3,000 nomismata, fifty prisoners, and fifty high-bred horses by the Agarenes. These terms, agreed upon by both sides, created a firm peace between Romans and Arabs for thirty years. After they had made the two general written treaties (and the oaths) and had given copies to each other, this highly acclaimed man (who has been mentioned in many contexts) returned to the Emperor—with many gifts as well.

356

When they learned of his, the inhabitants of the western regions —the Avar Khagan, the kings, rulers, and governors there, and the most eminent members of the western peoples—sent envoys with gifts to the Emperor, asking for confirmation of his peaceful love for them. He yielded to their request and acknowledged that he was quite definitely at peace with them. There was absolute freedom from care in both east and west.

ANNUS MUNDI 6170 (SEPTEMBER 1, 678—AUGUST 31, 679)

Bishop of Constantinople George: 6 years
6170. 670. 10. 23. 1.

In this year there was a severe earthquake in Mesopotamia. In it, the pulpit and the dome of the church at Edessa fell. Because of the Christians' zealous exertions, Muawiyah rebuilt it.

---

120. Besides being bandits and raiders, the Mardaites were also Christians.

ANNUS MUNDI 6171 (SEPTEMBER 1, 679—AUGUST 31, 680)

11. 24. 2.

In this year—the first indiction—Muawiyah the chief counselor of the Saracens died on the sixth of Artemisios.[121] He had been a general for twenty years, then caliph for twenty-four. His son Yezid succeeded him.

Also, the Bulgarian people attacked Thrace at this time. It is necessary to discuss the ancient history of the Onogondur Bulgars and the Kotrigurs. In the area on the north side of the Black Sea (in the Sea of Azov) there enters a great river called the Atel, which descends from the Ocean through the land of the Sarmatians. The Don leads into it; the Don itself springs from the Iberian gates in the Caucasus mountains. From the mingling of the Don and the Atel (which branches before the Sea of Azov) comes the Kouphis River,[122] which delivers itself up at the end of the Black Sea near Nekropela at the cape known as the Ram's Face. Sea and river are one and the same beyond the Sea of Azov, which leads into the Black Sea through the territory of the Cimmerian Bosporos.[123] The mourzoulin and other fish like it are caught in this river.

In the area east of the lake lie Phanagouria and the Hebrews living there.[124] The ancient Great Bulgaria stretches from the Sea of Azov along the Kouphis River, where the xyston, a Bulgarian fish, is caught. The Kotrigurs, who are related to the Bulgars, also live there.

During the period when Constantine was in the west, Krobatos, the lord of Bulgaria and the Kotrigurs, died. He left behind five sons, not at all imagining they would give up living by each other: for they were the masters of all they surveyed and were slaves to no other people. But a little while after his death these five sons separated from one another, along with the folk subject to each of them.

The first son, called Batbaian, kept the injunction of his father and has remained in his ancestral lands until the present day. The second brother, called Kotragos, crossed the Don River and settled across

357

121. May 6.
122. A river north of the Danube, which flows into the Black Sea.
123. The region of the Crimea or Cherson (see above, note 81).
124. Phanagouria (the medieval Russian Tmutarakan and modern Taman) is near the eastern shore of the Strait of Kerch, which connects the Sea of Azov and the Black Sea. Mention of Hebrews in this Khazar-dominated area is particularly interesting, because later in the eighth century the Khazar nobility converted from paganism to Judaism. They may well have been trying to enjoy the benefits of a high religion without coming under the cultural influence either of Byzantium or the Arabs.

from the first. The fourth and fifth brothers crossed the river Ister (that is, the Danube). One came to the land of the Avars in Pannonia, was subjected by the Avar Khagan, and remained there with his forces; the other reached the five cities by Ravenna and came under the control of Christians.

358   Now the third brother, called Asparukh, crossed the Dnieper and the Dniester and reached the Oglos[125] (these rivers are north of the Danube), settling between them and the Danube. He thought the location secure and invincible from all sides, for it was marshy ahead and surrounded by rivers in other directions. It provided his people, who had been weakened by their division, relief from their enemies.

After the Bulgars had been divided into five parts and thus diminished, the great Khazar people came from the far interior of Berzilia in first Sarmatia and became the masters of the whole northern coast of the Black Sea. They made Batbaian, the first brother and ruler of first Bulgaria, their subject and have taken tribute from him[126] until the present.

The Emperor Constantine was galled to learn that a foul, unclean tribe was living between the Danube and the Oglos, and that it had sallied forth to ravage the land near the Danube (that is, the land which is now ruled by the Bulgars, but then was held by Christians). He ordered all the thematic armies to cross over into Thrace, equipped an expeditionary force, and moved against the Bulgars by land and sea, attempting to dislodge them by force. He marshalled his army on the land by the Oglos and the Danube, anchoring his ships at a nearby promontory.

When the Bulgars saw his battle-line's numbers and density, they despaired of their salvation. They took refuge in the fastness which has been mentioned and, for the first three or four days, did not dare go outside this stronghold of theirs. But when the Romans did not join battle because of the swamp, the disgusting tribe guessed their empty vanity, regained its strength, and grew more courageous.

359   Since the Emperor was suffering severely from gout, he had to withdraw to Mesembria for his usual baths with five warships and men friendly to him. He left behind his generals and army, ordering them to use their lances to drag the Bulgars out of their stronghold, and to attack them if they came out. If not, then his men were to besiege them and hold them in their defensive position. However, the cavalry spread

125. The Oglos (or, as it is sometimes read, the Onglos) may in fact not be a river north of the Danube. The other possibility is that it may be the wedge-shaped strip of land between the Pruth and Seret Rivers north of the Danube. If the latter interpretation is correct, the word is to be derived from the Latin *angulus:* "angle."

126. And, by extension, from the people he ruled.

it about that the Emperor had fled; they were overcome by fear and ran away themselves, though none pursued.

When the Bulgars saw this, they did pursue, putting many to the sword and wounding others. They chased them to the Danube, crossed it, and came to Varna near Odyssos and its hinterland. They saw that it was securely located: from behind because of the river Danube and from the front and sides because of the mountain passes and the Black Sea.

When the Bulgars became the masters of the seven tribes of Sklavinoi in the vicinity, they resettled the Sebereis from the mountain passes before Bergaba to the lands to the east, and the remainder of the seven tribes to the south and west up to the land of the Avars. Since the Bulgars were pagan at that time, they bore themselves arrogantly and began to assail and take cities and villages under the control of the Roman Empire. The Emperor had to make peace with them because of this, and agreed to pay them an annual tribute. This was the fault of the Romans' disgrace over their great defeats. Folk far and near were amazed to hear that the Emperor, who had subjected everyone to himself, had been beaten by this newly arrived loathsome tribe. But he believed this had happened to the Christians because of God's will, and gladly planned to make peace.

He abstained from all warlike activity until his death, as he was eager to be the one chosen to unite God's holy churches everywhere. They had been divided since the time of Herakleios and since that of Sergios and Pyrrhos of evil belief. They had unworthily held the throne of Constantinople and had promulgated the doctrine of the one will and one energy of our Lord, God, and Savior Jesus Christ. This most Christian Emperor, eager to overturn their evil doctrines, convened an ecumenical synod of two hundred eighty-nine bishops at Constantinople. It secured the doctrines which had previously been confirmed at the preceding five ecumenical councils,[127] and this holy and most exact

360

127. The first five ecumenical councils are as follows:

i. The first council of Nikaia, called by Constantine I in 325. This council ruled against the doctrines of Arius, who taught that Christ was of different, and lesser, substance than God the Father. The council declared God the Father and God the Son consubstantial *(homoousios)* with each other.

ii. The first council of Constantinople, summoned by Theodosios I in 381. It confirmed the acts of the council of Nikaia, thus exterminating Arianism within the Empire (though many of the German tribes, converted to Christianity while Arianism was favored during the mid-fourth century, remained of that faith). It also promoted the see of Constantinople, the new imperial capital, to patriarchal status, and raised it to second in ecclesiastical rank after Rome, elevating it above the sees of Alexandria and Antioch.

iii. The council of Ephesos, summoned by Theodosios II in 431. Nestorios, the patriarch of Constantinople (428–431), followed the theological sixth ecumenical synod voted to promulgate the pious doctrine of the two wills and energies. The pious Emperor Constantine and his pious prelates had convened this council.

ANNUS MUNDI 6172 (SEPTEMBER 1, 680—AUGUST 31, 681)

Arab ruler Yezid: 3 years
6172. 672. 12. 1. 3.

In this year the sixth holy ecumenical council of two hundred eighty-nine bishops and fathers was convened in Constantinople, in accordance with the decision of the pious Emperor Constantine.

ANNUS MUNDI 6173 (SEPTEMBER 1, 681—AUGUST 31, 682)

A.D. 673
Roman Emperor Constantine: 17 years: year 13
Arab ruler Yezid: 3 years: year 2
Bishop of Constantinople George: 6 years: year 4

In this year Constantine removed his brothers Herakleios and Tiberius from the imperial power, and ruled alone with his son Justinian.

---

leanings of his native school of Antioch by stressing Christ's humanity and saying it was improper to call Mary *theotokos* (the Mother of God); he felt she should only be styled *Christotokos* (the Mother of Christ). This conflicted strongly with the views of Cyril, the patriarch of Alexandria. Also, both Alexandria and Rome were jealous of the upstart see of Constantinople; they united in declaring Nestorios' views heretical. The council of Ephesos, thanks in no small measure to the intimidation caused by Egyptian monks, ratified the Alexandrian theology (which put greater stress on Christ's divinity, and felt it perfectly proper that Mary should be deemed *theotokos*).

iv. The council of Chalcedon, convened by Marcian in 451. Rome and Constantinople now combined against the arrogance of the see of Alexandria after its victory at the council of Ephesos. Alexandrian monophysitism (the view that Christ had but one nature, the divine, after the incarnation) was condemned, causing a permanent rupture in the church. See also note 69.

v. The second council of Constantinople, called by Justinian I in 553. This council, which was an attempt to conciliate the monophysites, condemned as heretical the so-called Three Chapters: the works of Theodore of Mopsuestia, as well as some of those of Theodoretos of Cyr and Ibas of Edessa. Theodore was one of the men from whom Nestorios had derived his doctrines, while the other two theologians had written against Nestorios' foe Cyril of Alexandria, who was revered by monophysites and orthodox alike.

ANNUS MUNDI 6174 (SEPTEMBER 1, 682—AUGUST 31, 683)

14. 3. 5.

In this year Mukhtar the liar rebelled and, styling himself a prophet, became master of Persia. The Arabs were thrown into turmoil.

ANNUS MUNDI 6175 (SEPTEMBER 1, 683—AUGUST 31, 684)

Arab ruler Marwan: 1 year
15. 1. 6.

In this year Yezid died. The Arabs at Medina, troubled and aroused, made Abd Allah son of Zubayr their ruler. The Arabs in Phoenicia and Palestine assembled at Damascus, then went to Hasan, the emir of Palestine. They gave Marwan their right hands and made him ruler; he was caliph for nine months. After he died his son Abd al-Malik succeeded to the rule. He was caliph for twenty-one and a half years. He overpowered the rebels, killing Abd Allah son of Zubayr and Dahhaq.

ANNUS MUNDI 6176 (SEPTEMBER 1, 684—AUGUST 31, 685)

Arab ruler Abd al-Malik: 22 years
Bishop of Constantinople Theodore (again): 3 years
16. 1. 1.

In this year there was a famine and a great plague in Syria, and Abd al-Malik conquered its people. While the Mardaites were attacking Lebanon and the plague was at its height, Abd al-Malik sent envoys to the Emperor asking for the same peace terms which had been requested during the reign of Muawiyah. He agreed to pay the same 365,000 nomismata, the same three hundred sixty-five slaves, and likewise the same three hundred sixty-five high-bred horses.

ANNUS MUNDI 6177 (SEPTEMBER 1, 685—AUGUST 31, 686)

17. 2. 2.

In this year, after reigning for seventeen years, the pious Emperor Constantine died, and his son Justinian became Emperor.

It should be known that those who say it was not until four years later that the enactments expressed by the members of the sixth council became authoritative are vainly and foolishly speaking nonsense.[128] Since they speak falsely in every respect, they should be confuted and shown that in these matters they are not speaking the truth at all. For the exact chronological determination of the sixth holy ecumenical synod against the monothelites is that it was in the twelfth year of the reign of Herakleios' descendant Constantine: that is to say, in the 6172nd year since the creation of the world. Thereafter Constantine ruled for five years, and after he died his son Justinian held sole power for ten years. When Justinian was ousted Leontios held power for three years; after Leontios came Tiberius (also known as Apsimaros) for seven years, and then the ousted Justinian once more for six years.

As is found in the edicts which were promulgated in the second year of the last reign of Justinian (who had had his nose slit), the third edict is as follows: "We take the view that those who entered into second marriages up until the just-past fifteenth of January of the just-past fourth indiction (year 6199) shall be enslaved because of their sin, and those who do not reform from their sin shall submit to canonical condemnation." And after this there is another passage: "Those who (after their appointment) illegally join in one marriage—that is: priests, deacons, and subdeacons—shall be excluded from the sacred liturgy for a long period of time. They shall be penalized further by being restored to their own ranks,[129] and in no way shall they advance to higher ones unless it is clear beforehand that they have been released from their unlawful cohabitation."

Thus it quite clearly appears from this chronological determination that twenty-seven years elapsed from the sixth holy ecumenical council to the promulgation of these edicts. At the holy ecumenical synod George was patriarch of Constantinople and had held the patriarchate for three years; after the synod he was patriarch for another three years. After him came Theodore's three years, Paul's seven, Kallinikos' twelve, and Cyrus' two, so in these patriarchates twenty-seven years also passed. From the time when these edicts were promulgated to the first year of Philippikos' reign was five years. In the first year of Philippikos' reign occurred the insane synod which opposed the holy sixth ecumenical council. When Cyrus was ousted in the sixth year of his patriarchate, John became patriarch of Constantinople. He, Andrew the metropolitan of Crete, and Germanos the metropolitan of Kyzikos (along with everyone else around at that time) anathematized

128. A reference to the Council *in Trullo* (or Quinisextum) of 691–692, which supplemented the fifth and sixth ecumenical councils, especially in matters of church discipline.

129. That is, if they have been promoted since their illegal marriages. In the Greek church it is not improper for a priest to be married before his ordination.

the sixth holy ecumenical council, and had clearly subscribed to this course in advance.

When John died three years later, Germanos was translated from Kyzikos and became patriarch of Constantinople. In the thirteenth year of the reign of Leo he was exiled; Anastasios became patriarch for twenty-four years. After him Constantine was patriarch for twelve years, Niketas for fourteen, Paul for five, Tarasios for twenty-one, Nikephoros for eight, Theodotos for six, Antonius for sixteen, and John Lekanomantis for six years and one month.[130]

363 **ANNUS MUNDI 6178 (SEPTEMBER 1, 686—AUGUST 31, 687)**

A.D. **678**
Roman Emperor Justinian: 10 years: year 1
Arab ruler Abd al-Malik: 22 years: year 3
Bishop of Constantinople Theodore: 3 years: year 3

In this year Abd al-Malik sent envoys to Justinian to secure peace. It was arranged on these terms: the Emperor would keep the Mardaites' troops out of Lebanon and stop their attacks, and Abd al-Malik would give the Romans 1,000 nomismata, a horse, and a slave each day. Also, both sides would share equally the tribute from Cyprus, Armenia, and Iberia. The Emperor sent the magistrianos[131] Paul to Abd al-Malik to secure the arrangement. There were written sureties with witnesses; the magistrianos, who was treated with honor, returned.

The Emperor sent messengers who seized 12,000 Mardaites, mutilating the Roman state. For all the cities in the heights from Mopsuestia to fourth Armenia, which are now inhabited by the Arabs, had grown weak and depopulated from the Mardaites' attacks. After they were transplanted, Romania has suffered all sorts of evils at the hands of the Arabs up until the present day.

In the same year Abd al-Malik sent Muawiyah's brother Ziyad to

130. This chronological discussion was inserted into the chronicle some time after Theophanes' death in 818; by its description of John Lekanomantis' patriarchate as having lasted six years and one month, it can be dated to 840. Theodotos was patriarch of Constantinople from 815 to 821, Antonius from 821 to 834, and John Lekanomantis from 834 to 843.

131. This is the Greek equivalent of the Latin *agens in rebus. Agentes in rebus* served as dispatch-carriers and inspectors of the imperial post; some of the more prominent members of this civil service corps held administrative posts at the imperial court. *Agentes in rebus* had jurisdictional privileges which put them beyond the authority of local courts, and were also allowed to charge fees for their services: two reasons why appointments to membership in this corps were eagerly sought.

Persia against the rebel Mukhtar the liar, but Mukhtar killed him. When Abd al-Malik heard of this he went to Mesopotamia, but Saïd rebelled against him. He came back, persuaded Saïd to open Damascus (which he had previously overrun), and then assassinated him.

As he was but sixteen, Justinian was not one to follow traditional practice. He ran things without advice, and sent a Roman force to Armenia under his general Leontios. He killed the Saracens there and subjected it to the Romans, as he did Iberia, Albania, Boukania, and Media. Making them tributary, he sent the Emperor a large sum of money. When Abd al-Malik learned of this he overpowered Kirkesion and subjected Theopolis.

364 **ANNUS MUNDI 6179 (SEPTEMBER 1, 687—AUGUST 31, 688)**

Bishop of Constantinople Paul: 7 years
2. 4. 1.

In this year there was a famine in Syria, and many men entered Romania.

The Emperor went to Armenia and there received the Lebanese Mardaites, putting an end to his stout wall.

He also broke the peace with the Bulgars, utterly confounding his own father's appropriate edicts. He ordered the thematic cavalry to cross to Thrace, as he wanted to take prisoners among the Bulgars and the Sklavinoi.

ANNUS MUNDI 6180 (SEPTEMBER 1, 688—AUGUST 31, 689)

6180. 680. 3. 5. 2.

In this year Justinian campaigned against Sklavinia and Bulgaria. Advancing to Thessalonike, he thrust back as far as possible the Bulgars he encountered. He conquered large hosts of Slavs (some in battle, but others went over to him) and settled them in the Opsikion,[132] sending them across by way of Abydos.

While he was withdrawing, the Bulgars stopped him on the road at the narrow part of a mountain pass; he was barely able to get through, and his army took many casualties.

In the same year Abd Allah the son of Zubayr sent his brother Mu'sab against Mukhtar, who engaged him but was routed and fled to Syria. Mu'sab overtook and slew him. Abd al-Malik attacked, overcame, and killed Mu'sab, and subjected all of Persia.

132. This theme occupied the northwestern quadrant of Anatolia, being west of the theme of the Armeniacs and north of that of the Anatolics.

ANNUS MUNDI 6181 (SEPTEMBER 1, 689—AUGUST 31, 690)

A.D. 681
Roman Emperor Justinian: 10 years: year 4
Arab ruler Abd al-Malik: 22 years: year 6
Bishop of Constantinople Paul: 7 years: year 3

365

In this year Abd al-Malik sent Hajjaj to Mecca against the son of Zubayr; Hajjaj killed him there. After he subjected to Abd al-Malik the territory which had opposed him, he burned the house of his idol along with the idol they worshiped; thanks to that, Abd al-Malik appointed Hajjaj general of Persia. Persia, Mesopotamia, and the great Arabia of Medina were subjected to Abd al-Malik, and the Arabs' civil war ended.

ANNUS MUNDI 6182 (SEPTEMBER 1, 690—AUGUST 31, 691)

5. 7. 4.

In this year the Arabs' state was finally freed from all warfare. Once he had subjected everyone, Abd al-Malik made peace.

ANNUS MUNDI 6183 (SEPTEMBER 1, 691—AUGUST 31, 692)

6. 8. 5.

In this year, thanks to a lack of good sense, Justinian broke the peace with Abd al-Malik. He was foolishly anxious to resettle the island of Cyprus. A number of the Cypriots who made the effort drowned or died of sickness; the rest did return to Cyprus.

Also, Justinian would not accept the money Abd al-Malik sent, as it had a new type of stamp and had never been that way before.[133] When Abd al-Malik heard this, he satanically dissembled and called on Justinian not to break the peace, but rather to accept his money. Though the Arabs could not accept the Romans' impress on their own coins, they would give the Romans the correct weight of gold and there would not be any loss from the new Arab coinage. But Justinian thought Abd al-Malik's request was caused by fear. He did not understand that what the Arabs wanted was to stop the Mardaites' inroads, and then to break the peace with a pretext that seemed plausible. This is just what happened.

133. During the reign of Justinian II, Byzantine coinage began to feature an image of Christ, an image naturally unacceptable to the Muslims. Until this time the Arabs had closely imitated Byzantine models in their coinage; now they began an independent series of gold coins, minted on a lighter standard than the nomisma. After an intermediate series featuring a standing caliph on the obverse, by 696–697 Arab coinage was totally aniconic.

Abd al-Malik also sent orders to rebuild the temple at Mecca. He wanted to take way pillars from holy Gethsemane, but Sergios the son of Mansur (a Christian who was public finance minister and was very friendly with Abd al-Malik) and his co-leader of the Palestinian Christians, Patricius (surnamed Klausus), asked him not to do this, but to persuade Justinian through their request to send other columns in place of these. This was done.

ANNUS MUNDI 6184 (SEPTEMBER 1, 692—AUGUST 31, 693)

7. 9. 6.

366 In this year Justinian made a selection from the Slavs he had resettled. He levied 30,000 men, armed them, and named them the "special army." Their commander was named Neboulos. Justinian, confident in them, wrote to the Arabs that he would not abide by the peace which had been agreed upon in writing. Taking up his special army and all the thematic cavalry, he traveled by sea to Sebastopolis.

The hypocritical Arabs did not choose to break the peace, but imperial guilt and indiscretion forced them to do so. They armed themselves and went to Sebastopolis, though they first swore to the Emperor that they had not perverted what the two sides had agreed upon with oaths: God would be the judge and avenger of their charges.

But since the Emperor would not tolerate hearing any such thing, being instead eager for battle, they dissolved the written peace treaty and rushed against the Romans. They hung a copy of the treaty from a spear to go before them in place of a banner. Muhammad was their general as they joined battle. At first the Arabs were defeated, but Muhammad suborned the general of the Slavs allied to the Romans. He sent him a purse loaded with nomismata and, deceiving him with many promises, persuaded him to desert to the Arabs with 20,000 Slavs. Then Justinian massacred the remaining Slavs (and their wives and children) at Leukate, a precipitous place by the sea on the gulf of Nikomedeia.

ANNUS MUNDI 6185 (SEPTEMBER 1, 693—AUGUST 31, 694)

8. 10. 7.

In this year Sabbatios the prince of Armenia, after learning of the Roman defeat, surrendered it to the Arabs. Also, inner Persia (known as Khorasan) came under their control. A dangerous man, Sabinos by name, rose up there and killed many Arabs—almost including Hajjaj 367 himself—but was finally drowned in a river. From then on the Agarenes, growing bolder, ravaged Romania.

ANNUS MUNDI 6186 (SEPTEMBER 1, 694—AUGUST 31, 695)

A.D. **686**
Roman Emperor Justinian: 10 years: year 9
Arab ruler Abd al-Malik: 22 years: year 11
Bishop of Constantinople Kallinikos: 12 years: year 1

In this year there was an eclipse of the sun at the third hour of the fifth of Hyperbataios (a Sunday),[134] with the result that some bright stars appeared.

Muhammad attacked Romania; he had with him the Slavs who had fled, as they had experience of Romania. He took many prisoners.

There was a slaughter of pigs in Syria.

Justinian gave heed to the palace buildings; he built the triklinos of Justinian[135] and outwalls for the palace.

He made the sakellarios and chief eunuch Stephen the Persian (a lord and a powerful man, but bloodthirsty and cruel) his adviser. Stephen was not content with mercilessly harassing the workmen, but even stoned them and their leaders. After the Emperor went abroad, this wild beast even dared to whip Justinian's mother, the Augusta Anastasia, as if she were a child. During this time he worked many evils throughout the community, which made the Emperor hated.

In a similar fashion, Justinian put an abbot named Theodotos (who had formerly been a solitary monk at Stenon in Thrace, and was terrible and wild) in charge of the affairs of the public finance ministry. Theodotos rashly, vainly, and unjustifiably put into effect schemes, confiscations, and tax assessments against a great many leaders of the state and important men, not only from the governing class, but also from among the property-owners of the city. He hanged them and lit chaff-heaps under them. There is still more: by imperial order the prefect shut up a great many men in prisons and kept them under guard for years. All this exacerbated the people's hatred of the Emperor.

368 The Emperor demanded that the patriarch Kallinikos make a prayer so he could tear down the metropolitan's church dedicated to the Mother of God, which was near the palace. Justinian wanted to erect a fountain and build seats for the Blue faction so its members could receive the Emperor there. The patriarch said, "We have a prayer over the construction of a church, but we have not inherited a prayer over the demolition of a church." But since the Emperor pressured him and absolutely demanded the prayer, the patriarch said,

134. Actually, this appears to be the eclipse of October 5, 693: Newton, *op. cit.*, 543–544.
135. A reception hall.

"Glory to God the long-suffering at all times: now, forever, and through eons upon eons. Amen." When they heard this, they tore down the church and built the fountain. They rebuilt the metropolitan's church at Petrin.

ANNUS MUNDI 6187 (SEPTEMBER 1, 695—AUGUST 31, 696)

10. 12. 2.

In this year Muhammad attacked fourth Armenia, took many prisoners, and then withdrew.

In the same year Justinian was removed from the imperial power in this way: he ordered the patrician and general Stephen (surnamed Rhousios) to kill the populace of Constantinople, and to begin with the patriarch. Now Leontios, who was a patrician and general of the Anatolic theme, and was distinguished in battle, had spent three years in prison. Although he had been condemned, he was suddenly released and appointed general of Hellas.[136] He was ordered to embark on three warships and leave the city that very day.

That night, while he was preparing to sail from the city, he was steadied by his friends, who had come to him at the harbor of Sophia (or Julian) near Mauros. Among those who went to him were his true friends Paul (a monk of the monastery of Kallistratos) and Gregory the Kappadokian (who was a kleisouriarch[137] and later a monk and abbot of the monastery of Florus). They had watched over him carefully while he was in prison, since they thought he would become Roman Emperor.

Leontios said to them, "While I was in jail, you strongly supported me for the imperial power. Now my life is coming to an end in evil circumstances, for in the future I will constantly be expecting death."

They said, "Should you not hesitate, your bid for power will at once be fulfilled. Only listen to us, and follow us." Leontios took the men and such arms as he had and went to the Praitorion in great secrecy. They pounded on the doors, claiming the Emperor had come to administer some business there.

When the underofficer at that time had been notified, he immediately came and opened the door. He was overpowered, clubbed down, and bound hand and foot by Leontios. Once he had got in, Leontios opened the prisons, releasing the many noble men who had been

369

136. This is the first mention in Byzantine history of the organization of the theme of Hellas ("Greece"—which was not the name of the Roman province for the area). It may have come into being as a result of Justinian II's earlier campaigns against the Slavs in the Balkans.
137. An officer in charge of guarding a mountain pass.

jailed: they had been shut in for as long as six or eight years. Most of them were soldiers, and Leontios armed them and went out into the Forum with them. He cried, "All you Christians, go to Hagia Sophia!" and sent men to each region, ordering them to cry out the same thing. Once roused, the masses hastily assembled at the church's font.

Along with his two friends the monks and some of the more important men who had got out of jail, Leontios went to the patriarch at his residence. They found him troubled because of what had been commanded of Stephen Rhousios, and persuaded him to come down to the font and speak as follows: "This is the day which the Lord made!"

And all the people lifted up their voices: "Let Justinian's bones be exhumed!"[138] Then they all ran out to the hippodrome. When it was day they led Justinian into the hippodrome through the Sphendone, slit his nose, cut his tongue, and exiled him to the Cherson. The mob seized the public finance minister Theodotos the monk and the sakellarios Stephen the Persian, bound them by the feet, and dragged them through the Mese.[139] They carried them into the Forum of the Ox and burned them alive. Thus did they acclaim Leontios Emperor.

ANNUS MUNDI 6188 (SEPTEMBER 1, 696—AUGUST 31, 697)

Roman Emperor Leontios: 3 years
1. 13. 3.

In this year the Emperor Leontios maintained a policy peaceful in all respects.

370   ANNUS MUNDI 6189 (SEPTEMBER 1, 697—AUGUST 31, 698)

2. 14. 4.

In this year Khalid attacked Romania, took many captives, and withdrew. Also, Sergios son of Barnoukios, the patrician of Lazika, revolted and put it under Arab rule.

ANNUS MUNDI 6190 (SEPTEMBER 1, 698—AUGUST 31, 699)

6190. 690. 3. 15. 5.

In this year the Arabs attacked and conquered Africa, settling in it a garrison from their army. When Leontios learned of this he dispatched the patrician John, a competent man, with the entire Roman

138. A Byzantine curse, equivalent to, "Down with Justinian!"
139. The main street of Constantinople.

navy. When he arrived at Carthage he forced open the harbor's chain, routed his opponents, and drove them away. He freed the African cities and left behind his own garrison. He then referred these matters to the Emperor and, once he had received his orders, wintered in Africa.

On learning of this, the Arab leader sent a larger and more powerful expedition against him. In battle he drove John and his army from the harbor. Once he had entered it from outside, he camped in force within its small circuit.

John went back to Romania, as he wanted to get reinforcements from the Emperor. He had come as far as Crete, however, when the army was suborned by its officers. Because it was afraid and disgraced, it did not want to refer matters to the Emperor, and turned to a wicked plot. It dug up Apsimaros, the drungarios[140] of the Kibyrhaiotai,[141] and chose him as Emperor, renaming him Tiberius.

While Leontios was cleansing the Neoresian harbor in Constantinople, the bubonic plague descended on the city and destroyed a great number of people in four months.

371   Apsimaros and his expedition arrived and anchored at Sykai across from the city. For a time no-one in the city wanted to betray Leontios, but at the single wall of Blakhernai foreign officers (who had been entrusted with the keys of the land wall because of their frightful oath at the holy table) plotted to betray the city and carried out their perfidy. The soldiers of Apsimaros' naval force entered the citizens' houses and stripped the property-owners of their possessions.

Apsimaros slit Leontios' nose and ordered him into the monastery of Delmatos under guard. Since Leontios' officers and friends had clung to him even unto death, Apsimaros beat and exiled them and confiscated their property. He appointed his true brother Herakleios sole general of all the thematic cavalry outside the city, as he was quite competent. He sent Herakleios to Kappadokia to traverse the passes and administer and command the action being taken against Apsimaros' enemies.

140. A rank approximately equivalent to colonel.
141. The theme of the Kibyrhaiotai comprised the southwestern coast of Asia Minor; many of the thematic troops settled there seem to have owed naval, rather than land, military service.

ANNUS MUNDI 6191 (SEPTEMBER 1, 699—AUGUST 31, 700)

A.D. 691
Roman Emperor Apsimaros: 7 years: year 1
Arab ruler Abd al-Malik: 22 years: year 16
Bishop of Constantinople Kallinikos: 12 years: year 6

In this year Apsimaros held the imperial power.

Also, Abd ar-Rahman rebelled in Persia, became its master, and drove Hajjaj from it.

ANNUS MUNDI 6192 (SEPTEMBER 1, 700—AUGUST 31, 701)

2. 17. 7.

In this year there was a great plague.

Joining Hajjaj in Persia, Muhammad campaigned against Abd ar-Rahman with a host of Arabs. Once they had attacked and killed him, they entrusted Persia to Hajjaj once more.

The Romans overran Syria, advancing as far as Samosata. They foraged through the surrounding country, killing many Arabs (200,000, as they say). They took a large amount of booty and many Arab prisoners and withdrew after giving the Arabs a bad scare.

372 ANNUS MUNDI 6193 (SEPTEMBER 1, 701—AUGUST 31, 702)

3. 18. 8.

In this year Abd Allah attacked Romania; he besieged Taranton but withdrew without having accomplished anything. He rebuilt and garrisoned Mopsuestia.

ANNUS MUNDI 6194 (SEPTEMBER 1, 702—AUGUST 31, 703)

4. 19. 9.

In this year Baanes (surnamed Heptadaimon) brought fourth Armenia under Arab rule.

Apsimaros exiled to Kephalenia Philippikos the son of the patrician Nikephoros, since he had dreamed he would become Emperor. He said that in a dream he had seen an eagle shading his head.[142] When the Emperor heard that he immediately exiled him.

142. The eagle is the Byzantine symbol of the imperium, a tradition going back to Roman days. A vision of an eagle would have been thought by all concerned to be a portent of coming power.

ANNUS MUNDI 6195 (SEPTEMBER 1, 703—AUGUST 31, 704)

5. 20. 10.

In this year the leaders of Armenia rebelled against the Saracens and killed the Saracens there. They sent messengers to Apsimaros, who brought the Romans into their country. But Muhammad's campaign against them killed many. Once he had resubjected Armenia to the Saracens, he gathered the Armenian grandees together and burned them alive.

At around this time Azar attacked Kilikia with 10,000 men. The Emperor's brother Herakleios met him, killed most of his men, and sent the rest to the Emperor in bonds.

ANNUS MUNDI 6196 (SEPTEMBER 1, 704—AUGUST 31, 705)

6. 21. 11.

In this year Azid the son of Khounei attacked Kilikia. While he was besieging the fortress of Sision the Emperor's brother Herakleios arrived; in his attack he killed 12,000 Arabs.

Justinian, who was in Cherson, declared that he intended to become Emperor again. The property-owners there were afraid of danger from the Empire; they planned to kill him or send him to the Emperor, but he learned of this and was able to escape. He fled to Daras and asked for an interview with the Khazar Khagan. When the Khagan learned of this he received Justinian with great honor and gave him as a wife his own sister Theodora.

After a short time Justinian went down to Phanagouria to make his home there, as the Khagan had asked of him. When Apsimaros heard about this he sent a message to the Khagan promising to give him many presents if he would send Justinian alive: or if not, his head would do. The Khagan yielded to this request and set guards on Justinian, under the pretext of preventing plots against him by men of his own nation. The Khagan ordered Papatzun (who was going to Phanagouria from his court) and Balgitzin (the governor of Bosporos) to kill Justinian when asked.

One of the Khagan's house-slaves told this to Theodora, and it became known to Justinian. He summoned Papatzun to visit him at his own residence, strangled him with a cord, and dealt with Balgitzin in the same way. Then he immediately sent Theodora back to Khazaria, while he himself secretly fled to Tomi. He found a merchantman which had just been fully loaded, boarded it and, sailing past Assada, came to Symbolon near Cherson.

He sent a secret message to Cherson which roused Barisbakourios, Barisbakourios' brother (known as both Salibas and Stephen), Moropaulos, and Theophilos. With them he sailed past Cherson's lighthouse. They had sailed past Nekropela (the mouth of both the Dnieper and the Dniester) when the sea grew stormy, so that everyone despaired of being saved. Justinian's man Myakes said to him, "You are going to die, my lord! Make a deal with God for being saved, so that if He restores your rule to you, you will not take vengeance on your enemies."

Justinian answered him angrily, "If I spare any of them, *then* may God drown me!"

374   He escaped the heavy sea without harm and entered the Danube River. He sent Stephen to Tervel the lord of Bulgaria to gain his support for Justinian's reconquest of the Empire of his forefathers. He promised to give Tervel many gifts, even his own daughter as wife. Tervel promised on oath to obey and cooperate with him in every way, and received him with honor. He raised his entire army, Bulgars and Slavs.[143] In the following year, after they had been equipped, they approached the imperial city.

ANNUS MUNDI 6197 (SEPTEMBER 1, 705—AUGUST 31, 706)

A.D. 697
Roman Emperor Apsimaros: 7 years: year 7
Arab ruler Abd al-Malik: 22 years: year 22
Bishop of Constantinople Kallinikos: 12 years: year 12

In this year Abd al-Malik the Arab ruler died and his son Walid came to power.

In the same year Justinian reached the imperial city with Tervel and his Bulgars. His camp extended from the Charisian gate to Blakhernai. For three days his troops talked with the men in the city, but were reviled by them, as they would not accept any agreement.

But Justinian and a few comrades got into the city without battle through a pipe, which threw Constantinople into confusion. After taking the town, for a short time he quartered himself in the palace of Blakhernai.

ANNUS MUNDI 6198 (SEPTEMBER 1, 706—AUGUST 31, 707)

Roman Emperor Justinian (again): 6 years
Arab ruler Walid: 9 years

143. This passage shows that the Turkic Bulgars had not yet been assimilated by the more numerous Slavs over whom they ruled.

Bishop of Constantinople Cyrus: 6 years
1. 1. 1.

375   In this year Justinian regained the imperial power. He gave Tervel many presents (including imperial regalia) and sent him off in peace.

Apsimaros had abandoned the city and fled to Apollonias. He was pursued, seized, and brought to Justinian. Herakleios was brought in bonds from Thrace along with all the officers who were his comrades. Justinian hanged them all on the wall. He also sent men to the interior who routed out many more officers and killed them, those who had been active against him and those who had not alike. He triumphally paraded Leontios and Apsimaros through the whole city in chains.

While the horse-races were going on and Justinian was sitting on the throne, they were publicly dragged before him and thrown down like his slaves. He trampled on their necks until the end of the first heat, while the people shouted, "You have attacked an asp and a basilisk, and have trampled down a lion and a dragon."[144] Then he sent Leontios and Apsimaros to the Kynegion[145] and beheaded them.

Justinian blinded the patriarch Kallinikos and exiled him to Rome. In his place he appointed Cyrus (a solitary monk on the island of Amastris), since Cyrus had predicted his restoration. Justinian destroyed an uncountable number of political and military figures; many he gave bitter deaths by throwing them into the sea in sacks. He invited others to a fine meal and hanged some of them when they got up; others he cut down. Because of all this everyone was terrified.

Justinian sent an expedition to bring back his wife from Khazaria, and many ships sank. When the Khagan heard this he told Justinian, "You fool, would it not have been proper to send two or three ships to get your wife, and not to have killed such a host? Or do you think you are taking her by force? Know also that you have had a son: send a man and get them." Justinian dispatched the cubicularius Theophylaktos, who brought back Theodora and Justinian's son Tiberius. He crowned them and they ruled with him.

144. Psalm 91, verse 13, a particularly apt choice: "asp" puns on Apsimaros' name, and "lion" on that of Leontios. "Basilisk" is also a pun; it has two meanings in Greek, one being a dragon-like beast, the other a petty king.

145. An amphitheater close by the eastern tip of Constantinople, not quite half a mile northeast of Hagia Sophia. Executions were often performed there.

ANNUS MUNDI 6199 (SEPTEMBER 1, 707—AUGUST 31, 708)

Bishop of Jerusalem John: 30 years
2. 2. 2. 2 [sic].

376   In this year Walid robbed the holy catholic church of Damascus out of the envy the sinner felt toward the Christians because of this church's surpassing beauty. He also stopped the use of Greek in the public record books of the departments, ordering them to be written in Arabic instead: that is, except for numbers, since it is impossible to write the number "one," the number "two," the number "three," "eight and a half," or "three in the feminine gender" in their language. Because of this their scribes are Christians even to the present day.

ANNUS MUNDI 6200 (SEPTEMBER 1, 708—AUGUST 31, 709)

A.D. **700**
Roman Emperor Justinian: 6 years: year 3
Arab ruler Walid: 9 years: year 3
Bishop of Constantinople Cyrus: 6 years: year 3
Bishop of Jerusalem John: 30 years: year 3

In this year Justinian broke the peace between the Romans and Bulgars. He made all the thematic cavalry cross into Thrace, outfitted a naval expedition, and moved against Tervel and the Bulgars. On reaching Ankhialos he anchored his fleet in front of the city and, absolutely unsuspicious, ordered the cavalry to camp inland without close guard. While the army scattered like sheep over the camp to gather provisions, from the mountains the Bulgars' lookouts spied the Romans' thoughtless behavior. They came together like wild beasts and made a sudden, strong attack which destroyed the Roman flock. Besides the Romans who were killed, they took many prisoners, horses, and weapons.

Justinian and the survivors took refuge in the fortress and kept its gates shut for three days. He was the first to hamstring his horse, and ordered everyone to do the same.[146] He placed trophies on the wall, secretly boarded his ship that night, and sailed away, returning to the city in disgrace.

146. To keep them from falling into the hands of the Bulgars.

ANNUS MUNDI 6201 (SEPTEMBER 1, 709—AUGUST 31, 710)

4. 4. 4. 4.

377   In this year Maslama and Abas attacked Tyana because they were furious at the fate of Maiuoma's army, which had been slaughtered by Marianos. They besieged Tyana and wintered there. The Emperor sent two generals—Theodore Karteroukas and Theophylaktos Salibas —against it with an army (and some farmer-soldiers to help it) to drive them away. But the two generals squabbled with each other, engaged the Arabs in a disorderly way, and were routed. Many thousands were destroyed, and many taken prisoner. The Arabs, once they had taken the army's baggage-train and food-supply, could lay siege to Tyana until they captured it. They had been short of food, and had intended to withdraw.

Once they saw this battle, the inhabitants of Tyana despaired. They got a pledge that they would not be harmed and went out to the Arabs; they abandoned their city, which has been a wasteland until the present. The Arabs did not abide by the treaty, but exiled them to the desert; they also enslaved many of them.

ANNUS MUNDI 6202 (SEPTEMBER 1, 710—AUGUST 31, 711)

6202. 702. 5. 5. 5. 5.

In this year Abas attacked Romania, took many prisoners, and withdrew. He also began to build Garis near Heliopolis.

ANNUS MUNDI 6203 (SEPTEMBER 1, 711—AUGUST 31, 712)

6. 6. 6. 6.

In this year Uthman attacked Kilikia and took many fortresses on terms. Also, Kamakhon and its surrounding area were betrayed to the Arabs.

Because of a slight he remembered, Justinian sent the patricians Mauros and Stephen (surnamed Askemitos) to Cherson. He armed a large expedition, because he remembered the Chersonites, Bosporans, and inhabitants of the remaining areas there had been plotting against him. This expedition was made up of all his warships, triremes, transports, merchantmen, and other naval craft. They were obtained by a requisition on the senators, artisans, members of the circus factions, and all office-holders living in the city.

Justinian dispatched the patricians with orders to put everyone inhabiting these cities to the sword and not to save anyone. He also gave them Helias, a spatharios who was in his debt, to install as gover-

378   nor of Cherson. They reached Cherson and, as no-one opposed them, took its cities and put everyone to the sword except the children; because of their youth they were spared and saved for slavery.

The soldiers sent the Tudun (the governor of Cherson by virtue of his being the Khagan's personal representative), Zoïlos (a leading citizen because of his lineage and birth), and forty other leading men of Cherson (kin and all) in bonds to the Emperor. They fastened seven other leading citizens of Cherson on wooden spits and roasted them over a fire. They bound twenty others with their hands behind their backs and tied them to a warship, then filled it with stones and drowned the men in the deeps.

When Justinian learned what had happened he was furious because the children had been saved, and commanded his men to report to him at once. Since the expedition departed in October and was at sea at the time of the rising of the star known as Tauroura,[147] it was entirely sunk: around 73,000 sailors died. Justinian was not dismayed when he learned of this, but rather filled with joy, as he was now at the peak of his madness. He kept bellowing threats that he would kill every male in Cherson: he threatened to send out another expedition, mow down everyone, and smash them to bits.

When the inhabitants of the cities heard this, they looked to their own safety. As they were compelled to oppose the Emperor, they sent messages to the Khagan in Khazaria, asking for an army to protect them. Under these circumstances, Helias the spatharios and Bardanes the exile[148] (who by this time had been recalled from Kephalenia and was in Cherson with the expedition) also rebelled. When he learned of these developments, Justinian dispatched the patrician and minister of public finance George (surnamed Syros), John the prefect, and Christopher the turmarch of the Thrakesian theme[149] with a few war-

379   ships and three hundred armed men. He also gave them the Tudun and Zoïlos, whom he intended to restore in Kherson as before, and he ordered them to justify themselves to the Khagan through an envoy. They were to bring Helias and Bardanes to the Emperor.

But after they crossed to Cherson, the inhabitants of the city

---

147. "The Bull's Tail." Despite the fact that he was a monk, Theophanes took astrology and its premonitions seriously, as is demonstrated here and elsewhere.

148. This is Philippikos, whose exile is mentioned in *annus mundi* 6194. He ruled as Philippikos; Bardanes, an Armenian name, might not have been acceptable to the Greek-speaking population of the Empire. There was precedent for this sort of name change; the Emperor who reigned as Zeno (474–491), e.g., was born with the uncouth Isaurian appellation Tarasikodissa.

149. The western part of the original Anatolic theme is now detached from the large administrative unit to become a separate theme of its own.

would not talk with them. On the next day the city dwellers persuaded Justinian's officers to enter the city alone and slammed shut the gates. They put the minister of public finance and the prefect to the sword, but gave the Tudun, Zoïlos, the turmarch, and the three hundred soldiers to the Khazars, who sent them to the Khagan. When the Tudun died on the way, the Khazars killed the turmarch and the three hundred soldiers as a funeral-rite.

Then the Chersonites and the dwellers in the rest of the cities renounced Justinian and acclaimed Bardanes Philippikos (who was in exile there) as Emperor. When he learned of this Justinian went madder yet. He killed the spatharios Helias' children on their mother's breast and made her marry her own cook, who was an Indian. Then he readied another naval force under the patrician Mauros Bessos. He gave him rams, catapults, and all sorts of siege-engines for attacking fortified positions, and commanded him to raze Cherson's walls and the entire city, and not to spare a single soul. He made even more clear what would be done to Mauros as a means of repairing failure.

Mauros crossed and with a ram overthrew the Kentenaresion gate and the one near it known as Syagros. But then the Khazars arrived, and there was a truce in the fighting. Bardanes fled to the Khagan. Justinian's expedition was unsuccessful, but did not dare return to the Emperor; its members renounced him and acclaimed Bardanes as 380 Emperor. The Khagan demanded that they promise not to betray him, and that each of them give the Khagan a nomisma. They immediately gave him the pledge and the money and received the Emperor Philippikos.

When the expedition lingered and did not return, Justinian guessed the reason. He departed (with him were the Opsikians and some of the Thrakesians) for Sinope to find out exactly what was going on in Cherson. In his examination he discerned the rebel expedition arming against the city[150] and, charging forward like a lion, rushed toward the city himself. But since Philippikos got there ahead of him and had taken it, he went to Damatrys,[151] where he camped with his men.

Philippikos immediately dispatched the patrician Mauros and the spatharios John (surnamed Strouthos[152]) against Tiberius. He also sent out a raiding-party against Justinian at Damatrys, and another man against Barisbakourios, who had fled.

Mauros and Strouthos went to Blakhernai. They found Tiberius

---

150. Constantinople.
151. A town about twenty miles east of Chalcedon.
152. "The Ostrich," or, perhaps, "The Sparrow"—two very different physical types.

holding with one hand the leg of the altar's holy table in the church of the Mother of God, and with the other the True Cross. Round his neck were protective amulets. His father's mother Anastasia was sitting outside the chapel; she fell at Mauros' feet and begged him not to kill her grandson Tiberius, as he had done no wrong. But while she was clutching his feet and tearfully entreating, Strouthos went into the chapel and took Tiberius away by force. He took the True Cross away from him and put it on the holy table; the amulets he fastened round his own neck. They took the boy to the small porch above the monastery of Kallinike, stripped him, stretched him out in the doorway like a sheep, and cut his throat. They ordered him buried in the church of the holy Anargyroi[153]—known as that of Pauline.

Barisbakourios, the chief patrician and count of the Opsikion, was overpowered and killed. Helias and his army went to Damatrys and entered into talks with the army there. They gave Justinian's army a promise of no ill-treatment, whereupon everyone abandoned Justinian, leaving him all alone and going over to Philippikos. Then the spatharios Helias angrily burst forward and seized Justinian's neck. He cut off his head with the dagger with which he was girded and sent it to Philippikos by way of the spatharios Romanos. Through the same spatharios Philippikos sent it to the western lands, even to Rome.

Before Philippikos had become Emperor, a heretic solitary monk who could see the future went to him in the monastery of Kallistratos and said, "The Empire will devolve on you." Philippikos was upset, but the monk said, "If God ordains it, how can you oppose it? I tell you this: the sixth synod was evil. Cast it out, and your reign will be mighty and long-lasting."

With an oath, Philippikos agreed to do this. When Leontios succeeded Justinian, Philippikos went to the monk, who told him, "You should not be eager: this *will* come to pass." And when Apsimaros became Emperor, Philippikos again went to him, and again he told Philippikos, "You should not be eager: it is still alive for you." But when Philippikos confided in one of his friends, the man told Apsimaros. He cudgeled and tonsured Philippikos, put him in irons, and exiled him to Kephalenia. When Justinian became Emperor, he recalled him once more.

Once he had become Emperor, Philippikos convened a false assembly of bishops to cast out the holy sixth ecumenical council, following the plan of the false abbot and monk. At the same time the profane fellow went blind.

Nevertheless, he stayed in the palaces, not a bit concerned. He had

381

---

153. Sts. Kosmas and Damian. They were healer-saints, who accepted no fees: thus their sobriquet, "those who take no money."

found a lot of money and expensive property collected by the previous Emperors (especially Justinian) through confiscations and various pretexts, and senselessly and vainly squandered it. In his speech he was reckoned eloquent and sensible, but his actions were impious and incompetent and showed him to be altogether disreputable. He was both a heretic and an adulterer. He ousted the patriarch Cyrus from his church and appointed his fellow mystic and fellow heretic John.

382   **ANNUS MUNDI 6204 (SEPTEMBER 1, 712—AUGUST 31, 713)**

A.D. **704**
Roman Emperor Philippikos: 2 years: year 1
Arab ruler Walid: 9 years: year 7
Bishop of Constantinople John: 3 years: year 1
Bishop of Jerusalem John: 30 years: year 7

In this year Philippikos drove the Armenians from his territory and made them settle in Melitene and fourth Armenia. Maslama took Melitene, other fortresses, and many prisoners. George the bishop of Apamea was resettled in Martyropolis.

Philippikos was not ashamed to move insanely against the sixth holy ecumenical council, and was eager to overturn the holy doctrines it had secured. He found that John, whom he had made bishop of Constantinople when he condemned his predecessor Cyrus, was of his opinion (Philippikos had imprisoned Cyrus in the monastery of the Khora). Also of his party were Germanos[154] (who later held the throne of Constantinople, but was at that time bishop of Kyzikos), Andrew (who was bishop of Crete), Nicholas (who knew a great deal about medicine and was at that time quaestor[155]), Elpidios the deacon of the great church, Antiokhos the chartophylax, and many others of similar stripe. They anathematized in writing the holy sixth synod.

When the Bulgars sneaked down through Philea to Stenon, they killed a large number of people and advanced all the way to the city. They found many men in transit and rich marriage feasts in progress; these were numerous and fine, with intricately wrought silver pieces

154. It is interesting to note that, according to Theophanes, Germanos subscribed to Bardanes Philippikos' council which briefly overturned the antimonothelite third Council of Constantinople, but proved a champion of orthodoxy against iconoclasm after he became patriarch of Constantinople.
155. In classical Roman times, the quaestor's chief concern had been with financial matters. In the Byzantine Empire, he was an imperial commissioner responsible for dealing with people coming from the provinces to the capital, sending home those without a valid excuse for coming to Constantinople, and also for dealing with the city's unemployed. In addition, the quaestor's court was responsible for dealing with certain judicial areas, including forgery.

and other trappings. They reached the Golden Gate after capturing all of Thrace, and then returned unharmed to their own country with uncountable flocks. In like fashion the Arabs took Mistheia and other fortresses, working destruction on many families and countless flocks.

383 ANNUS MUNDI 6205 (SEPTEMBER 1, 713—AUGUST 31, 714)

2. 8. 2. 8.

In this year Abas attacked Romania; he took Pisidian Antioch, then withdrew with many prisoners.

On the twenty-eighth of Peritios[156] there was a strong earthquake in Syria.

The two years of Philippikos' reign had passed in this way. After his birthday races had been held (with the Greens winning), the Emperor decided on the sabbath of Pentecost to enter the public bath-house of Zeuxippos on horseback (and to bring food and musical instruments) to wash himself there and breakfast with citizens of ancient lineage.

At the advice of George (surnamed Bouraphos) the patrician and count of the Opsikion, Rufus the protostrator of the Opsikion and the patrician Theodore Myakios suddenly entered the city through the Golden Gate with the regiments of that theme which they had in Thrace. This was while Philippikos was taking his siesta; they rushed into the palace and caught him napping, spiriting him away to the oratory of the Greens. Though no-one knew it, they blinded him there. On the next day (that is, Pentecost), when the people had gathered in the great church, the protoasekretes[157] Artemios was crowned and renamed Anastasios. On the Saturday after Pentecost Theodore Myakios was blinded, and on the next Saturday George Bouraphos; they were exiled to Thessalonike.

ANNUS MUNDI 6206 (SEPTEMBER 1, 714—AUGUST 31, 715)

A.D. **706**
Roman Emperor Artemios: 2 years: year 1
Arab ruler Walid: 9 years: year 9
Bishop of Constantinople John: 3 years: year 3
Bishop of Jerusalem John: 30 years: year 9

In this year Maslama raided Romania; after plundering Galatia, he withdrew with prisoners and booty. Still unafraid, Artemios appointed competent generals—men who were also skilled politicians—for the

156. February.
157. The chief of the imperial chancery. He renamed himself after another bureaucrat-turned-Emperor: Anastasios I (491–518).

384 thematic cavalry. Even while the Arabs were arming themselves against Romania by both land and sea, the Emperor sent officers (led by Daniel of Sinope) to Walid in Syria to discuss peace terms. He ordered Daniel to make a precise examination of the Arabs' move against Romania and their forces. After Daniel had gone and returned, he reported to the Emperor on their great expedition heading against the imperial city by land and sea.

Then the Emperor commanded each man to be able to pay his own way for three years' time, and ordered those unable to do so to abandon the city. He made sails and began to build warships, Greek-fire-carrying biremes, and huge triremes. He restored the land and sea walls, and installed arrow-shooting engines, stone-throwing engines, and catapults on the gates. He stored up a great amount of produce in the imperial granaries and secured it as best he could, and strengthened the city to the best of his ability.

ANNUS MUNDI 6207 (SEPTEMBER 1, 714—AUGUST 31, 715[158])

Arab ruler Suleiman: 3 years
Bishop of Constantinople Germanos: 15 years
2. 1. 1. 10.

In this year Walid died, with Suleiman succeeding to the rule.

In this same second year of Artemios (who was also called Anastasios)—the thirteenth indiction—on August 11 Germanos was translated from the metropolis of Kyzikos to Constantinople. On that occasion a decree of transfer was announced: "By the decision and determination of the pious priests and deacons, of all the pious clergy, of the holy senate, and of the Christ-loving people of this God-guarded imperial city, divine grace (which ministers to sickness and fulfills the incomplete) translates the most holy president of the metropolitanate

385 of the Kyzikenes so he can become bishop of this God-guarded and imperial city." This translation took place in the presence of Michael (a holy priest who was legate of the apostolic throne) and of other priests and bishops, and occurred during the reign of Artemios.

Artemios learned that the Saracens' expedition had sailed from Alexandria to Phoenicia to cut cypress-wood. He chose swift-sailing ships from his own forces and embarked in them regiments from the theme of the Opsikion, ordering them to rendezvous at Rhodes. As their general and chief he appointed John the deacon of the great church (known as "papa Ioannakis"), who was at that time minister of

158. See the discussion of Theophanes' chronology in the introduction, p. xviii.

public finance. He gave his officers instructions as they embarked: they were to go to Phoenicia to burn the timber and the Agarenes' equipment they found there.

Although all the officers obeyed eagerly, the troops of the Opsikion would not acquiesce in this; they renounced the Emperor and put John to the sword. Thereupon the expeditionary force broke up, with its components sailing off to their own homelands while the evildoers proceeded against the imperial city. They were leaderless until they came to Adramyttion. There they found a man named Theodosios, who was a native of that place. He was a tax collector, a good quiet easy man and a private citizen. They urged him to become Emperor, but he fled and hid in the mountains. When they found him they acclaimed him Emperor, compelling him to accept.

When Artemios learned this he posted friendly officers in the city along with the expeditionary force he had organized; once he had armed them, he went to Nikaia and securely established himself there. The rebels reached and roused the whole theme of the Opsikion, as well as the Gothogreeks.[159] They seized a number of merchant ships large and small, and came to Chrysopolis by both land and sea. Constantinople's naval force was anchored in the harbor of St. Mamas;[160] they fought with each other daily for six months.

386

When Constantinople's force moved its base to the Neoresian harbor, Theodosios crossed to Thrace. Thanks to treachery, he took the city through the gate of Blakhernai's single wall. The outlaw troops of the Opsikion and the Gothogreeks ran through the citizens' houses during the night, sparing no-one and working great destruction.

They seized those of Artemios' officers who were in the city and Germanos the patriarch of Constantinople and took them to Nikaia to assure Artemios and his men. When Artemios saw them he lost hope and, requesting a promise that he not be harmed, gave himself up and donned monastic garb. Theodosios did not harm him, but did exile him to Thessalonike. Philippikos had ruled for two years and nine months, Artemios for one year and three months.

Leo, who was general of the Anatolic theme, fought on behalf of Artemios and was not subjected by Theodosios. Artavasdos the Armenian, the general of the Armeniac theme, conspired and cooperated with Leo, who agreed to give him his daughter as a wife. This he did.

159. These are the descendants of Gothic soldiers who settled in Anatolia during the fourth and fifth centuries. By the eighth century they are, as their name indicates, largely Hellenized.

160. St. Mamas is a suburb of Constantinople across the Golden Horn from the city, close to Galata.

ANNUS MUNDI 6208 (SEPTEMBER 1, 715—AUGUST 31, 716)

A.D. **708**
Roman Emperor Theodosios: 1 year: year 1
Arab ruler Suleiman: 3 years: year 2
Bishop of Constantinople Germanos: 15 years: year 2
Bishop of Jerusalem John: 30 years: year 11

In this year Maslama attacked Constantinople, sending Suleiman ahead with an army by land and Umar by sea. He marched behind them with a great deal of military equipment. When Suleiman and Bakr reached Amorion, they wrote to Leo the general of the Anatolics: "We know the Roman Empire is rightfully yours. Come to us; let us discuss peace terms." Suleiman observed that Amorion had no garrison and opposed the general because he backed Artemios. As he wanted to receive Maslama there, he laid siege to it. The Saracens began to acclaim the general Leo as Emperor as soon as he neared the city, and called on those within to do the same. When the Amorians saw that the Saracens were acclaiming him because they liked him, they did so themselves.

When the general learned that Suleiman intended to destroy the city because it had no garrison or officers, he asked the Arab, "If you want me to come to you to discuss peace, why are you besieging this town?"

Suleiman said to him, "Come, and I will withdraw." The general got a safe-conduct from him, then came to him with three hundred cavalrymen. When the Agarenes saw him they met him wearing their corselets and full coats of mail; he camped half a mile from their army. He went to them on three days, and they discussed peace terms and the Arabs' withdrawal from Amorion. The Arabs said, "Make peace, and then we will withdraw."

The general knew they wanted to seize him. He invited most of the important Saracens to a dinner, but while they were eating Suleiman sent out 3,000 armored Saracens to encircle him and guard him so he could not escape. When his sentries realized this, they told him, "A host of Saracen cavalry is surrounding us."

One of the Saracens, a cavalryman named Zubayr, came up to him and said, "A slave stole a great treasure and fled; that is why our cavalry is in action."

The general recognized the tricky ploy; he told them, "Do not be distracted. If he should come to our camp we will find him."

Although dismayed, through a man of his Leo was secretly able to tell the Amorians, "Fear God and do not give yourselves up: learn that Maslama is on his way." Their bishop went out to him, and Leo told him the same thing. When Suleiman learned the bishop had gone to him, he sent the general a message: "Give us the bishop." Because he was surrounded, Leo hid him and told one of Suleiman's men, "After we met he changed clothes and went to the mountains, either through the woods or by water."

When the Arabs made threats about the bishop, the general said, "He isn't here. However, you go off to the emir, and I will come too, and we can talk everything over." The Saracens let him go, thinking that when he had come to the emir they would seize him while he was in their midst. He rode off with two hundred men, as if hunting, and gave way to the left. The Saracens with him asked, "Where might you be going?"

He said, "I want to shift camp to the springs."

They said, "Your idea is not a good one, and we will not come with you."

Then the general told his own men, "They gave us this safe-conduct because they wanted to seize us, and through us to destroy the Christians. But they will not capture one of our remaining men or horses." He kept on going for ten miles and then encamped. On the next day he sent a domesticus[161] who was one of his grooms to the Arabs, whom he told, "You gave me a safe-conduct, but you want to capture me by treachery. That is why I have withdrawn."

Maslama was coming over the mountain passes, but Suleiman did not know it. His emirs and army rebelled against him: "Why are we besieging walls instead of raiding?" They struck their tents and withdrew.

Leo sent the turmarch Nikaias into Amorion with eight hundred soldiers and made most of the women and children leave. He himself went to Pisidia.

389

When Maslama reached Kappadokia the Kappadokians lost hope for themselves and went out to him, calling on him to accept them. Since Maslama had heard that the Emperor Theodosios hated his general, he wanted to entice Leo and make peace with him, and to subject Romania through him. He asked the Kappadokians, "Are you not subjects of this general?"

"Yes," said they.

"Would you do anything if he does it?"

"Yes."

Then he told them, "Go off to your towns, and do not be afraid of anything." He commanded his army to do no damage in the general's provinces. When the general learned this he realized Suleiman had told Maslama he had gotten away from him and withdrawn; he sent

161. That is, a bodyguard.

letters to Maslama: "I wanted to approach you, but when I came to Suleiman he tried to capture me. Now I am afraid to come to you."

Maslama told the general's man, "I know the general is playing games with me, because I have not damaged his provinces at all."

The general's man said to him, "That is not so; he is writing to you in very truth."

Then Maslama asked him, "What is the situation in Amorion, which he is near?"

"It is well, and under his control," he answered.

Maslama became angry and reviled him: "Why should you lie?"

He said, "It is just as I said; Leo has sent troops and a turmarch into Amorion and brought out the superfluous families." Maslama was distressed and angered at this, and drove the man away. He had planned to gain control of Amorion during the summer, take over the expedition, and then return to Asia to winter there. Again he interrogated the general's man, who told him on oath, "Everything I have said to you is true, and the turmarch went in there with a thousand troops.[162] Leo removed all the people's property and the families there without resources."

When Maslama heard this he wrote to the general, "Approach me; I will make peace, and will do everything you wish."

390   But the general saw that Maslama was near Masalaion, and that in another five days Maslama would have traversed his provinces. He sent out two men of consular rank and told Maslama, "I have received your letters and I accept your plan. Behold, I am on my way to you. But as you know, I am a general, and have to have my money and silver and army following me. Send me a safe-conduct for each of them. If affairs turn out as I want of you, well and good: then I will return without penalty and without being put into difficulty."

At Theodosiana Maslama told the men of consular rank, "I see your general is playing with me."

"Heaven forbid!" they said.

While they were returning to their general with the written pledge, Maslama (who had a large army and could not stay in one place) went to Akroïnos. Seeing that Maslama had gone past his provinces, Leo went to Nikomedeia. He met Theodosios' son and captured him, the entire imperial retinue, and the palace's leading figures. The general took counsel with his men; he took the Emperor's son to Chrysopolis as a prisoner.

Maslama went back to Asia and wintered there, as did Umar in Kilikia.

162. At the same time as Leo's man is insisting on his truthfulness to Maslama, he is exaggerating by two hundred men the number of troops Leo had put into Amorion.

When Theodosios learned what had happened he consulted the patriarch Germanos and the senate. Through the patriarch he received a pledge from Leo that he would not be harmed and that the church would not be disturbed, and on those terms entrusted the Empire to him. Theodosios and his son became clerics, and lived out the rest of their lives in peace.

Maslama came to Pergamon and besieged it; thanks to the devil's action and God's concession he took it. For, at the urging of a wizard, the inhabitants of the city brought out a pregnant woman who was near giving birth and cut her open. They took the fetus and boiled it in a three-legged pot. All those who wanted to fight dipped their right sleeves in this sacrifice, disgusting to God. Hence they were given over to their enemies.

391

ANNUS MUNDI 6209 (SEPTEMBER 1, 716—AUGUST 31, 717)

Roman Emperor Leo the Isaurian: 24 years
6209. 709. 1. 3. 3. 12.

In this year Leo became Emperor. He derived from Germanikeia, but actually from Isauria. With his parents he had been resettled in Thracian Mesembria by the Emperor Justinian during his first reign. When Justinian came there with the Bulgars during his second reign, Leo met him with a gift of five hundred sheep. Flattered, Justinian made him a spatharios on the spot and judged him a true friend.

Some men who were jealous of Leo falsely accused him of grasping for the imperial power. There was an inquiry about this, with the result that his accusers were disgraced, but from then on many began to speak of this notion. If, indeed, Justinian did not wish to harm Leo openly, he did begin to feel anger toward him.

He sent Leo to Alania with money to help the Alans against the Abasgians because the Saracens had conquered Abasgia, Lazika, and Iberia. Leo went to Lazika, and stored the money at Phasis. He took a few of the locals to Apsilia and, crossing the Caucasus Mountains, reached Alania. But Justinian now wanted to destroy him, and sent out a messenger who took the money back from Phasis.

The Alans received the spatharios with all honor, paid attention to his plans, and invaded and captured Abasgia. The lord of the Abasgians told the Alans, "As I have found, Justinian does not have anyone else who is as big a liar as this man. The Emperor made him go off to work with you against us, your neighbors. Leo has even lied to you about his promise of money, for Justinian sent a man and took it back. Give him to us and we will pay you 3,000 nomismata; also, we will not break off the friendship we have always felt."

392   But the Alans said, "We do not obey him on account of money, but because of our love for the Emperor."

The Abasgians sent them men again, saying, "Give him to us and we will give you 6,000 nomismata." As they wanted to learn the Abasgians' land thoroughly, the Alans agreed to take the 6,000 nomismata and give up the general. But they told Leo everything, and said to him, "As you see, the road to Romania is closed, and you do not know how to cross. Instead, let us turn round and agree with them to give you up. We will send our men off with them, learn their mountain passes, and raid and devastate their land to do your service."

So the Alans' envoys went to Abasgia and agreed to give up the spatharios; they received gifts of friendship from the Abasgians. The Abasgians sent back more envoys with the amount of money to get the spatharios. The Alans told Leo, "Just as we said before, these men have come to take you, and Abasgia awaits you. When we near their land, our agents will not stop going to them. Furthermore, in order to keep from giving away our goal, we will openly give you up. But when your party has left, we will secretly come back to kill them, and will hide you until our army is mustered and we can invade their land by surprise."

This, in fact, is what happened. The Abasgians' envoys took the spatharios and his men, bound them, and went off. The Alans and their lord Itaxes overtook the Abasgians from behind; they killed them and hid Leo. Once they had levied troops, they marched on Abasgia and unexpectedly penetrated its passes. They took a great number of pris-

393   oners and worked destruction on the Abasgians.

When Justinian heard that his goal had been accomplished even without his money, he sent letters to the Abasgians: "If you preserve our general and let him come through your territory unharmed, we will suffer all your errors." They were overjoyed to agree to this, and sent a message back to Alania: "We will give you our children as hostages; give us the spatharios so we can send him to Justinian." But Leo would not accept this; he said, "May God open me a gate so I can go away, as I will not do so through Abasgia."

After a certain time a force of Romans and Armenians invaded Lazika and besieged Arkhaiopolis, but retreated when they heard the Saracens were coming. About two hundred got cut off from them; these men moved north and raided in Apsilia and the Caucasus. When the Saracens overran Lazika, the army of the Romans and Armenians fled to Phasis. The two hundred men still in the Caucasus Mountains stayed there as brigands, since they had lost hope for themselves.

When the Alans learned this, they thought there was a Roman host in the Caucasus; rejoicing at this, they said to the spatharios, "The Romans are near—go to them." He took fifty Alans and crossed the peaks of the Caucasus with snowshoes (in May!). He found the men and joyfully asked them, "Where is your army?"

They said, "When the Saracens attacked, it went back to Romania. Since we could not get there, we have been on the way to Alania."

"What shall we do now?" he asked them.

"We cannot travel this land," they said.

The spatharios answered, "It is impossible to leave by any other route."

There was a fortress there called Sideron, in which was a commander named Pharasmanios, who was subject to the Saracens and at peace with the Armenians. The spatharios sent him a message: "Because you are at peace with the Armenians, make peace with me as well. Come under the Empire, and help us go down to the sea so we can cross to Trebizond."[163] Since Pharasmanios did not choose to do this, the spatharios sent out some of his men and some Armenians, ordering them to lay an ambush: "When they leave the fortress to work, overpower as many of them as you can and seize the gates from the men outside until we get there too." They went there to lay the ambush, and made a sudden attack when the garrison came out to work; they captured the gates and took many prisoners.

But Pharasmanios was still in the citadel with a few men; when the spatharios arrived, he tried to talk him into opening the gates in peace. He did not wish to do so, and fought. Since his citadel was strong, Leo could not take it.

When Marinos (the leader of the Apsilians) learned the fortress was under siege he grew fearful, as he thought the spatharios had a large army. He took three hundred men to the spatharios, and told him, "I will maintain you until you reach the coast." Once Pharasmanios had seen this state of affairs, he said to the spatharios, "Take my child as a hostage; I agree to serve the Empire."

Leo took his child, then told him, "What sort of servant of the Empire do you call yourself, when you are talking with us while shut up? We cannot withdraw until we have taken your citadel."

Then Pharasmanios said, "Give me your pledge."

The spatharios promised he would not treat him unjustly, and would enter the citadel with only thirty men. But he did not keep his promise, ordering the thirty who entered with him, "When we go in, seize the gates so all of us can get in." After this was done he ordered the citadel set afire. There was a great conflagration; the families came out, snatching up whatever they could of their property.

After they spent another three days there, the troops razed the fort's walls to the ground. With the Apsilian leader Marinos they went

163. A Byzantine port on the southern shore of the Black Sea.

395   to Apsilia, where the Apsilians received them with great honor. From there Leo went to the coast, crossed, and went to Justinian.

After Justinian was killed and Philippikos blinded, Artemios became Emperor; he appointed Leo general over the Anatolics. Artemios was ousted and Theodosios became Emperor; the Roman state was being demolished by barbarian inroads, by those who bore the guilt for Justinian's blood, and by Philippikos' impious actions. Leo fought on Artemios' side, opposing Theodosios. He had as conspirator and helper Artavasdos the general of the Armeniacs; after Leo became Emperor he married Artavasdos to his daughter Anna, and also appointed him curopalates.

Maslama, who had wintered in Asia, received Leo's promises but did not accept anything from him, since he knew Leo was playing games with him. When he came to Abydos, he sent a large army across to Thrace and set it in motion against the imperial city. He also wrote to the caliph Suleiman that he should bring up his army, which was already ready.

On August 15 Maslama put the city under siege, while also punishing the Thracian fortresses. He surrounded the land wall with a stockade, digging a great ditch and erecting above it a parapet-like wall of unmortared stone.

On September 1 of the first indiction Christ's enemy Suleiman and his emirs arrived with their expedition. He had front-line ships, fighting merchantmen, and warships; their number was 1,800, and they anchored from Magnaura to Kyklobion. After two days the south

396   wind began to blow; they left that area and sailed past the city. Some crossed to the suburbs of Eutropios and Anthemios,[164] while others anchored in Thrace from Galata to Kleidion.[165]

The Arabs' great ships were useless because they were weighed down by their cargo, and so they left behind about twenty merchantmen to guard their backs; these had about a hundred armored men to protect them. Good weather came while they were in the Bosporos, and its narrow passage was not very windy, so Maslama pushed his ships farther forward. With God's help, the pious Emperor[166] immediately sent fireships against them from the citadel, which turned them into blazing wrecks. Some of them, still burning, smashed into the sea wall, while others sank in the deep men and all, and still others, flaming

---

164. These districts are on the Asiatic coast of the Bosporos, about halfway between the Sea of Marmora and the Black Sea.

165. Galata is, of course, just across the Golden Horn from Constantinople. Kleidion is on the European side of the Bosporos, not far north of Galata.

166. Theophanes is plainly (and carelessly) copying from a contemporary source, for of his own free will he would never term Leo III, who began the iconoclastic controversy, "pious"!

furiously, went as far off course as the islands of Oxeia and Plateia.[167]

Because of this the spirits of the city's inhabitants were lifted, but their foes shivered in terror, recognizing how strong the liquid fire was. They had planned to anchor at the sea walls and to attack the battlements at the narrow neck of land on the same evening. But, at the intercession of His wholly chaste Mother, God shattered their plan.

On that same night the Emperor mysteriously drew up the chain,[168] but the enemy thought he wanted to entice them and would stretch it out again: they did not dare come in to anchor within the confines of Galata. Instead, they sailed to the bay of Sosthenios[169] and warded their fleet there. On October 8 their ruler Suleiman died, and Umar became caliph. The winter was very severe in Thrace, so that for a hundred days crystalline snow covered the earth. A great number of the enemy's horses, camels, and other beasts died.

When it was spring, Sufyan arrived with an expedition organized in Egypt; he had four hundred food-carrying merchantmen and warships. When he learned of the power of Greek fire, he bypassed Bithynia; after crossing over to the other shore, he anchored at the harbor of Kalos Agros. Yezid soon arrived with another expedition, which had been formed in Africa. He had two hundred sixty merchantmen, with both arms and supplies. Like Sufyan, he had learned about the liquid fire. He anchored at Satyros, Bryas, and as far away as Kartalimen.[170]

397

The Egyptians[171] of the two expeditions consulted among themselves. That night they took the merchant ships' light boats and, acclaiming the Emperor, fled to the city, so that the sea seemed entirely covered with wood from Hiereia to the city. The Emperor learned from them of the two fleets hidden in the bay. He readied fire-carrying siphons and put them aboard warships and two-storied ships, then dispatched them against the two fleets. Thanks to the cooperation of God through His wholly immaculate Mother's intercession, the enemy was sunk on the spot. Seizing booty and the Arabs' supplies, our men returned with joy and victory.

Under Mardasan, the Arabs' army once more came through the Gates, advancing up to Nikaia and Nikomedeia. The imperial officers

167. About twenty miles south of Constantinople.

168. A stout chain ran between Constantinople and Galata to protect the Golden Horn from enemy ships.

169. An inlet about halfway up the European coast of the Bosporos.

170. These are towns on the Asian shore of the Sea of Marmora; Kartalimen is more than thirty miles from Constantinople.

171. As opposed to the Arabs. Egypt, which had been under Muslim rule for only a little more than seventy years, was still a predominantly Christian land.

and their infantry (who had been hiding in Libon and Sophon like Mardaites[172]) suddenly attacked them; they broke them up and made them flee the spot.

Once the opposite shore[173] had gained a little security, a great number of small craft could emerge from the city and get food for it. Similarly, the small fishing boats at the islands and men on the walls around the city were not prevented from catching fish.

Since the Arabs were extremely hungry, they ate all their dead animals: horses, asses, and camels. Some even say they put dead men and their own dung in pans, kneaded this, and ate it. A plague-like disease descended on them, and destroyed a countless throng.[174] Also, the Bulgars attacked them and, as say those who know such things exactly, slaughtered 22,000 Arabs. Many terrible things happened to them at that time, so that from their own efforts they realized that God and His all-holy maiden Mother watched over this city and the Empire of the Christians. God's ability to fulfill prayer for those who truly call on Him cannot be blocked, even if, because of our sins, we learn only a little.

398

ANNUS MUNDI 6210 (SEPTEMBER 1, 717—AUGUST 31, 718)

Arab ruler Umar: 2 years
2. 1. 4. 13.

In this year the protospatharios Sergios, the governor of Sicily, heard that the Arabs were besieging the imperial city. At Sicily he crowned his own Emperor: a Constantinopolitan named Basil, the son of Gregory Onomagoulos. He was renamed Tiberius. He prepared defenses and created his own officers (with the advice of Sergios).

When the Emperor heard this he sent out his own chartularius[175] Paul, making him a patrician and general of Sicily. For support Leo gave him two spatharioi and a few men, orders to the western officers, and a state letter to the army. By night they boarded an outbound warship, and went somewhere near Kyzikos. They traveled from place to place by both land and sea, and reached Sicily unexpectedly. Sergios was amazed when he heard they had entered Syracuse. Knowing his own guilt, he fled to the Lombards, who were nearby in Calabria. The army was assembled and the state letter read: it assured the troops that the Empire endured and the city was in good spirits about its enemies. Also, it related the details about the two fleets. The men at once

172. That is, like mountain brigands.
173. Where the Arabs were.
174. If the preceding sentence is true, this is hardly surprising!
175. Privy secretary.

acclaimed Leo as Emperor and gave to his general Basil Onomagoulos and the officers he had appointed.

Paul decapitated Basil and his chief general; after he had cut off their heads, he sent them swathed in cloth to the Emperor by means **399** of his two spatharioi. He beat and tonsured the rest, slit some of their noses, and exiled them. In this way there was a great settlement of affairs in the west. Sergios asked the general for a pledge that he would not be harmed, and came to him after he got it. They pacified the entire western area.

Umar, who was ruling the Arabs, urged Maslama to retire. The Arabs pulled out in great disgrace on August 15. While their expedition was on its way back, a furious storm fell on them and scattered them: it came from God at the intercession of His Mother. God drowned some of them by Prokonnessos and other islands, and others on Apostrophoi and other promontories. Those who were left had got through the Aegean Sea when God's fearful wrath attacked them: a fiery shower descended on them, making the sea's water foam up. Once their pitch[176] was gone, the ships went to the bottom men and all. Only ten survived to report to us and the Arabs the magnitude of what God had done to them. Our men were able to seize five when they ran into them, but the other five escaped to tell Syria of God's might.

In the same year, because there had been a strong earthquake in Syria, Umar banned wine[177] from his cities and forced the Christians to apostasize. He exempted the apostates from taxation but killed those who refused, which made many martyrs. He promulgated a law that a Christian's testimony against a Saracen was not acceptable. He also sent a doctrinal letter to the Emperor Leo, thinking to persuade him to apostasize.

ANNUS MUNDI 6211 (SEPTEMBER 1, 718—AUGUST 31, 719)

3. 2. 5. 14.

In this year a still more impious son was born to the impious **400** Emperor Leo: Constantine, the forerunner of the Antichrist. On December 25 Leo's wife Maria was crowned in the triklinos of the Augusteion. She went to the great church alone—without her husband—and without ceremony. She prayed before going in to the altar, then went into the great baptistery. Her husband and a few of his intimates had preceded her in. While Germanos the chief prelate was baptizing Leo's successor (in both his evil and his rule) Constantine, the boy,

---

176. Which, of course, caulked the ships.
177. Islamic law always prohibited Muslims from drinking wine; Umar is attempting to apply the law to all his subjects, whether Muslim or not.

because he was so young, gave a terrible, foul-smelling harbinger: he defecated in the holy font, as say those who were accurate eyewitnesses.[178] This made the patriarch Germanos prophetically say, "This is a sign that in the future great evil shall befall the Christians and the church because of him." The leaders of the themes and senate received Constantine after his baptism. After the divine liturgy the Augusta Maria returned with her baptized son; she distributed largess all the way from the church to the Bronze Gate of the palace.

In the same year Niketas Xylinites wrote to Artemios in Thessalonike that he should go to Tervel and move against Leo with a Bulgarian alliance. Obeying Niketas, he went off to Tervel, who gave him an army and fifty centenaria[179] of gold. Artemios took them and moved on Constantinople, but when the city did not receive him favorably, the Bulgars handed him over to Leo and went home. The Emperor treated them kindly, but executed Artemios and Xylinites. He also confiscated the property of Xylinites, who was a magistros and had acquired quite a lot. Since the patrician Sisinnios (surnamed Rhendakis) had been with Artemios, the Bulgars likewise beheaded him. They also gave the Emperor the archbishop of Thessalonike, who was decapitated with Artemios. Leo executed Isoes the patrician and count of the Opsikion, Theoktistes the protoasekretes, and Niketas Anthrax the officer of the walls because they were Artemios' friends and colleagues. After he had slit the noses and confiscated the property of the rest, he exiled them.

401

ANNUS MUNDI 6212 (SEPTEMBER 1, 719—AUGUST 31, 720)

A.D. 712
Roman Emperor Leo: 24 years: year 4
Arab ruler Yezid: 4 years: year 1
Bishop of Constantinople Germanos: 15 years: year 6
Bishop of Jerusalem John: 30 years: year 15

In this year—the third indiction—Constantine was crowned by his father Leo in the tribunal of the nineteen Akkubita.[180] The blessed patriarch Germanos made the usual prayers.

In the same year, after having been caliph of the Arabs for two years and four months, Umar died and Yezid became caliph. In Persia a rebel who was himself named Yezid the son of Muhallab rose up

178. This is the origin of the derisive title Kopronymos ("Dung-name") by which Constantine V is sometimes known.
179. One centenarium equals one hundred pounds.
180. A ceremonial banquet-hall, built by Constantine I, on the western side of the palace complex.

against him, and many inhabitants of Persia went over to him. Yezid dispatched Maslama, who killed Yezid the son of Muhallab and resubjected Persia.

ANNUS MUNDI 6213 (SEPTEMBER 1, 720—AUGUST 31, 721)

5. 2. 7. 16.

In this year there appeared a Syrian false Christ who deceived the Hebrews by saying he was the Christ, the Son of God.

ANNUS MUNDI 6214 (SEPTEMBER 1, 721—AUGUST 31, 722)

6. 3. 8. 17.

In this year the Emperor forced the Hebrews and the Montanists[181] to be baptized. The Hebrews ate and partook of the holy gift but, as they had not been baptized of their own free will, washed off their baptism and defiled the faith. The Montanists settled matters for themselves through an oracle. They set a day on which they went into their heretical churches and incinerated themselves.

ANNUS MUNDI 6215 (SEPTEMBER 1, 722—AUGUST 31, 723)

7. 4. 9. 18.

In this year a Jewish wizard who made his headquarters at Phoenician Laodikeia came to Yezid. He told him that he would rule the Arab state for forty years if he would condemn the honored and revered icons in the Christians' churches throughout his entire empire. The senseless Yezid believed him and promulgated an all-embracing edict against the holy icons. But by the grace of our Lord Jesus Christ and the intercession of His uncorrupt Mother and all the saints, Yezid died in the same year, no sooner than his satanic doctrine had been heard by the masses.

But the Emperor Leo caused us many evils, because he shared this malignant, illegal, and evil doctrine. He found a partisan for his stupidity: a man named Beser, who had been a Christian prisoner in Syria and had apostasized from his faith in Christ and converted to the Arabs' doctrine. He had been freed from his servitude to them not

181. A heretical Phrygian sect, originating in the second century and savagely persecuted since the days of Justinian I. They were ecstatics, and saw themselves as new vehicles for the Holy Spirit. They denied the power of priests to forgive sins incurred after baptism, and confused the persons of the Trinity, to the distress of the orthodox.

long before, and had reached the Roman Emperor. Leo favored him because he was physically strong and because he agreed with Leo's wicked doctrine; he was a comrade in this great evil the Emperor worked. Also, the totally impure bishop of Nakoleia, who lived with Leo, wickedly concurred with his natural stupidity.

ANNUS MUNDI 6216 (SEPTEMBER 1, 723—AUGUST 31, 724)

Arab ruler Hisham: 19 years
8. 1. 10. 19.

I have come to discuss the matter of the blessed Stephen, the pope of Rome,[182] and how he fled to the Frankish land for his salvation.

This famous Stephen had withstood many evils from Astulph the king of the Lombards. He fled to the Franks: to Pepin, the majordomo and viceroy in charge of administering the Frankish people and all their affairs. For it was a custom among them that their lord (that is, the king) reigned by virtue of his family, but administered nothing and did nothing but senselessly eat and drink. He passed his time at home, but on May 1 he sat before the entire tribe, bowed low to them and was bowed to by them, was brought the customary gifts and gave them in return, and then lived by himself until the next May. He had an official called a majordomo, who administered all affairs according to his own will and that of the tribe. Those of the royal house were called "kristatai," which means "those with hair down their backs," for they had hair growing down along their backs like swine.[183]

At any rate, Stephen was being harassed by Astulph's cruelty and rudeness. All at once he turned on him, and went to the Frankish lands to accomplish whatever he could. Once he had gone, he invested Pepin, a man who was quite eminent at that time, with the royal power. Not only did he have leadership over affairs from the king, but had fought the Arabs who had crossed from Africa to Spain and dared range themselves against the Franks (the Arabs have held Spain until the present). By the Eridanos river[184] Pepin met them with his army

403

182. For Arab affairs, Theophanes' chronology is quite accurate. This is not the case in regard to western events. Stephen II was pope from 752–757; his flight to the Franks took place in the winter of 753–754.

183. This is Theophanes' confused description of the coiffure of the Merovingian kings of the Franks; they wore their hair long as a badge of royalty.

184. Again, Theophanes' chronology is vague. The battle of Tours took place in 732 or 733, and was won by Pepin's father Charles Martel ("the hammer"). Interestingly, the monk correctly states the name of the Arab commander who opposed the Franks.

94

and killed their commander Abd ar-Rahman and a host not easy to count.

Pepin's people marveled at and loved him not only because of this, but also from other exploits. When Stephen freed him of his false oath to the king, tonsured the ex-king and shut him into a monastery with honor and rest, Pepin was the first man to become the leader of his people who did not do so by virtue of his family. This Pepin had two sons, Charles and his brother Carloman.

In the same year died Yezid, who had been caliph for four years; his brother Hisham succeeded him. He began to build palaces in every city and town, to sow crops, and to create gardens and fountains. He also attacked Romania, but withdrew after squandering many of his men.

Stephen the pope of Rome fled to the Franks.

404   ANNUS MUNDI 6217 (SEPTEMBER 1, 724—AUGUST 31, 725)

Bishop of Rome,[185] *Gregory: 9 years* [186]
9. 2. 1.[185] *11. 20.*

In this year the impious Emperor began to frame an order[187] condemning the august, holy icons. When Gregory, the pope of Rome,

185. As Rome has the highest status among the patriarchates, the regnal years of the popes precedes those of the patriarchs of Constantinople (see note 9).

186 This papal reign is a conflation of the papacies of Gregory II (715–731) and Gregory III (731–741).

187. This is one of the most vexing passages in Theophanes. The word rendered "order" here is in Greek λόγον (nominative, λόγος), a term with a bewildering multiplicity of possible meanings. Followed here are the conclusions of Milton V. Anastos, *Cambridge Medieval History*, 4, part 1 (second edition, Cambridge, England, 1966), 61–104, 835–848, and his article "Leo III's Edict Against the Images in the Year 726–27 and Italo-Byzantine Relations Between 726 and 730," *Polychordia: Festschrift Franz Dölger zum 75. Geburtstag* (Amsterdam, 1968), III, 5–41 and especially 8–9. Using Latin sources and later Byzantine hagiographical writing, Anastos convincingly demonstrates the correctness of his interpretation. The opposing viewpoint, wherein this passage is to be construed as meaning that in 726 the Emperor began *discussion* of the issue of the icons, but did not take formal action against them until January, 730 (the date of the dismissal of the iconophile patriarch Germanos), is championed by George Ostrogorsky, "Les débuts de la querelle des images," *Mélanges Charles Diehl* (Paris, 1930), I, 235–255, and *History of the Byzantine State*, 162–164.

Related to the issue of the outbreak of iconoclasm is the transfer by the Byzantine Empire of Illyricum, southern Italy, and Sicily from papal jurisdiction to that of the patriarch of Constantinople (although Steven Runciman, *The Eastern Schism: A Study of the Papacy and the Eastern Churches during the XIth and XIIth Centuries* [Oxford, 1955], 20, ascribes it to "the general Isaurian

learned this he stopped the tribute from Italy and Rome and wrote Leo a doctrinal letter to the effect that it was not proper for the Emperor to issue a command concerning the faith or to make innovations in the ancient doctrines of the church, which had been established by the holy fathers.

In the same year a raging torrent overflowed and got into Edessa, where it destroyed many people.

ANNUS MUNDI 6218 (SEPTEMBER 1, 726—AUGUST 31, 727[188])

10. 3. 2. 12. 21.

In this year Maslama attacked and took Kappadokian Caesarea.
There was a plague in Syria.
The caliph's camels became a burnt-offering in the church of St. Helias.
Hisham's son Muawiyah attacked Romania, went here and there, and withdrew.
In the same year—the ninth indiction—for some days during summer a smoke, as if from a burning oven, arose from the depths of the sea between the islands of Thera[189] and Therasia. Little by little it thickened and petrified from the heat of the fiery combustion, and the smoke became entirely incandescent. With the thickening of its earthy nature it sent forth great lumps of pumice like hilltops: they reached all Asia Minor, Lesbos, Abydos, and the coast of Macedonia, so the whole face of this sea was full of floating lumps of pumice.

From the midst of the huge conflagration an island came up from the bowels of the earth and was joined to the island called Hiera. It had not existed at all before but, just as Thera and Therasia were once

scheme for tidying the administration of the Empire"). As with the question of iconoclasm's beginning, there is a problem in dating the ecclesiastical shift. Anastos, "The Transfer of Illyricum, Calabria and Sicily to the Jurisdiction of the Patriarchate of Constantinople in 732–33," *Silloge bizantina in onore di Silvio Giuseppe Mercati* (Rome, 1957), 14–31, puts the transfer in the years mentioned in his article's title, as does Runciman, loc. cit. Vénance Grumel, "L'annexion de l'Illyricum, de la Sicile et de la Calabre au patriarcat de Constantinople," *Recherches de science religieuse*, 40 (1952), 191–200, argues that the shift did not take place until the early 750s during the reign of Constantine V; Ostrogorsky, *History of the Byzantine State,* 170, concurs with him. On balance, the earlier date seems preferable, linking this transfer to the confiscation of the papal patrimonies by Leo III (Theophanes, *annus mundi* 6224:de Boor, 410, this translation, 101).

188. See the introduction's discussion of Theophanes' chronology, p. xviii.

189. Thera is itself a volcanic island; a previous explosion more than 2,000 years before this time may well have given rise to the legend of Atlantis.

405 thrown up, so was this one then: during the time of God's foe Leo.

Leo deduced that God was angry at him, but still more shamelessly incited battle against the august, holy icons. He had as an ally Beser, who had denied God and was his match in this sort of nonsense. Both of them were totally ignorant and stupid; from this sprang many evils.

The masses of the imperial city, dismayed at their newfangled teachings, intended to attack Leo. They killed some of the Emperor's men who had destroyed the icon of the Lord on the Bronze Gate, with the result that Leo caused many of them (especially those distinguished by noble birth or rhetorical skill) to be punished for their piety by mutilation, lashes, exile, and fines. This brought an end to the schools and pious education which had prevailed since the time of Constantine the Great, who is among the saints. The Saracen-minded[190] Leo condemned them and many other fine things.

At this time the men of the themes of Hellas and the Cyclades islands, impelled by holy zeal, entered into agreements with each other and rebelled against Leo in a great sea-campaign. Kosmas was with them as their candidate for the crown; Agallianos (the turmarch of the theme of Hellas) and Stephen led their army. They neared the imperial city on April 18 of the tenth indiction and engaged the Byzantines, but were defeated because their ships were consumed by the artificial fire. Some men went to the bottom of the sea, among them Agallianos, who drowned himself in his armor, but the survivors went over to the victors. Kosmas and Stephen were beheaded, the impious Leo was strengthened in his evil ways, and his faction stepped up its persecution of piety.

At around the summer solstice of this tenth indiction (after the evil victory of Leo's partisans) a body of Saracens attacked Bithynian Nikaia. It had two emirs: Amr went ahead with 15,000 light-armed men to surround the unprepared city, while Muawiyah followed with an-

406 other 85,000. Even after a long siege and the partial destruction of the walls, they could not enter Nikaia's sacred precinct of the honored and holy fathers because of its inhabitants' prayers, which were acceptable to God. The images of the fathers were set up there, and have been honored until the present by their fellow believers.

Constantine, one of Artavasdos' grooms, saw an icon of the Mother of God. He picked up a stone and threw it at the icon, and when it fell he broke it and trampled it. In a dream he saw our Mistress standing beside him. She said, "Do you think you have done Me any sort of good turn? Actually, this will rebound on your own head." On the next day the Saracens attacked the wall and battle was joined. Like a good soldier, this miserable fellow ran to the wall. He was hit by a

190. That is, opposed to icons.

stone shot from a catapult, which smashed his head and face; thus he received a repayment worthy of his impiety.

After the Arabs accumulated a large body of prisoners and booty, they withdrew. God reveals this to the impious: not because of his piety did Leo prevail over his fellow citizens, as he boasted, but for a divine reason and an ineffable judgement. The city of the holy fathers[191] beat back the Arabs' might by the images in it (which most definitely were honored) and their intercession. The impious fellow not only was mistaken about the natural reverence due the revered icons, but also about the intercession of the wholly sacred Mother of God and of the saints. Like his teachers the Arabs, the totally bloody man loathed their remains.

From that time on he shamelessly harassed the blessed Germanos (the patriarch of Constantinople) and found fault with all the Emperors, chief prelates, and Christian folk who had preceded him, on the ground that they had been idolaters because of their reverence for the august, holy icons. Because of his faithlessness and uncouthness he did not withdraw his statement on natural reverence.

407 ANNUS MUNDI 6219 (SEPTEMBER 1, 727—AUGUST 31, 728)

11. 4. 3. 13. 22.

In this year Muawiyah took the fortress of Ateous, then withdrew.

ANNUS MUNDI 6220 (SEPTEMBER 1, 728—AUGUST 31, 729)

12. 5. 4. 14. 23.

In this year the son of the Khagan (the ruler of Khazaria) attacked Media and Armenia. On encountering the Arab general in Armenia, he killed him and his host. He ravaged the land of the Armenians and that of the Medes and returned after terrorizing the Arabs.

ANNUS MUNDI 6221 (SEPTEMBER 1, 729—AUGUST 31, 730)

13. 6. 5. 15. 24.

In this year Maslama attacked the land of the Turks.[192] When they met one another in battle men fell on both sides. Maslama became fearful and withdrew in flight through the mountains of Khazaria.

In the same year the lawbreaking Emperor Leo raged against the

191. Nikaia was the site of the first ecumenical council, and would be that of the seventh council in 787.
192. That is, the Khazars.

true faith. He brought in the blessed Germanos and began to entice him with coaxing words. The blessed chief prelate told him, "We have heard there will be a condemnation of the holy and revered icons, but not during your reign." When the Emperor forced him to say during whose reign, he said, "During the reign of Konon."

The Emperor said, "In fact, my baptismal name is Konon."

The patriarch said, "Heaven forbid, my lord, that this evil should come to pass through your rule. For he who does it is the forerunner of the Antichrist and the overthrower of the incarnate and divine dispensation." Because of this the tyrant became angry; he put heavy pressure on the blessed man, just as Herod once had on John the Baptist. But the patriarch reminded him of his agreements before he became Emperor: he had given Germanos a pledge secured by God that he would in no way disturb God's church from its apostolic laws, which God had handed down. But the wretch was not ashamed at this. He watched Germanos and contended with him, and put forth statements to the effect that if he found Germanos opposing his rule, he would condemn the holder of the throne[193] like a conspirator and not like a confessor.

In this Leo had Germanos' pupil and synkellos[194] Anastasios as an ally. He was on good terms with Anastasios because Anastasios agreed with his impiety: the successor to the throne was an adulterer. The blessed patriarch was not unaware that Anastasios was crooked; imitating his Master, he wisely and gently reminded him of what betrayal entailed, as if to another Iscariot. But when he saw Anastasios had inalterably gone astray, he turned to him so that Anastasios stepped on the back of his robe. When Anastasios went in to the Emperor, Germanos said, "Don't hurry, for you will enter the gate through which the chariots come."

Anastasios was troubled by this statement, as by other things he had heard, but was unaware of its prophetic nature. It came true at last after fifteen years, in the third year of Constantine the persecutor (the twelfth indiction). This persuaded everyone that it had been foretold to the senseless man by divine grace. For once Constantine had reconquered the Empire after the revolt of his brother-in-law Artavasdos, he beat Anastasios and paraded him backwards in the hippodrome with other enemies of the Emperor. Naked and seated on an ass, he was brought in through the gate the chariots used, because with the Em-

193. That is, the patriarchal throne.
194. A synkellos was originally a monk who lived with his bishop (literally, one who shared a cell), whose function was to be a witness to the purity of his life. In the Orthodox Church, synkelloi became patriarchal advisers with considerable powers, and had seats and votes of their own at church councils.

peror's enemies he had renounced Constantine and crowned Artavasdos, as will be revealed in its own place.

In Byzantium the champion of pious doctrines—the holy and marvelous priest Germanos—was in his prime, fighting against the wild
beast who bore the name Leo and against his henchmen. In the elder
Rome Gregory, a holy and apostolic man who held the same throne
as had the prince Peter, caused Rome, Italy, and all the west to secede
from both political and ecclesiastical obedience to Leo and his Empire.
In Syrian Damascus the priest and monk John Chrysorrhoas (the son
of Mansur), an excellent teacher, shone in his life and his words.[195]

But since Germanos was under his control, Leo expelled him from
his throne. Through letters Gregory openly accused Leo of what was
known to many, and John subjected the impious man to anathemas.
On January 7 of the thirteenth indiction—a Saturday—the impious
Leo convened a silentium[196] against the holy and revered icons at the
tribunal of the nineteen Akkubita. He even summoned the holy patriarch Germanos, thinking he could persuade him to subscribe to opposing the holy icons. But in no way would the noble servant of Christ
obey Leo's abominable, wicked doctrine. He rightly taught the true
doctrine, but bade farewell to his position as chief prelate. He gave up
his surplice[197] and, after many instructive words, said, "If I am Jonah,
cast me into the sea. For, Emperor, I cannot make innovations in the
faith without an ecumenical conference." He went off to the Platanaion
and went into seclusion at his ancestral home, having been patriarch
for fourteen years, five months, and seven days.

On the twenty-second of this same January they chose Anastasios,
who was misnamed the pupil and synkellos of the blessed Germanos,
since he agreed with Leo's impiety. He was appointed false bishop of
Constantinople because of his all-embracing hunger for power. As I
said before, Gregory the pope of Rome refused to accept Anastasios
and his libelli[198] and, through letters, condemned Leo for his impiety;
he also split off Rome and all Italy from his rule.

The tyrant was furious, and stepped up his persecution of the holy
icons. Many clerics, monks, and pious laymen were endangered because of their true concept of the faith and were crowned with the
crown of martyrdom.

409

195. This is the famous theologian John of Damascus, who, being safe
under the rule of the Arabs, could fulminate as he wished against iconoclasm
without fearing imperial reprisals. "Chrysorrhoas" means "flowing with
gold."
196. An assembly of leading secular and church officials.
197. The garment which was a symbol of his office.
198. The "pamphlets" in which his statement of faith was contained.

ANNUS MUNDI 6222 (SEPTEMBER 1, 730—AUGUST 31, 731)

Bishop of Constantinople Anastasios: 24 years
14. 7. 6. 1. 25.

In this year Maslama attacked Romania; when he reached Kappadokia, he took the fortress of Kharsianon by treachery.

ANNUS MUNDI 6223 (SEPTEMBER 1, 731—AUGUST 31, 732)

15. 8. 7. 2. 26.

In this year Maslama attacked the land of the Turks but grew fearful and withdrew after he had reached the Caspian Gates.

ANNUS MUNDI 6224 (SEPTEMBER 1, 732—AUGUST 31, 733)

16. 9. 8. 3. 27.

410 In this year the Emperor betrothed the daughter of the Khagan (the ruler of the Skythians[199]) to his son Constantine. Converting her to Christianity, he renamed her Irene. She became eminent for her piety and, after closely examining the holy scriptures, condemned their impiety.

Hisham's son Muawiyah attacked Romania; he moved all the way up to Paphlagonia and returned with many prisoners.

The Emperor was furious at the pope and at the defection of Italy. He armed a great expedition and, appointing as its commander Manes the general of the Kibyrhaiot theme, sent him against the pope and the Italians. But the irreverent fellow was put to shame when the expedition reached the Adriatic Sea. Thereupon Leo the enemy of God raged all the more, for he was under the control of his Arabic heart. He levied a third more tribute on the people of Sicily and Calabria.[200] He also ordered the patrimony of the saints and princes of the apostles[201] (who are honored in the elder Rome), which from ancient times had paid three and a half talents of gold to the churches, to pay them to the public account. He even ordered male babies observed and registered, as Pharaoh once had those of the Hebrews: not even his teachers the Arabs themselves did this to the Christians in the east.

199. That is, the Khazars. Byzantine historical writers often used this archaic name to describe the nomads of the northern steppes; on occasion its vagueness can cause modern writers considerable confusion. It seems a reasonable conclusion, however, that the Byzantine authors and their readers generally knew about whom they were talking.

200. These areas were still under the control of the Byzantine Empire, despite the pope's detachment of the rest of Byzantine Italy from imperial rule.

201. That is, the patrimony of Peter.

ANNUS MUNDI 6225 (SEPTEMBER 1, 733—AUGUST 31, 734)
17. 10. 9. 4. 28.

In this year there was a plague in Syria, and many died.

ANNUS MUNDI 6226 (SEPTEMBER 1, 734—AUGUST 31, 735)
Bishop of Rome Zachariah: 21 years[202]
18. 11. 1. 5. 29.

In this year Theodore son of Mansur was exiled to the desert. There was a sign in the sky which shone like a burning brand. Muawiyah devastated Asia.

ANNUS MUNDI 6227 (SEPTEMBER 1, 735—AUGUST 31, 736)
19. 12. 2. 6. 30.

In this year Hisham's son Suleiman attacked the land of the Armenians, but accomplished nothing.

ANNUS MUNDI 6228 (SEPTEMBER 1, 736—AUGUST 1, 737)
20. 13. 3. 7.

In this year Muawiyah attacked Romania. On his way back he fell off his horse and gave up the ghost a few days later.

411 ANNUS MUNDI 6229 (SEPTEMBER 1, 737—AUGUST 31, 738)
21. 14. 4. 8.

In this year Hisham's son Suleiman took many prisoners from Asia. Among them he captured a Paphlagonian who said he was Tiberius son of Justinian. In order to honor his own son and terrify the Emperors,[203] Hisham sent this fellow to Jerusalem with the appropriate imperial honors, soldiers, banners, and scepters. Hisham ordered him to tour all Syria so everyone could see and marvel at him.

202. Zachariah was pope from 741 to 752; Theophanes' chronology is still very confused.
203. Leo and his son Constantine.

ANNUS MUNDI 6230 (SEPTEMBER 1, 738—AUGUST 31, 739)

22. 15. 5. 9.

In this year Hisham's son Suleiman attacked Romania. He stormed the fortress known as Sideroun and captured Eustathios the son of the patrician Marianos.

ANNUS MUNDI 6231 (SEPTEMBER 1, 739—AUGUST 31, 740)

23. 16. 6. 10.

In this year—the eighth indiction—in May Suleiman attacked Romania with 90,000 men. There were four generals: of them, Ghamr led 10,000 light-armed troops to surprise the land of Asia; behind him, Malik and Battal had 20,000 cavalry near Akroïnos; after them came Suleiman with 60,000 men near Kappadokian Tyana. While the Arabs in Asia and Kappadokia withdrew unharmed after destroying a large number of men, women, and beasts of burden, Malik's and Battal's forces were completely subdued and defeated by Leo and Constantine. Most of them, including their two commanders, were lost while under arms. But 6,800 of their warriors resisted, fled to Synnada, and survived. They joined Suleiman in his return to Syria. In the same year many of them fell in Africa with their commander, whose name was Damaskenos.

412 ANNUS MUNDI 6232 (SEPTEMBER 1, 740—AUGUST 31, 741)

24. 17. 7. 11.

In this year (the twenty-fourth of the reign of the tyrant and great lawbreaker Leo the Syrian) the markets in Damascus were burned by the Hierakitai, who were hanged.

Also, in September there was a flood at Edessa.

In the same year—the ninth indiction—at the eighth hour of Wednesday, October 26, there was a strong and terrifying earthquake at Constantinople. Many churches and monasteries were toppled, and many people died. The statue of Constantine the Great on the Attalid gate fell, as did the gate itself. So did Arkadios' monument on the column of Xerolophos, the statue of Theodosios the Great on the Golden Gate,[204] the city's land walls, towns and villages in Thrace, and

204. Arkadios was Emperor in the East from 395 to 408; his father Theodosios I ("the Great") ruled the East from 379 to 395, and was the last man briefly to rule both the eastern and western halves of the Roman Empire. Xerolophos ("dry hill") was in southwest Constantinople; Arkadios' statue and column stood in the center of a forum also named for him.

in Bithynia Nikomedeia, Prainetos, and Nikaia (in Nikaia one church was preserved). In some places the sea withdrew from its own boundaries. Aftershocks continued for twelve months.

Seeing the fallen walls of the city, Leo discussed this with the people: "You do not have the means to rebuild the walls, but we will command our government officials to levy a miliaresion extra per solidus.[205] The state will take this money and rebuild the walls." From that time on it was customary to give the officials two keratia.[206]

According to the Romans, this year was 6,248 years after the creation of the world (from the time of Adam); according to the Egyptians (that is, the Alexandrians), 6,232. It was 1,063 years after Philip of Macedon.[207] Leo had ruled from March 25 of the fifteenth indiction to June 18 of the ninth indiction, and was Emperor for twenty-four years, two months, and twenty-five days. God suffered his son and successor (in his impiety and in his imperium) to rule from the same June 18 of the ninth indiction to September 14 of the fourteenth indiction: thirty-four years, three months, and two days. Thus, as we said before, on June 18 of the ninth indiction Leo died a physical death to match his spiritual death, and his son Constantine became Emperor.

Such evils as befell the Christians during the reign of the impious Leo were made clear in the preceding chapters. They concerned the orthodox faith, and also (in political administration) Leo's love of money and his plan for base profit in Sicily, Calabria, and Crete. There was rebellion in Italy because of his wicked beliefs, and there were earthquakes, famines, plagues, and popular revolts. I must keep silent over part of this, but it is important to set forth the illegal actions of his impious and totally miserable son one after the other, as they were still more unholy and hateful to God. I do this in the spirit of one who loves truth—since omniscient God is supervising this—and so it may be a clear aid for men in the future and for those wretched, arrogant manikins who are now stumbling into the loathsome and evil doctrine of this supreme lawbreaker.[208]

Constantine's actions were impiously carried out from the tenth indiction—the first year of his reign—to the fourteenth indiction—the year of his end. For he was a totally destructive bloodsucking wild beast

413

205. κατὰ ὁλοκοτίνιν, not κατὰ νομίσμα; solidus is an older term for nomisma.

206. One-twelfth of a nomisma.

207. Philip of Macedon ruled that land 359–336 B.C. Actually, *annus mundi* 6232 begins 1,076 years after his death. However, it begins 1,063 years after the death of his son and successor, Alexander the Great (336–323 B.C.).

208. While Theophanes was writing, Leo V (813–820) was returning to iconoclasm, a return which would result in the monk's exile. For the significance of this passage, see the discussion in the introduction, pp. x–xi.

who used his power tyranically and illegally. First, he sided against our God and Savior Jesus Christ, His altogether immaculate Mother, and all the saints. He was deceived by wizardry, licentiousness, blood sacrifices of horses, dung, and urine. Effeminacy and summoning demons pleased him, and ever since he was a boy he had partaken of absolutely every sort of soul-destroying practice. What can I say? When, with his wickedness, the altogether abominable one took over his father's rule, from the beginning he craved such evil, and openly threw his flame into the air.

Christians felt no little fear when they saw this, so from the beginning everyone immediately began to hate him because of his audacity. But they were well-inclined to Artavasdos the curopalates and count
414 of the Opsikion (who was married to Constantine's sister Anna), and wanted to give him the imperial power because he was orthodox.

In the same year the Arabs' ruler Hisham killed the Christian prisoners in every city under his control. Among them was Eustathios, the blessed son of the famous count Marianos. He was tortured for a long time but would not renounce his true faith, and was shown to be a true martyr at Harran, a notable Mesopotamian city. There his precious, holy remains cure all sorts of ills, doing so by divine grace. Through martyrdom and bloodshed many others also died in Christ.

ANNUS MUNDI 6233 (SEPTEMBER 1, 741—AUGUST 31, 742)

A.D. 733
Roman Emperor Constantine: 35 years: year 1
Arab ruler Hisham: 19 years: year 18
Bishop of Rome Zachariah: 21 years: year 8
Bishop of Constantinople Anastasios: 24 years: year 12

In this year Constantine, the persecutor of the laws handed down from the fathers, became Emperor by divine judgment because of the multitude of our sins. On June 27 of the previous tenth indiction he had gone out to the Opsikian theme against the Arabs, and was at Krasos.

Artavasdos was in Dorylaion with the army of the Opsikion, and they watched each other suspiciously. Constantine sent Artavasdos a message asking him to send his sons to the Emperor on the grounds that he wanted to see them because they were his nephews, but his aim was to seize and imprison them. Artavasdos recognized his treachery and lost hope for himself, as he knew Constantine's boundless wickedness. He harangued his army, brought them over, and with his whole host attacked Constantine.

He killed with a sword-stroke the Saracen-minded patrician Beser, who had advanced to meet him. But Constantine found himself beside a horse whose master had been laid low, mounted it, and fled to Amorion. He went to the regiments of the Anatolic theme (at that time commanded by Lankinos), which saved him. He promised them a great deal, and immediately sent a message to Sisinniakos (who was at that time general of the Thrakesian theme), whose men he persuaded to ally with him. After that there were terrible battles between the supporters of the two men, as each of them had been acclaimed Emperor.

415

By means of the silentarius[209] Athanasios, Artavasdos sent a message about what had happened to the patrician and magistros Theophanes, who was in the city as his legate. Since he was devoted to Artavasdos, he assembled the people by the upper gates of the great church. Through Athanasios and his letters, Artavasdos convinced everyone that he had been proclaimed Emperor by the thematic troops because the Emperor had died.

Then all the people, including Anastasios (misnamed patriarch), anathematized and renounced Constantine, since he was an accursed wretch and God's enemy. They politely accepted his slaughter if it would wash them clean of his great evil, and acclaimed Artavasdos Emperor, since he was orthodox and fought for the holy doctrines.

At once Monotes sent a message to his son Nikephoros (who was in Thrace as general at that time) to muster his army there to protect the city. He shut the walls' gates, put guards on them, and overpowered Constantine's friends, whom he beat, harassed, and jailed.

After Artavasdos and the army of the theme of the Opsikion entered the city, Constantine overran Chrysopolis with two thematic armies (I mean, the Thrakesians and Anatolics). But since he was not able to accomplish anything further, he withdrew to winter in Amorion.

When the Arabs learned of the civil war between these men they took many prisoners in Romania; Suleiman was their general.

Artavasdos replaced the holy icons all through the city. Anastasios (misnamed patriarch) took hold of the precious and lifegiving Cross and swore to the people: "By Him Who was nailed on this, the Emperor Constantine said to me, 'One should not conclude it was the Son of God (Who is called Christ) Whom Mary bore, but only a mere man. For Mary gave birth to Him like my mother Maria gave birth to me.'"[210] When the people heard this they rejected Constantine.

---

209. Silentarii were doorkeepers at imperial audiences and at silentia (see above, note 196).

210. This theological position has strong Nestorian overtones (see above, notes 55 and 127).

ANNUS MUNDI 6234 (SEPTEMBER 1, 742—AUGUST 31, 743)

Bishop of Antioch Stephen: 2 years
2. 19. 9. 13. 1.

416   In this year the Arabs' ruler Hisham died. He had left the holy church of Antioch a widow for forty years, as the Arabs kept it from having a patriarch. Hisham had had as a friend a Syrian monk named Stephen: Stephen was rather uncultured, but pious. Hisham urged the eastern Christians to choose Stephen if they wished to be allowed to have a patriarch. They thought the opportunity God-sent, chose him for the throne of the city of God,[211] and have not been hindered up to the present.

In this year Hisham's son Walid took power over the Arabs. To him Constantine sent the spatharios Andrew and Artavasdos the logothete[212] Gregory; both of them were seeking terms for an alliance.

There was a severe drought and an earthquake in the area where the mountains in the desert of Saba meet each other, and villages were gulped down into the ground.

In the same year Kosmas the patriarch of Alexandria and his city became orthodox, emerging from the wicked doctrines of the monothelites, which had held sway since the time of Cyrus, Alexandria's bishop during the reign of Herakleios.

A host of Arabs under Ghamr attacked Romania, took many prisoners, and withdrew.

In June a sign appeared in the northern sky.

Walid ordered the tongue of the holy metropolitan of Damascus, Peter, cut out, because he openly condemned the impiety of the Arabs and Manichaeans.[213] Then he exiled Peter to Arabia Felix, where he died: a martyr for Christ. Those who tell of this say it is fully assured because they heard it themselves.

Peter's emulator and namesake, Peter of Maiouma, was at this time shown to be a voluntary martyr for Christ. When he became ill he summoned some important Arabs, who were his intimates because

211. Another name for Antioch is Theopolis—the city of God.

212. Originally, logothetes were accountants. As Byzantine bureaucracy evolved and many late-Roman offices disappeared during the crises of the seventh and eighth centuries, logothetes began to fill their functions, and the title came to mean "minister."

213. Manichaeism was a dualistic religion combining elements of Zoroastrianism, Christianity, Judaism, and Buddhism founded by the Persian prophet Mani in the third century A.D. It associated the material world with the evil power in the universe; thus, observant Manichaeans lived lives of great asceticism. Manichaeism was rarely able to find a state to support it; its followers were persecuted minorities wherever they lived.

417 he was chartularius in charge of the payment of public taxes. He told them, "You should gain a reward from God for visiting me, even if you friends are outside the faith. I want you to be my eyewitnesses that this is the situation: everyone who does not believe in the Father, the Son, and the Holy Spirit, in consubstantiality, and in the Trinity in Unity which rules life, has maimed his soul and deserves eternal punishment. Even your false prophet Muhammad is such a person, and a forerunner of the Antichrist. If you are convinced by my testimony about the heaven and earth, abandon his mythology today, lest you be punished with him: for I feel goodwill toward you." When they heard his theological disquisition on these and other matters they were struck with amazement and fury, but thought it good to be patient, since they believed he was delirious from his illness. After he recovered from it, though, he began to cry out even more arrogantly, "Anathema to Muhammad, to his false writings, and to everyone who believes in him." Then he was shown to be a martyr, and submitted to punishment from the sword.

Our holy father John has honored him with eulogies. John is well-called "Chrysorrhoas" because the brilliant grace of the Spirit gleams golden in him, both in his words and in his life. The impious Emperor Constantine hurled annual anathemas at him because of his surpassing orthodoxy.

In place of John's patronym "Mansur" (which means, "he who has been washed clean"), Constantine, in his Jewish arrogance, renamed the new teacher of the church "Manzeros."[214]

In the same year Walid resettled the Cypriots in Syria.

Artavasdos appointed his son Niketas his chief general, then sent him to the Armeniac theme. Through Anastasios the patriarch, he also crowned his son Nikephoros.

In May of the same year Artavasdos went to Asia; when he got there he plundered it and levied troops. Constantine moved against Artavasdos as soon as he learned of this. He caught up with Artavasdos near Sardis, engaged him in battle, routed him, and chased him all the way to Kyzikos. When he got to Kyzikos, Artavasdos boarded a warship and got safely to the city.

418 In August of the same eleventh indiction his son Niketas the chief general attacked Constantine but was routed and fled to Modrine. This battle killed the patrician Teridates the Armenian (a noble soldier who was Artavasdos' cousin) and other officers. There were no small losses on either side: the Armenians and Armeniacs fought against the men fighting for Constantine: Thrakesians and Anatolics. At this time the devil, that evil prince, stirred up madness and mutual slaughter against

214. A Greek form of the Hebrew word *mamzer*—"bastard."

the Christians, so that children were shamelessly made to murder their parents and brothers their brothers. The factions mercilessly burned each other's property and homes.

ANNUS MUNDI 6235 (SEPTEMBER 1, 743—AUGUST 31, 744)

Arab ruler Walid: 1 year
3. 1. 10. 11.[215] *2.*

In this year a sign appeared in the north, and dust fell in various places. There was also an earthquake at the Caspian Gates.

On Thursday, April 16, Walid was killed by the Arabs after he had ruled for one year. Yezid Leipsos seized the rule. He dispersed a large sum of money and conquered Damascus, receiving from the Arabs in Damascus, Persia, and Egypt recognition as their ruler. As soon as he heard of this, Muhammad's son Marwan, who was administering Armenia, overran Mesopotamia. He seemed to be fighting for Walid's sons and against Yezid. After five months Yezid died, leaving behind his brother Ibrahim as his successor in Damascus. At his command Marwan, who commanded the forces in Mesopotamia, went to Edessa, and from there to a camp called Garis in the vicinity of Damascus and Antilebanon. He engaged Suleiman there by the river Lita (that is, the Kakos), routed him, and killed 20,000 men. Only Suleiman and a few others got away safe to Damascus. Once Suleiman was in Damascus, he killed the sons of Walid, for whom Marwan had seemed to be fighting. He left Damascus after appropriating an adequate amount of money. Then Marwan also overran Damascus, and killed many of its prominent citizens and those who had aided in the murder of Walid and his sons; others he mutilated. He transferred all its money and treasures to Harran, a Mesopotamian city.

In September of the twelfth indiction Constantine came down near Chalcedon and crossed over into Thrace. Sisinnios the general of the Thrakesian theme crossed by way of Abydos and laid siege to Constantinople's land walls. Constantine went from the Charsianesian gate to the Golden Gate, showing himself to the masses, then withdrew once more to camp at St. Mamas.

The inhabitants of the city began to run out of supplies. They sent out the asekretes Athanasios and his aide Artavasdos to get them by ship. But the Kibyrhaiots' fleet came on them outside Abydos, overcame them, and brought them to the Emperor. He gave the food to his troops and forthwith blinded Athanasios and Artavasdos. After this

415

---

215. This is an error for the fourteenth year of patriarch Anastasios of Constantinople.

Artavasdos[216] decided to open the gates of the land wall and join battle with Constantine. In the battle Artavasdos' forces were crushingly defeated and many died, Monotes among them. Artavasdos prepared two-storied ships which bore Greek fire and sent them to St. Mamas against the Kibyrhaiots' fleet. But while they were approaching, the Kibyrhaiots' ships sallied forth and drove them away.

Famine grew severe in the city, so that a modius[217] of barley sold for twelve nomismata, a modius of pulse for nineteen, and even one of millet or lupine for eight. Five pounds of olives sold for a nomisma, and a xestes[218] of wine for half a nomisma. Since the people were **420** dying, Artavasdos had to let them leave the city. Some, though, he stopped after looking at their faces. Because of this, some people covered their faces and put on women's clothing; others wore monastic garb and hairshirts. In this way they were able to escape and leave.

Niketas the chief general gathered together his army, which had dispersed from Modrine, and advanced to Chrysopolis. When he wheeled round, the Emperor crossed to pursue him, and overtook him at Nikomedeia. He overwhelmed Niketas and his adjutant the bishop Marcellinus, whom he at once ordered cut down. He bound the chief general and showed him to his father Artavasdos on the wall.

On the evening of November 2, Constantine suddenly moved his troops against the land wall in battle array and took the city. While it was still possible, Artavasdos and the patrician Baktangios boarded a naval vessel for the theme of the Opsikion. They went to the fortress of Pouzanes, in which they shut themselves up. The Emperor overcame them; he blinded Artavasdos and his two sons, but decapitated Baktangios in the Kynegion and hung his head on the Milion for three days.

Thirty years later the malicious and heartless Emperor ordered Baktangios' wife to go to the monastery of the Khora (for Baktangios was buried there), dig up his bones, carry them in her own cloak, and throw them into the memorial of Pelagios with the suicides. Oh, his inhumanity!

Constantine also executed many other prominent men who had been on Artavasdos' side. He blinded countless men, and cut off the hands or feet of others. He urged the foreign officers who had entered Constantinople with him to go into houses and rob the citizens of their property, and showed the city a countless number of other evils.

He held horse-races: through the gate by which the horses entered he brought in Artavasdos and his sons and friends in bonds, along with

216. This is the pretender once more, not his aide.
217. A measure of volume, about two gallons.
218. A measure of volume, a bit less than a pint.

421 Anastasios (misnamed patriarch), who was seated backwards on an ass and then publicly beaten. Although Constantine brought him in and paraded him at the races, he seated him on the throne of holiness once more after terrifying and frightening him, since he was of the same party as the Emperor.

By the just judgment of God, forty days later Constantine blinded his cousin Sisinnios, who was general of the Thrakesian theme and for long had struggled on his behalf. As it has been written, he who helps the impious man falls into his hands.

ANNUS MUNDI 6236 (SEPTEMBER 1, 744—AUGUST 31, 745)

A.D. 736
Roman Emperor Constantine: 35 years: year 4
Arab ruler Marwan: 6 years: year 1
Bishop of Rome Zachariah: 21 years: year 11
Bishop of Constantinople Anastasios: 24 years: year 15
Bishop of Antioch Theophylaktos: 7 years: year 1

In this year a great comet appeared in Syria.

Thabit and Dahhaq of the Kharijites rebelled against Marwan, who overcame and killed them—and a force of 12,000 soldiers—in the mountains of Emesa.

In the same year, at the request of the Christians of the east, Marwan allowed Theophylaktos, an Edessan priest, to be chosen patriarch of Antioch, since Stephen had died. Theophylaktos was adorned with spiritual gifts, and especially with discretion. With universal letters, Marwan commanded that he should be honored by the Arabs.

In Emesa, Marwan hanged one hundred twenty Kalbites[219] and killed Abbas in prison; Abbas had shed a great deal of Christian blood and had overrun and conquered many places. For this purpose Marwan sent him an Ethiopian, who went in to him and smothered him. The Ethiopian had bags filled with quicklime, which he put round Abbas' head and nostrils. Marwan had devised this as a just punishment for a sorcerer. Many evils which have befallen Christians have sprung from wizards and summoners of demons. Also, Abbas had a share in Walid's blood.

219. There was a great deal of factional strife in the Arab dominions between the northern tribal grouping of the Kalb and the southern Arab members of the Qais grouping. Marwan was favored by the latter faction, and moved his capital from Damascus to Harran, where the Qais were dominant. This led to rebellion among the Kalbites in Syria, a revolt which Marwan crushed.

422　**ANNUS MUNDI 6237 (SEPTEMBER 1, 745—AUGUST 31, 746)**

5. 2. 12. 16. 2.

In this year Suleiman once more assembled his army and attacked Marwan. He was defeated after throwing away 7,000 soldiers, but saved himself by fleeing to Palmyra, and from there to Persia. The Edessans, Heliopolitans, and Damascenes also rebelled, shutting their cities against Marwan. He sent an army under his son against Dahhaq, while he himself went to Emesa, which he took in four months. Dahhaq had come from Persia with a very large force. Marwan engaged him in Mesopotamia; after many of Dahhaq's men had been killed, Marwan captured and executed him.

At this time Constantine took Germanikeia and attacked Syria and Doulikhia; he found his opening because of the Arabs' civil war. By treaty he expelled the Arabs from these cities without arms; he took some maternal relatives of his and resettled them in Byzantium, as he did with many Syrian monophysitic heretics. Most of these have lived in Thrace until the present day. In the fasion of Peter Knapheus, they keep on crucifying the Trinity in the trisagion.[220]

From August 10 to 15 it was misty, cloudy, and dark.

Once he had conquered and taken Emesa, Marwan killed all of Hisham's relatives and freedmen. He destroyed the walls of Heliopolis, Damascus, and Jerusalem, killed many important people, and mutilated the people who remained in those cities.

ANNUS MUNDI 6238 (SEPTEMBER 1, 746—AUGUST 31, 747)

6. 3. 13. 17. 3.

In this year, at the fourth hour of January 18, there was a strong earthquake in Palestine, Jordan, and all Syria. Many tens of thousands —a countless number—died, and both churches and monasteries fell, especially in the desert round the holy city.

In the same year there was a plague. It sprang from Sicily and

423　Calabria and, spreading like fire, came to Monemvasia, Greece, and the islands which lie off it. It lasted the entire fourteenth indiction, scourging the impious Constantine and restraining his fury against the holy churches and the revered icons even if, like Pharaoh of old, he re-

220. Peter Knapheus ("the fuller") was patriarch of Antioch from 476 to 477 and again from 485 to 489; he was a monophysite. The trisagion ("thrice-holy") is the hymn which begins, "Holy, holy, holy is the Lord God of Hosts." In the late fifth century at Antioch the monophysites added, "Who was crucified for us," to the hymn. This was seen by the orthodox as a heretical expression, as they denied that God could suffer on the cross, saying the Passion was of Christ's humanity alone.

mained uncorrected. The bubonic plague reached the imperial city in the fifteenth indiction.[221]

Suddenly and in some unseen fashion, a great number of small oily crosses began to appear on men's cloaks, on the holy garb of the churches, and on their curtains.[222] People grew distressed and dismayed because they were perplexed by this kind of sign. The wrath of God mercilessly destroyed not only the folk in the city, but also those in all its suburbs. Many men had delusions and, as it seemed, while they were delirious they thought they were traveling with strange, harsh-faced men, and that those who met them hailed and talked with these people like friends. Those who indicate what these sick people said definitely state this. The sick folk also saw these people entering houses, killing some of their inhabitants, and wounding others with swords. Most of the things they said happened just as they had seen.

In the spring of the first indiction the plague got even worse, and in summer it was burning everywhere at once, so that whole houses were shut up and there was no-one to help bury the corpses. Because the times were very critical, it was planned to put oblong wooden panniers on beasts of burden so as to carry away the dead; similarly, they were piled one atop the other on wagons. In this way all the cemeteries—both in the city and in the suburbs—were filled, as, in fact, were many dry cisterns and pools. Even many vineyards were dug up, and not only those, but the orchards within the old walls were also pressed into service to bury human bodies. Thus they barely met this

424 need. Every household was harmed by the disaster, which took place because of the attack the rulers impiously made on the holy icons.

An Agarene expedition presently came to Cyprus from Alexandria while a Roman fleet was there. The general of the Kibyrhaiot theme suddenly attacked the Arabs in the harbor and captured the mouth of the harbor. They say that, although there were 1,000 warships, only three got away.

ANNUS MUNDI 6239 (SEPTEMBER 1, 747—AUGUST 31, 748)

7. 4. 14. 18. 4.

In this year Gregory was killed by the Kharijites. Also, as I said before, Marwan won his victory.

---

221. Reading ιε´ (15) for ε´ (5).
222. A western chronicler, Paul the Deacon, records similar circumstances surrounding an outbreak of plague in Liguria (northwestern Italy) around A.D. 566 in his eighth-century *History of the Lombards* (book II, chapter iv).

ANNUS MUNDI 6240 (SEPTEMBER 1, 748—AUGUST 31, 749)
8. 5. 15. 19. 5.

In this year the people of the interior of Persia—known as Khorasanians or Black-cloaks[223]—moved against Marwan and his entire dynasty, who had ruled after Muhammad the false prophet up until Marwan: that is, the line of him who was known as the son of Umayya.[224] Ever since the murder of Walid the Arabs had been fighting among themselves and giving each other no rest. The sons of Ekhim and Ali, who were relatives of the false prophet, were fugitives in hiding in lesser Arabia. When Ibrahim became their leader they met and sent one of their freedmen, Abu Muslim, to some of the leading men in Khorasan, asking the Khorasanians to ally with them against Marwan.

The Khorasanians met in the presence of a man named Qahtabah. They took counsel among themselves and incited the slaves to rise against their masters, killing many in one night. Once armed with the weapons, horses, and money of these men, they had a powerful position. However, they were divided into two tribes, Qaisites and Yemenites. Realizing this, Abu Muslim stirred up the Yemenites, who were more powerful, against the Qaisites. Once he had killed them, he went to Persia with Qahtabah. He attacked ibn-Sayyar and, after he won, took over all ibn-Sayyar's men, perhaps as many as 100,000. Then Abu Muslim came upon ibn-Hubayrah, who was encamped with 200,000 men, and drove him off. Abu Muslim overtook Marwan, who had 300,000 men, at the Zab River, and in his attack killed a countless throng. As is written,[225] one man was seen pursuing a thousand, and two making ten thousand run. Marwan, seeing that his men were being overwhelmed in this way, went to Harran; after he crossed the river he cut the bridge, which was made of boats. He took up all his money and his retinue and fled to Egypt with 3,000 men who had been born in his household.

425

ANNUS MUNDI 6241 (SEPTEMBER 1, 749—AUGUST 31, 750)
9. 6. 16. 20. 6.

In this year Marwan was pursued, overtaken, and killed by the Black-cloaks after a severe battle. Their leader was Salim the son of Ali,

---

223. This [Maurophoroi] is Theophanes' conventional term for the Abbasids and their backers. Black was the Abbasid color; they rose to power by gaining the backing of the followers of Ali's murdered descendants, and wore black as a token of their mourning for the slain Alids.

224. The Umayyad caliphate ruled the Arabs from 661 to 750.

225. Once more, Deuteronomy 32:20.

one of the fugitives who had sent out Abu Muslim. The rest of them assembled at Samaria in the village of Trakhonitis; by lot they assigned the rule to Abu-l-Abbas, after him to his brother Abd Allah, and after him to Isa ibn Musa. They arranged that Abd Allah (son of Ali and Salim's brother) should be general of Syria, Salim should rule Egypt, and that Abu-l-Abbas' brother Abd Allah should take from him a mandate to rule Mesopotamia. Abu-l-Abbas, who was also the ruler of them all, settled in Persia. He and his Persian allies transferred from Damascus the capital and all the treasure which had been carried off (and which Marwan had increased).

426   Marwan's surviving sons and relatives went from Egypt to Africa, and from there crossed the border between Libya and Europe at the Straits of Gibraltar. They have lived in European Spain until the present day.[226] There were some men previously settled there whom Muawiyah had shipped into exile; they were relatives of Marwan's kin and their co-religionists.

Conquering Marwan took six years. In the struggle the notable cities of Syria had their walls torn down (except for Antioch, since Marwan planned to keep it as a place of refuge). He destroyed countless numbers of Arabs, because he paid close attention to military matters. He was a follower of the heresy of the Epicureans (that is, the Automatists), having adopted this impiety from the pagan Greeks who lived in Harran.[227]

On January 25 of the same third indiction a son was born to the Emperor Constantine of the daughter of the Khagan of Khazaria. Constantine named him Leo.

In the same year there was an earthquake and a great and fearful collapse in Syria. Thanks to it, some of the cities were wholly razed, others partially, and others were shifted—walls, buildings, and all—from the mountains to the plains below, moving as much as six miles or even a bit more. Eyewitness observers say the land of Mesopotamia was torn asunder to a depth of fully two miles, and from this depth new earth, very white and sandy, was brought up. As they say, an immacu-

226. The Umayyad emirate (caliphate after 929) of Spain endured until 1031.

227. Epicurus (342–270 B.C.), despite the modern connotations attaching to his name and doctrines, did not advocate a life of sensuality. He urged the cultivation of man's higher faculties, and advocated materialism and freedom from fear. Ambrose Bierce's definition of "epicure" is perhaps not out of place: "An opponent of Epicurus, an abstemious philosopher, who, holding that pleasure should be the chief aim of man, wasted no time in gratification of the senses." Theophanes' reference to "automatism" stems from the Epicurean belief in immutable natural laws. Harran was a center of surviving paganism well into Islamic times.

late mule-like beast came up from the midst of this and, speaking in a human voice, foretold the attack of a people from the desert upon the Arabs, which indeed took place.

At the festival of holy Pentecost in the following year—the fourth indiction—the impious Emperor Constantine crowned his son Leo Emperor by means of his partisan Anastasios, misnamed the patriarch.

427 ANNUS MUNDI 6242 (SEPTEMBER 1, 750—AUGUST 31, 751)

Arab ruler Muhammad: 5 years
10. 1. 17. 21. 7.

In this year the Khakideis rebelled against the Persian Black-cloaks, who killed 40,000 of them in the mountains of Emesa. The Persians did the same thing to the Qaisites in Arabia. When the embalmed head of Marwan arrived, most of the rebellions stopped.

In the same year Theophylaktos, the holy patriarch of Antioch, died on the twenty-ninth of Daisios.[228]

ANNUS MUNDI 6243 (SEPTEMBER 1, 751—AUGUST 31, 752)

Bishop of Antioch Theodore: 6 years
11. 2. 18. 22. 1.

In this year the new conquerors killed most of the Christians who were "kinsmen"[229] of the previous rulers. They overpowered them by treachery at Palestinian Antipatris.

In the same year Constantine took Theodosiopolis and Melitene, and took captives from the Armenians.

Theodore son of Vicarius, who sprang from lesser Arabia, was chosen patriarch of Antioch.

ANNUS MUNDI 6244 (SEPTEMBER 1, 752—AUGUST 31, 753)

12. 3. 19. 23. 2.

In this year the impious Constantine, buoyed up by his arrogance, devised many measures against the church and the orthodox faith. He convened a silentium for each measure and treacherously persuaded the people to follow his own will, preparing the way in advance for his plan for absolute impiety.

228. June 29.
229. Theophanes is using this word as an indication of favor or client status rather than as an implication of a true blood relationship.

ANNUS MUNDI 6245 (SEPTEMBER 1, 753—AUGUST 31, 754)

13. 4. 20. 24. 3.

In this year Anastasios, who had ruled the throne of Constantinople in an unholy fashion, died after suffering piteously in body and soul from what is known as an intestinal obstruction. He vomited fecal matter from his mouth, paying an appropriate price for his disregard of God and his teacher.

In the same year the impious Constantine convened at the palace of Hiereia an illegal assembly to oppose the holy and revered icons. It had two hundred thirty-eight bishops, of whom the leaders were Theodosios bishop of Ephesos (the son of Apsimaros) and Pastillas of Perge. They promulgated doctrines which seemed good to themselves, although no-one was present from the catholic thrones: I mean those of Rome, Alexandria, Antioch, and Jerusalem. Beginning on February 10, they continued until August 8 of the same seventh indiction.

428

Then the enemies of the Mother of God went to Blakhernai, where Constantine ascended the pulpit. He had a monk named Constantine, who was bishop of Syllaion. After praying, the Emperor said, "Many years to the ecumenical patriarch Constantine!" On the twenty-seventh of the same month the Emperor went to the Forum with his unholy president Constantine and the rest of his bishops. In the presence of all the people they declared their evil-doctrined heresy, anathematizing the holy Germanos, George of Cyprus, and John Chrysorrhoas of Damascus, who were holy men and venerable teachers.

ANNUS MUNDI 6246 (SEPTEMBER 1, 754—AUGUST 31, 755)

Bishop of Constantinople Constantine: 12 years
14. 5. 21. 1. 4.

In this year Muhammad—also known as Abu-l-Abbas—died after ruling for five years. His brother Abd Allah was in Mecca, the Arabs' place of blasphemy. He wrote to Abu Muslim in Persia to guard the capital for him, as it had been allotted to him. Abu Muslim learned that Abd Allah (son of Ali and brother of Salim), the chief general of Syria, had seized the capital for himself and was on his way to conquer Persia. The Persians opposed Abd Allah, but the inhabitants of Syria were devoted to him and fought on his side. Abu Muslim raised his army and engaged Abd Allah near Nisibis, where he defeated him and killed many of his men. Most of them were Slavs[230] and Antiochenes. Only

230. See above, under *anni mundi* 6185 and 6186. The Slavs who had deserted to the Arabs at that time were settled in Syria.

Abd Allah got away, and after a few days he asked for a safe conduct from the other Abd Allah (Muhammad's brother), who had come to Persia in great haste from Mecca. This Abd Allah imprisoned the other in a tumbledown shack. He ordered its foundations dug out from under it, and thus secretly killed him.

429

He prevented Abu Muslim from venting his wrath on the Syrian Arabs, although they had revolted against the Black-cloaks and captured many places in Palestine and the seacoast, including Emesa. Abu Muslim had been planning to attack them with his soldiers; now he became angry at Abd Allah and went to the Persian interior with his host. Very much afraid of him, Abd Allah recalled him with persuasive speeches, summonses, and the loathsome symbols of their rule—I mean, the false prophet Muhammad's staff and sandals. He asked Abu Muslim to come one day's journey toward him so he could give Abu Muslim the same sort of thanks he would his father. Deceived, Abu Muslim approached him with 100,000 cavalrymen, but when he joined Abd Allah, Abd Allah killed him with his own hands. Abu Muslim's mob was dispersed on the same day; they went off after having been given honors not easy to reckon. In this way Abd Allah solidified his rule.

ANNUS MUNDI 6247 (SEPTEMBER 1, 755—AUGUST 31, 756)

Arab ruler Abd Allah: 21 years
Bishop of Rome Paul: 7 years[231]
15. 1. 1. 2. 5.

In this year Niketas the bishop of Heliopolis was anathematized by the entire church.

The Emperor Constantine resettled in Thrace the Syrians and Armenians he had brought from Theodosiopolis and Melitene; they have spread the Paulician heresy.[232] In the same way, he brought men and their families from the islands, Greece, and the southerly regions,

231. Paul I, actually pope 757–767.
232. The Paulicians were a dualist, semi-Christian sect originating in eastern Anatolia; their doctrines probably ultimately derived from Manichaeism. Persecuted by Christians, they often took refuge with the Muslims, who used them as a buffer against the Byzantine Empire. In the ninth century their bandit-state grew to formidable power, and ravaged much of Byzantine Asia Minor before finally being extinguished in 872 by Basil I (867–886). Those Paulicians transplanted to the Balkans maintained their own doctrines; they survived into the late eleventh century to harass Alexios I (1081–1118), who persecuted them without mercy. These Balkan Paulicians also inspired the Bosnian Bogomils, and probably the Cathari of northern Italy and the Albigensians of southern France.

because there were few property-owners in the city. He had them settle there, thickly studding it with them.

In the same year the Bulgars sought tribute because of the fortresses which had been built. The Emperor dishonored their envoy, so they came out in force, advancing as far as the Long Walls and even making an attack on the imperial city. After they had worked much destruction and taken prisoners, they withdrew, unharmed, to their own country.

430 ANNUS MUNDI 6248 (SEPTEMBER 1, 756—AUGUST 31, 757)

16. 2. 2. 3.

In this year there was an earthquake—no small one—in Palestine and Syria on March 9.

Theodore the patriarch of Antioch was exiled. Because of the Arabs' jealousy, they falsely accused him of revealing their affairs to the Emperor Constantine by letters. Salim put him in an out-of-the-way place: the land of the Moabites, which was also his native land. Salim also commanded that no new churches should be built, that the cross should not be displayed, and that Christians should not enter into religious discussions with Arabs.

He attacked Romania with 80,000 men, but after he had entered Kappadokia he heard Constantine was arming against him. He grew afraid and withdrew without accomplishing anything. In his retreat he took only the few Armenians who had gone over to him.

ANNUS MUNDI 6249 (SEPTEMBER 1, 757—AUGUST 31, 758)

17. 3. 3. 4.

In this year Abd Allah increased the taxes on the Christians, so that all monks, solitary monks, and pillar-sitters (who are pleasing to God) had to pay taxes. He also sealed the churches' treasuries and brought in Hebrews to sell them; they were purchased by freedmen.

ANNUS MUNDI 6250 (SEPTEMBER 1, 758—AUGUST 31, 759)

18. 4. 4. 5.

In this year Constantine captured the Macedonian Sklavinias and subjected the rest of them.[233]

In the same year some of the Persian Black-cloaks who were of the

---

233. These are the small, tribal statelets of the Slavs who settled the Balkans after the collapse of the Avars (see above, note 105).

magian religion[234] were overcome by a trick of the devil's. They sold their property and, naked, climbed up onto walls and threw themselves off so that, as they thought, they could fly to heaven. But they had nothing worth mentioning for citizenship there; instead, they came back to earth, shattering their limbs. Through Salim, Abd Allah killed the leaders of the heresy in Beroia and Khalkis: they number sixteen.

ANNUS MUNDI 6251 (SEPTEMBER 1, 759—AUGUST 31, 760)

19. 5. 5. 6.

431   In this year the Arabs, out of envy of the Christians, for a short time prevented them from being public scribes. However, they once more had to use the Christians for these matters because of their own inability to record the decisions.

    The Arabs attacked Romania and took many prisoners. At Melas they joined battle with Paul the general of the Armeniacs; they killed him and a host of soldiers, and brought back many heads and forty-two important men in bonds.

    The Emperor attacked Bulgaria; the Bulgars met him when he came to the pass at Bergaba. They killed many of his men, among whom were the patrician Leo (the general of the Thrakesian theme) and another Leo, the logothete of the drome.[235] They took the weapons of many of the men they killed. Thus the Emperor's troops ingloriously retreated.

ANNUS MUNDI 6252 (SEPTEMBER 1, 760—AUGUST 31, 761)

20. 6. 6. 7.

    In this year there was an error in the calculation of Easter. The orthodox in the east celebrated it on April 6, while the erring heretics did so on April 13.

    In the same year the head of the holy John the forerunner and Baptist was moved from the monastery of Spelaion to his famous church in Emesa. A way down to it was built, whereat the faithful have adored it until the present, and have honored it for both its physical and spiritual sweet smell. It gives out cures to all those who come to it with faith.

    In the same year a brilliant apparition appeared in the east for ten days, and again in the west for twenty-one.

234. That is, Zoroastrians. Persia was by no means entirely converted to Islam by the middle of the eighth century.

235. A post approximately equivalent to prime minister.

In Lebanon, a Syrian named Theodore raised a rebellion against the Arabs in the villages outside Heliopolis. When he attacked them, many fell on both sides. Routed at last, he fled, and all the Lebanese who were with him were killed. There were also insurrections and wars in Africa, and there was a solar eclipse on Saturday, August 15 at the tenth hour.[236]

Some of the Black-cloaks at Dabekon rose up, saying the caliph's son was God because it was he who fostered them: this was the doctrine they promulgated. The Black-cloaks entered the house of their heresy and killed sixty of its leaders. Some also went to Basra, where they took many prisoners and a large sum of money.

432 **ANNUS MUNDI 6253 (SEPTEMBER 1, 761—AUGUST 31, 762)**

21. 7. 7. 8.

In this year the Qaisites rebelled against the Black-cloaks because of a dispute over their wives. Some of the Black-cloaks had been staying at a house in which dwelt three brothers, whose wives they wanted to drown. But the three brothers, thus incited, killed and buried the Black-cloaks and, once engaged, also killed the rest of their party. Selikhos sent out his armies, which cunningly got ahead of the rebels. He captured them and executed many; the three brothers were hanged.

At the festival of Easter Selikhos entered the cathedral during the holy service. While the metropolitan was standing by him and reciting, "Your people and your church entreat you," Selikhos took him away to prison. Another priest finished the holy service. This caused considerable fear, and if the metropolitan (the blessed Anastasios) had not appeased Selikhos with courtesy and humble speeches, a great evil would have taken place at that time.

In the same year the persecutor Constantine whipped to death a monk at Blakhernai—Andrew, who was called Kalybites—in the hippodrome at St. Mamas. Andrew had accused Constantine of impiety and of being a new Valens, and had called him a Julian.[237] Constantine ordered his body thrown in the river, but his sister stole it and buried it in the marketplace of Leukadios.

236. This is actually the eclipse of August 15, 760: Newton, op. cit., 544.
237. Julian (361–363) tried to restore paganism as the state religion of the Roman Empire; Valens (Emperor in the East, 364–378) was an Arian (see above, note 127) who persecuted the orthodox in his half of the Empire.

ANNUS MUNDI 6254 (SEPTEMBER 1, 762—AUGUST 31, 763)

Bishop of Rome Constantine: 5 years[238]
22. 8. 1. 9.

In this year an apparition appeared in the east, and Fatima's son was killed.

The Bulgars rose up and murdered their rulers, whom they hanged on a rope. They elevated an evil-minded man named Teletzes, who was thirty years old. Many Slavs fled and went over to the Emperor, who settled them at Artana. On June 15 the Emperor went to Thrace. He also sent a fleet by way of the Black Sea; it had about eight hundred warships, each of which carried about twelve horses. When Teletzes heard of the movement against him, he made allies of 20,000 men from neighboring tribes, and secured himself by putting them in his strongpoints.

433

The Emperor advanced to camp at the fortress of Ankhialos. Teletzes and his host from the tribes appeared on Friday, June 30 of the first indiction. The two sides joined battle and cut each other up badly, the battle raging from the fifth hour until evening. Large numbers of Bulgars were killed, others were overcome, and still others went over to the Emperor. He was exalted by the victory, and held a triumphal procession at the city because of it. He and his army entered Constantinople under arms; the people acclaimed him as he dragged along the overpowered Bulgars with wooden instruments of torture. He ordered the people to put them to death outside the Golden Gate.

The Bulgars revolted against Teletzes and killed him and his officers, then elevated Sabinos, the brother-in-law of their old ruler. He immediately sent a message to the Emperor, seeking to make peace. But the Bulgars convened a council which firmly opposed him, saying, "Thanks to you, the Romans will enslave Bulgaria." They rebelled, and Sabinos fled to the fortress of Mesembria and went over to the Emperor. The Bulgars raised another ruler for themselves, whose name was Paganos.

ANNUS MUNDI 6255 (SEPTEMBER 1, 763—AUGUST 31, 764)

23. 9. 2. 10.

In this year two brothers from the desert and Basrathon rebelled against Abd Allah. He dispatched an army which killed them and 80,000 of their men.

238. This is either a badly misplaced reference to pope Constantine (708–715) or, more probably, a reference to the antipope Constantine (767–768). The pope's regnal year now appears in front of that of the patriarch of Constantinople, while that of the patriarch of Antioch disappears.

In the same year the Turks emerged from the Caspian Gates, killed many people in Armenia, took many prisoners, and withdrew.

Kosmas (surnamed Komanites), a bishop of the Syrian Epiphaneia which is near Apamea, apostasized from the orthodox faith and came into accord with Constantine's heretical opposition to the holy icons. He did this because the citizens had lodged an accusation against him with Theodore the patriarch of Antioch over his loss of church property which he was unable to produce. With common will and unity of purpose, Theodore the patriarch of Antioch, Theodore of Jerusalem, Kosmas of Alexandria,[239] and the bishops under them, each in his own city, anathematized him on the day of holy Pentecost after the reading of the holy gospel.

In the same year it was bitterly cold after the beginning of October, not only in our land, but even more so to the east, west, and north. Because of the cold, the north shore of the Black Sea froze to a depth of thirty cubits a hundred miles out. This was so from Ninkhia to the Danube River, including the Kouphis, Dniester, and Dnieper Rivers, the Nekropela, and the remaining promontories all the way to Mesembria and Medeia. Since the ice and snow kept on falling, its depth increased another twenty cubits, so that the sea became dry land. It was traveled by wild men and tame beasts from Khazaria, Bulgaria, and the lands of other adjacent peoples.

By divine command, during February of the same second indiction the ice divided into a great number of mountainous chunks. The force of the wind brought them down to Daphnousia and Hieron, so that they came through the Bosporos to the city and all the way to Propontis, Abydos, and the islands, filling every shore. We ourself were an eyewitness and, with thirty companions, went out onto one of them and played on it. The icebergs had many dead animals, both wild and domestic, on them. Anyone who wanted to could travel unhindered on dry land from Sophianai[240] to the city and from Chrysopolis to St. Mamas or Galata. One of these icebergs was dashed against the harbor of the acropolis, and shattered it. Another mammoth one smashed against the wall and badly shook it, so that the houses inside trembled along with it. It broke into three pieces, which girdled the city from Magnaura to the Bosporos, and was taller than the walls. All the city's men, women, and children could not stop staring at the icebergs,

434

435

---

239. Although Theophanes knows the names of the patriarchs of Alexandria and Jerusalem here, he does not have any information on the years in which they reigned. Theodore of Antioch's exile, mentioned above in *annus mundi* 6248, was not permanent, for he remained patriarch of that city until 773, despite Theophanes' ignorance of this fact.

240. Sophianai is on the Asiatic coast of the Bosporos, about three miles northeast of Chrysopolis, the town directly across from Constantinople.

then went back home lamenting and in tears, at a loss as to what to say about this phenomenon.

In March of the same year a great many stars were seen falling from the sky, so that everyone who saw them suspected this was the end of the age. There was also a bad drought, and even springs dried up.

The Emperor brought in the patriarch and asked him, "But why would it harm us if we were to call the Mother of God 'the mother of Christ'?"

The patriarch embraced him, saying, "Have mercy, lord, that title should not have crossed your mind. Do you not see that Nestorios was declared infamous and was anathematized by the entire church?"[241]

In reply the Emperor said, "I asked because I wanted to learn; in any case, the decision is yours."

ANNUS MUNDI 6256 (SEPTEMBER 1, 764—AUGUST 31, 765)

A.D. 756
Roman Emperor Constantine: 35 years: year 24
Arab ruler Abd Allah: 21 years: year 10
Bishop of Rome Constantine: 5 years: year 3
Bishop of Constantinople Constantine: 12 years: year 11

In this year the Turks once more sallied forth into the area of the Caspian Gates and Iberia. They battled with the Arabs, and many on both sides lost their lives.

By the following knavery Abd Allah took away the rule from Isa ibn Musa, to whom, as was said above, the third lot (to rule after Abd Allah) had fallen. He saw that Isa was suffering from a headache and dizziness, and persuaded him that he would cure him if Isa would implant in his nostrils a sneezing potion concocted by Abd Allah's physician, whose name was Moses and who was a deacon of the church of Antioch. Moses had already been bribed into concocting a bitter, numbing drug. Abd Allah talked Isa into accepting the nasal plug; according to plan, he had been reassured by eating with Abd Allah. But when the passages in his head were filled, he was robbed of all his senses and their ruling energies, and lay down without a sound. Then Abd Allah summoned his race's leaders and chiefs and said, "What do you think of this fellow who will rule you?" They unanimously rejected him and gave guarantees to Abd Allah's son Muhammad (who was surnamed Mahdi), then brought the unconscious Isa to his home.

436

241. Nestorian Christians denied that Mary could rightly be called "the Mother of God" (see above, note 127).

When he recovered after three days, Abd Allah consoled him with false excuses, but requited the insult with a hundred talents of gold.

In the same year Paganos, the lord of Bulgaria, sent a message to the Emperor, asking for an interview with him. Once he had received a safe conduct, Paganos and his boyars came down to the Emperor. The Emperor sat with Sabinos beside him, and reproached the Bulgars' disorder and their hatred of Sabinos. They made peace on terms which seemed good.

But the Emperor secretly sent men into Bulgaria who seized Sklabounos the ruler of the Sebereis, a man who had worked many evils in Thrace. Christianos, an apostate from Christianity who headed the Skamaroi, was also captured. His hands and feet were cut off at the mole of St. Thomas. They brought in doctors who cut him open from his groin to his chest in order to ascertain the constituent parts of a man, and then he was burned.

The Emperor suddenly sallied forth from the city. Because of the deceitful peace, he found the passes unguarded, and penetrated Bulgaria as far as Tzikas. After he set fire to the villas he found, he withdrew in flight; he had accomplished nothing noble.

ANNUS MUNDI 6257 (SEPTEMBER 1, 765—AUGUST 31, 766)

25. 11. 4. 12.

In this year—the fourth indiction—on November 20 the impious and utterly unholy Emperor Constantine grew furiously angry at everyone who feared God. He ordered Stephen the new chief martyr, a solitary monk at the monastery of St. Auxentios in the mountains near Damatrys, to be dragged out. Stephen's enemies (scholarii and members of the other imperial guards regiments), who shared Constantine's ignorance, seized him, bound his feet with cord, and dragged him from the Praitorion to the monastery of Pelagios. There they tore his precious body limb from limb and threw it into the pit of the suicides. They did this because he had advised many people about monastic life and persuaded them to despise imperial dignities and money. This famous man had surpassed everyone by spending about sixty years in his cell, and was distinguished by his many virtues.

When many officers and soldiers were accused of venerating icons, Constantine subjected them to various punishments and bitter tortures. From everyone under his rule he demanded a general pledge that they would not venerate an icon. After that, he made the misnamed patriarch Constantine ascend to the altar, hold up the precious and lifegiving Cross, and swear there was no one who gave icons veneration. At the same time the Emperor talked him into becoming

437

a married man instead of a monk, and into partaking of the meats at the imperial table and appearing where they sang to the kithara. But soon justice gave the patriarch into the hands of the bloodstained one.

On June 21 the Emperor moved against the Bulgars. He outfitted 2,600 warships from all the themes and sent them to Akhelon. But after they had anchored by the shore, the north wind began to blow; almost all of them were beaten to bits, and a large army drowned. Because of this, the Emperor ordered the corpses gathered up in baskets and buried. On July 17 he ingloriously re-entered the city.

438

On August 21 of the same fourth indiction he denounced and dishonored the monastic way of life, summoning each of the abbots to the hippodrome to take a wife in hand. Thus they all came to the hippodrome, where they were spat upon and cursed by all the people. Similarly, on the twenty-fifth of the same month nineteen important officers were brought to and paraded in the hippodrome on the grounds that they had wickedly plotted against the Emperor; in fact, they were not falsely accused. But Constantine was jealous of them because they were handsome, strong, and praised by everyone, and of some of them because of their piety and because they had gone to the solitary monk who was mentioned before, and had condemned his suffering.

These were the leaders of the men he executed: the patrician Constantine was also logothete of the drome; he was surnamed Podopagouros. His brother Strategios was a spatharios and commander of the excubitores. Antiokhos had been logothete of the drome and was general of Sicily. David had been a spatharios under Beser, and was count of the theme of the Opsikion. Theophylaktos Ikoniates was a protospatharios and general of Thrace. Christopher was a spatharios under Himerios. The patrician Bardanes' son Constantine was a spatharios and imperial protostrator. Theophylaktos was an officer under Marinakes . . . there were also others.

At the hippodrome the Emperor mistreated them and made all the people spit on them and denounce them, then passed sentence on them. He beheaded the two brothers (I mean Constantine and Strategios) in the Kynegion, although all the people deeply mourned them. The Emperor grew angry when he learned that. He beat the prefect Prokopios and replaced him on the grounds that he agreed with the above. The others the Emperor blinded and exiled. Full of madness, he annually sent men to their places of exile and ordered them given up to a hundred strokes with an ox-hide whip.

On August 30 of this same fourth indiction the evilly-named Emperor became furious at the patriarch, who was of his party and was also his namesake. Constantine found some clergymen, monks, and laymen who were the patriarch's initiates and friends and primed them to say, "We heard the patriarch speaking against the Emperor with Podopagouros." The Emperor sent them to Constantine the patriarch at the patriarchal residence to accuse him; as part of their denial of him, the Emperor made them swear on the precious Cross, "We heard this abuse from the patriarch." Then the Emperor sent them away and sealed up the patriarchal residence. He exiled the patriarch to Hiereia, and later to the Prince's Island.

ANNUS MUNDI 6258 (SEPTEMBER 1, 766—AUGUST 31, 767)

Bishop of Constantinople Niketas: 14 years
26. 12. 5. 1.

In this year Abd Allah ibn Ali died when the tower in which he was imprisoned fell on him.[242] While the other Abd Allah was caliph, he showed the Christians under his control many evils. He took the crosses from their churches, and prevented them from celebrating night-festivals and studying their letters.

The Kharijites (which means "zealots") among the Arabs raised an insurrection in the desert of Palmyra. But their actions were as manifestly evil toward God's churches as toward the unbelievers.

He who was ruling the Christians by the ineffable decision of God (just as the mad Ahab had ruled Israel) did far worse to the orthodox bishops, monks, laymen, rulers, and subjects under his control than did the madness of the Arabs. He totally renounced the intercession of the holy Virgin and Mother of God and that of all the saints, on the grounds that it gave no aid and was unscriptural. But all aid for us springs from this intercession.

If Constantine heard of some notable person making an offering for the health of his body or soul and, as was usual, being honored by the pious, that person was threatened with death, confiscation, exile, or torture on the grounds of impiety. Relics containing a great deal of God's grace were a treasure for their owners, but he took them away so they were never seen again.

The unholy Emperor even did this to the precious remains of the martyr Euphemia, who was acclaimed by everyone. He threw them into the depths of the sea, coffin and all, as he could not bear to see Euphemia showering countless gifts on all the people and reflecting on his stupid opposition to the intercession of the saints. But, according to testimony, God preserved from him the bones of the virtuous;

242. See above, under *annus mundi* 6246.

440 He kept them safe and revealed them once more at the island of Lemnos. In a dream He commanded that what lay there should be lifted up and preserved. During the reign of the pious rulers Constantine [VI] and Irene (in the fourth indiction) the relics returned to their sacred precinct with suitable honors. Because he was an enemy of the church, Constantine [V] had appropriated this sacred precinct and turned it into an armory and a latrine. But Constantine [VI] and Irene cleansed and resanctified it to condemn his atheism and demonstrate their piety. We observed this amazing and noteworthy marvel in the company of our most pious rulers and the holy patriarch Tarasios twenty-two years after the death of the lawbreaker. We were taken along, although unworthy of such a great privilege.

By the decision of the Emperor, Niketas, a Slavic eunuch, was illegally chosen patriarch of Constantinople on November 16 of the fifth indiction.

There was a drought; no pure water fell from heaven, and it entirely abandoned the city. The reservoirs and the bath-houses were empty, and not only those, but also the spring-fed rivers which had formerly flowed at all times. When the Emperor saw this he began to restore the aqueduct of Valentinian,[243] which had been used until the time of Herakleios but had been torn down by the Avars. He collected skilled workmen from various places and brought them to Constantinople: from Asia and Pontos 1,000 homebuilders and two hundred plasterers, from Greece and the islands five hundred tile makers, and from Thrace 5,000 workmen and two hundred potters. He put overseers and one patrician in charge of them. When the work was done in this way, water reached the city.

In the same fifth indiction Constantine appointed generals of his party who were worthy workmen for his wickedness. They were Michael Melissenos in the theme of the Anatolics, Michael Lakhanodrakon in the theme of the Thrakesians, and Manes, who was named for evil,[244] in that of the Bukellarii. And who is competent to relate in full all their unholy deeds, which we have recorded here and there in their own places? For I do not plan to write one by one every action

441 of theirs done to aid their ruler: the universe itself, I think, would not have room for the books that would be written, and it is more congenial to speak evangelically.

243. This is actually the aqueduct constructed by Valens (see above, note 237), who was Valentinian's brother; Valentinian ruled in the west from 364 to 375. The aqueduct was rebuilt during the reign of Justin II (565–578). The Avars presumably destroyed it in the siege of Constantinople in 626.

244. This is the Greek form of the name Mani (see above, note 213), which to a devout Christian was synonymous with evil. *Manes* in Greek can also mean "madman."

ANNUS MUNDI 6259 (SEPTEMBER 1, 767—AUGUST 31, 768)

Bishop of Rome Stephen: 3 years
27. 13. 1. 2.

In this year—the sixth indiction—on October 6, Constantine the misnamed patriarch was brought from the Prince's Island. The tyrant Constantine beat him so badly he could not walk. He ordered him put on a litter and brought in to sit in front of the sanctuary at the great church. With him was an asekretes who lifted up a document on a sheet of paper, on which were written Constantine's crimes. By imperial order all the people of the city assembled there to watch while the sheet was read in their hearing. After each chapter the asekretes hit Constantine in the face, while the patriarch Niketas sat watching on his throne. Once this was done, they brought Constantine up onto the pulpit and stood him upright. Niketas took the sheet of paper and sent down bishops who took away Constantine's surplice and anathematized him. They renamed him Skotiopsis[245] and expelled him from the church backwards.

On the following day there was a horse-race. They shaved his face and cut off his beard, the hair on his head, and his eyebrows, then, clothing him in silk and a sleeveless garment, mounted him backwards on an ass which bore a packsaddle. He held onto its tail. They brought him into the hippodrome by way of the gate through which the horses enter, while all the people and members of the factions cursed him and spat on him. His nephew Constantine, who led the ass, had his nose slit.

When the ex-patriarch went by the members of the factions, they came down to spit on him and throw dust on him. They brought him to the Emperor's part of the hippodrome, threw him from his ass, and trampled on his neck. Then he was seated across from the members of the factions, where he listened to their mockery until the end of the races.

442   On the fifteenth of the same month the Emperor sent patricians to him. They asked, "What do you have to say about our faith and the synod we convened?"

As he was impious in his heart, he answered, "You believe correctly, and the synod did well," thinking he could again propitiate the Emperor by this.

But they answered him at once. "We wanted to hear this from your own polluted mouth. Henceforward go into darkness and into anathema." Thus he received his sentence, and was beheaded in the Kynegion. They tied his head by the ears[246] and hung it on the Milion for

245. "Of darkened vision."
246. As he had been shaved bald, he had no hair left to tie to anything.

three days as a spectacle for the people. They dragged his corpse, its feet tied together by a cord, through the Mese to the cemetery of Pelagios and threw it in with the suicides. Three days later they also brought his head there, and threw it in too. Oh, the senselessness, cruelty, and heartlessness of this savage wild beast![247]

Was the wretch not ashamed by the holy font? For Constantine took two of his children into his arms from his third wife.[248] In every way he was beastlike and savage of manner. From that time on, he vented more spleen on the holy churches. He sent out men who brought the famous stylite Peter down from his rock. Because he would not abandon his doctrines, Constantine bound his feet and ordered him dragged through the Mese and thrown alive into the cemetery of Pelagios. He bound others in bags, fastened them with stones, and ordered them thrown into the sea. He devised all sorts of punishments for the pious: blindings, nose slittings, whippings. In the city Constantine did these deeds by himself and through the members of his party: I mean the patrician Antonius (who was domesticus of the scholae[249]), the magistros Peter, and the palace guard regiments, which the Emperor had trained. In the outlying themes he acted through the aforementioned generals.

He himself enjoyed kithara-playing and drinking-bouts, and educated the men around him to foul language and dancing. If someone who had fallen ill or felt a pain let fall the prayer usual for Christians ("Mother of God, have mercy on me!"), or was seen making a night-prayer, or regularly attending church, or living piously, or not using oaths shamelessly, he was punished as an enemy of the Emperor and known as an unmentioned one. Constantine made the common property of his faction's soldiers monasteries which had been established for the glory of God and as houses of refuge for those who needed salvation. Thus he gave the monastery of Dalmatos, which was the leader of the coenobitic houses[250] of Byzantium, to his soldiers so they could live in it. He also toppled from their foundations the monastery of Kallistratos, that of Dios, that of Maximinus, and other holy houses for monks and nuns.

He condemned to death useful men, important in the army or in

443

---

247. That is, Constantine V.

248. Third marriages were frowned upon by canon law in the Orthodox Church, and fourth marriages even more so; these were reckoned a sin worse than fornication. Leo VI (886–912) precipitated a great scandal when, as he was three times a widower without male issue, he married his mistress Zoe Karbonopsina ("Black-eyed Zoe") after she bore him a son, the future Constantine VII (913–959).

249. Commander of a regiment of the imperial guards.

250. Monastic establishments where the monks lived as an organized community.

government, who undertook the monastic way of life—and especially those who had been near him and witnessed his licentiousness and unspeakable actions, as he suspected their statements would disgrace him. Because of this, as was said before, he killed Strategios the brother of Podopagouros when he learned Strategios, who did not approve of his illegal acts of unnatural lust, had told them to the blessed Stephen (the solitary monk at the church of St. Auxentios) and had received the medicine of salvation. Thus Constantine, who had taken the comely Strategios as partner (for because of his licentiousness he loved to have such people by him), accused him of plotting with the monk.

At this time Constantine made the city prosper, for he was a new Midas who heaped up treasures of gold by stripping the farmers bare. Because of tax demands, men were compelled to sell God's abundance cheaply.

In the same year the misnamed patriarch Niketas scraped off the mosiac-work icons of the small consistory in the patriarchal residence, and took down those in the building's great consistory, which were painted on wood. He painted over the faces of the rest of the icons, and did the same thing in the Abramaion.

ANNUS MUNDI 6260 (SEPTEMBER 1, 768—AUGUST 31, 769)

28. 14. 2. 3.

In this year the Emperor, that trigamist, crowned his third wife Eudokia Augusta in the tribunal of the nineteen Akkubita. This was on Saturday, April 1 of the seventh indiction. On the next day, which was April 2, the Sunday of holy Easter, he appointed his two sons by her, Christopher and Nikephoros, Caesars in the same tribunal. The patriarch gave the prayers, then the Emperor put their robes and Caesars' crowns on them. In the same way he made Niketas, their last brother, nobilissimus,[251] and put a gold robe and crown on him. Then the Emperors went all the way to the great church, distributing consular largess: newly minted third-nomisma pieces, half-nomisma pieces, and nomismata.

444

ANNUS MUNDI 6261 (SEPTEMBER 1, 769—AUGUST 31, 770)

29. 15. 3. 4.

In this year there was a reconciliation in Syria: of man toward man, woman toward woman, and likewise child toward child. Abd Allah

251. A title of high honor between Caesar and curopalates in rank, and restricted to the imperial family.

ordered all his subjects to shave their beards and wear cubit-and-a-half turbans. He besieged Kamakhon all summer long but withdrew in disgrace without having accomplished anything.

On November 1 of the eighth indiction Irene came from Athens. She went from Hiereia to the imperial city with a large number of different kinds of warships equipped with silk mantlings. The city's leading men and their wives met and escorted her. On November 3 the patriarch entered the palace to betroth the Emperor Leo to Irene in the church of Pharos. On December 17 the Empress Irene was crowned in the triklinos of the Augusteion. She went to the oratory of St. Stephen in Daphne and received the crowns of marriage with Constantine's son the Emperor Leo.

ANNUS MUNDI 6262 (SEPTEMBER 1, 770—AUGUST 31, 771)

Bishop of Rome Hadrian: 27 years
30. 16. 1. 5.

445

In this year ibn Wakkas attacked Romania, taking many prisoners. The Romans invaded and plundered fourth Armenia. Palestinian Germanikeia was rebuilt.

In the same year Lakhanodrakon, imitating his teacher, collected at Ephesos every monk and nun under the jurisdiction of the Thrakesian theme. Bringing them to the plain known as Tzoukanisterin, he told them, "Let he who wishes to obey the Emperor and us put on white clothing and take a wife at this hour; those who do not want to do so shall be blinded and exiled to Cyprus." His speech and action were simultaneous, and on that day many martyrs were revealed and many who abandoned their vocations were lost: to these Drakon was friendly.

On January 14 of the same ninth indiction a son was born to the Emperor Leo and Irene. He was named Constantine, as his grandfather Constantine was still alive.

ANNUS MUNDI 6263 (SEPTEMBER 1, 771—AUGUST 31, 772)

31. 17. 2. 6.

In this year ibn Wakkas attacked Romania. He advanced from Isauria to the fortress of Sykes, which he besieged. When the Emperor heard of this, he wrote to Michael the general of the Anatolics, Manes of the Bukellarii, and to Bardanes of the Armeniacs, who all moved to seize the rugged pass which was ibn Wakkas' exit-route. Under its general the protospatharios Petronas, the Kibyrhaiots' naval force reached Sykes' harbor and anchored there. When he saw this, ibn

Wakkas lost hope for himself. But he encouraged and inspired his troops, who sallied forth against the mounted thematic troops while shouting their war-cry and put them to rout. He killed many of them and captured all the territory roundabout, then withdrew with much plunder.

In the same year Michael Lakhanodrakon, the general of the Thrakesian theme, sent out his secretary Leo (surnamed Kouloukes) and Leo Koutzodaktylos (an abbot) to sell all the monastic communities (both for men and women) and all their holy gear, books, and beasts, as well as whatever was under their management. He turned over to the Emperor the price these things brought. Whatever monastic books or books of the fathers he found, he burned. If it seemed someone had the remains of a saint in an amulet, he also consigned that to the flames and punished the person who had it for impiety. He whipped many monks to death, while others he put to the sword; he blinded a countless number. He set fire to some monks' beards by anointing them with oil, and thus burned their faces and heads; he sent others into exile after many tortures. Finally, he would not allow one single man in his entire theme to assume monastic garb. And when the Emperor, who hated the good, learned this, he wrote Lakhanodrakon his thanks: "I have found you a man after my own heart; you are acting as I wish." The rest imitated him and did the same sort of thing.

ANNUS MUNDI 6264 (SEPTEMBER 1, 772—AUGUST 31, 773)

32. 18. 3. 7.

In this year Abd Allah sent a large army to Africa under Moulabit.

Al-Fadal Badinar invaded Romania and took five hundred prisoners. The Mopsuestians encountered his men, attacked them, and killed a thousand Arabs.

Abd Allah went to Jerusalem; after fasting, he ordered the Christians and Jews tattooed on their hands. Many of the Christians fled to Romania by sea.

Sergios Kourikos was captured outside Sykes, as was Sergios Lakhebaphos in Cyprus—he was legate for that area.

ANNUS MUNDI 6265 (SEPTEMBER 1, 773—AUGUST 31, 774)

33. 19. 4. 8.

In this year—the twelfth indiction—Constantine set in motion against Bulgaria an expedition of 2,000 warships. He boarded the scarlet[252] warships with the intention of entering the Danube, and left

252. Again, the imperial color—cf. note 54.

447 the generals of the thematic cavalry behind, outside the passes. If they could, they were to invade Bulgaria while the Bulgars were occupied with him. But when he had gone as far as Varna, he grew fearful and planned to retreat. The Bulgars, however, had also grown fearful when they saw him, and sent a boyar, Tzigatos, to ask for peace. The two sides agreed with each other that the Bulgars should not sally forth against Romania, nor should the Emperor make it his business to invade Bulgaria. They made written agreements with each other on these terms. The Emperor withdrew; after he entered the city he released the units from the themes to the fortresses he had built.

In October of the eleventh indiction [sic], the Emperor received from his secret friends in Bulgaria a message that the lord of Bulgaria had sent out boyars with a 12,000-man army to capture Berzitia and transfer its population to Bulgaria. Constantine did not want it known that he was going to move against the Bulgars, because the lord of Bulgaria's envoys had come to him. While they were still in the city, he pretended he was moving against the Arabs, and his banners and equipage even crossed over.[253] But once he had sent away the envoys and learned from his spies that they had left, he quickly raised his army and set out. He assembled units from the thematic armies and the Thrakesians and joined the optimatoi[254] to the palace guards, levying 80,000 men. When he came to a place called Lithosoria,[255] he fell on the Bulgars without sounding his trumpets and routed them: a great victory. He returned to the city in triumph, with much booty and many prisoners. He called the war a noble one, since he had invaded successfully without any opposition, slaughter of Christians, or Christian blood shed.

253. To the Asiatic side of the Bosporos.
254. The optimatoi (a word derived either from the Latin *optimi* [the best troops] or, more probably, the Latin *Optimates* [a band of nobles]) were unusual in that, while organized on the thematic model in their territory in the northwest corner of Asia Minor, they were normally an army service unit rather than a fighting force. In the early days of the seventh century they had indeed been an elite, being ranked by the military author who goes under the name of Maurice as equals to the *foederati*, who were definitely first-class troops. They were probably degraded to noncombatant status after backing Artavasdos against Constantine V during the former's rebellion after the death of Leo III; this muster of them by Constantine V appears to have been one of the rare times they were allowed to bear arms thereafter, and was an emergency measure only.
255. "Heap of stones."

ANNUS MUNDI 6266 (SEPTEMBER 1, 773—AUGUST 31, 774[256])

34. 20. 5. 9.

In this year two hundred eighty heads which had come from Africa were paraded in Syria.

Since the Emperor had broken the peace with the Bulgars, he once more prepared a large naval force. He brought 12,000 cavalrymen to it and sent all the admirals of the naval force with it, though he himself stayed with the cavalry out of fear. When the expedition reached Mesembria a strong north wind blew up; almost all the ships were smashed to pieces, and many men were killed. The Emperor withdrew without having done anything.

448

Telerigos the lord of Bulgaria knew the Emperor had learned of his plans from his own men; he wrote to Constantine: "I am of a mind to flee to you, but send me a guarantee that I will not be harmed. Also, tell me who your friends here are, so I can encourage them to come with me." Out of simplicity, Constantine wrote back, and Telerigos got rid of them all once he had learned. When Constantine learned this he tore out many of his gray hairs.

ANNUS MUNDI 6267 (SEPTEMBER 1, 774—AUGUST 31, 775)

35. 21. 6. 10.

In this year—the thirteenth indiction—the Emperor Constantine sallied forth against the Bulgars in August. At that time his legs were terribly burnt by a God-sent plague, unknown to his doctors, which caused a severe fever. He was overcome by its overpowering inflammation at Arkadiopolis, and retreated, carried in a bed on his subjects' shoulders. He came to Selymbria, boarded ship, and on September 14 of the fourteenth indiction reached the castle of Strongylon. Pitiably dying in his warship, he cried out: "I have been given to unquenchable fire while still alive." Her implacable enemy demanded hymns to the Virgin and Mother of God. Thus did the autokrator give up his life; he had ruled thirty-four years, two months, and twenty-six days after his father's death. He was defiled by the blood of many Christians, by invocations of demons and sacrifices to them, by persecution of the holy churches and the true and blameless faith, and by the murder of monks and the parceling out of monasteries. He had done all sorts of wicked deeds, no less than had Diocletian[257] and the tyrants of old.

256. See the introduction's discussion of chronology, p. xviii.
257. Diocletian (284–305), at the instigation of his Caesar Galerius, began a great persecution of Christianity in 303. Carried on by some of his successors, this persecution continued until 313.

In the same month the Arabs' ruler Abd Allah also died. By divine providence these two terrible beasts, who had so long divided the
449 human race, died at the same time. Their sons Leo and Mahdi became the rulers.

Also in the same year, Theodotos the king of the Lombards fled to the Emperor in the imperial city.[258]

ANNUS MUNDI 6268 (SEPTEMBER 1, 775—AUGUST 31, 776)

A.D. 768
Roman Emperor Leo: 5 years: year 1
Arab ruler Mahdi: 9 years: year 1
Bishop of Rome Hadrian: 27 years: year 7
Bishop of Constantinople Niketas: 14 years: year 11

In this year Mahdi sent a large force under Abasbali against Romania. He forced open the cave of Kasin with smoke, captured the men in it, and withdrew.

The Emperor Leo began to dip into the money his father had left behind for him, and to propitiate the army and the people in the city. For a little while he seemed to be pious, and a friend to the Mother of God and the monks. Because of this, he appointed metropolitans to many of the leading thrones from among the abbots. He levied many soldiers from the themes to strengthen the imperial guards. This roused the officers of the thematic forces, who entered the city with a large host of soldiers and asked Leo to raise his son Constantine to the imperial dignity.

But he, as was proper for Emperors, replied, "He is my only son, and I am afraid to do so, lest humanity's fate befall me. Because he would be so young, you would kill him and choose someone else." But they agreed to assure Leo on oath that no-one would become Emperor save his son, even if God should will that he die. Because the army assembled in the hippodrome to demand this from Palm Sunday to Maundy Thursday, he ordered them to swear it on holy gear. All the people—the thematic troops, senators, palace guards, and all the citizens and artisans—swore on the precious and lifegiving wood not to accept anyone as Emperor save Leo, Constantine, and their seed. By their own hands they made written agreements, just as they had sworn.

On the next day, the holy sabbath, the Emperor went to the
450 tribunal of the nineteenth Akkubita and appointed his brother Eudokimos nobilissimus. While still alive, his father had appointed An-

258. Properly, Desiderius. The Lombard king was fleeing the conquering armies of Charlemagne, who destroyed the Lombard kingdom in 774.

thimos.[259] Then the Emperor went to the great church with the two Caesars, the three nobilissimi, and the young Constantine. As was customary for Emperors, Leo changed his clothing, then mounted to the pulpit with his son and the patriarch. All the people came in and put their written agreements on the holy table. The Emperor spoke as follows: "Well, brothers, I am fulfilling your request and giving you my son as Emperor. Lo, receive him from the church and from Christ's hand."

They cried out in a loud voice, "Be our surety, Son of God, that we have received our lord Constantine the Emperor from Your hands, to protect and die for him."

On the following day, the great Sunday of Easter, April 24 of the fourteenth indiction, at daybreak the Emperor and the patriarch went to the hippodrome. The holy sacrament was brought in while all the people watched; the patriarch performed the prayer while the Emperor crowned his son. Thus the two Emperors went on to the great church with the two Caesars and three nobilissimi. After the Emperors had gone ahead, the Empress Irene also went; the scholae attended her with the scepters. She went up through the Bronze Gate's stairway to the upper gate, although she did not go into the middle of the portico.

In May of the same indiction the Caesar Nikephoros (the Emperor's brother) was denounced to Leo on the grounds that he had plotted against him with some of the Emperor's spatharioi, grooms, and other servants. The Emperor convened a silentium at Magnaura and put to the army what had been reported about Nikephoros. With one accord they shouted that both Caesars should be exiled from the Emperor's heart, since they (who always broke their oaths) were paying no mind to what they had sworn to their father: that after his death his children would not be wronged. The Emperor beat and tonsured the revolutionaries, exiling them to the vicinity of Cherson under guard and in safekeeping.

451

ANNUS MUNDI 6269 (SEPTEMBER 1, 776—AUGUST 31, 777)

2. 2. 8. 12.

In this year Thumama son of Baka invaded Romania, took many prisoners, and withdrew.

Telerigos, the lord of the Bulgars, fled to the Emperor. Leo made him a patrician and married him to a cousin of his own wife Irene. The Emperor received Telerigos favorably and honored him after he had been baptized at the holy font.

259. Another younger brother of Leo IV.

ANNUS MUNDI 6270 (SEPTEMBER 1, 777—AUGUST 31, 778)

3. 3. 9. 13.

In this year Thumama rebelled, enthroning himself at Dabekon.

The Emperor loosed the Romans' armies: 100,000 men invaded Syria. They were led by Michael Lakhanodrakon of the Thrakesians, Artavasdos the Armenian of the Anatolics, Karisterotzes of the Armeniacs, and Gregory Mousouliakos of the Opsikion. They surrounded Germanikeia and seized all the camels of Mahdi's uncle Isbaali, who was there. They would also have taken Germanikeia had Isbaali not bribed Lakhanodrakon not to do so. He withdrew from the fortress to harass its villages, then returned to the fortress after capturing some Syrian Jacobite heretics.

Thumama sent out from Dabekon emirs with an army. When they joined battle with the Romans, as they say, five emirs and 2,000 Arabs fell. But the Arabs got away with their equipment, for Sunday was beginning. The Emperor held May Day at Sophianai; he sat on a throne there with his son, and in this way the generals celebrated their victories. Leo forced the Syrian heretics to cross to Thrace and settled them there.

452

ANNUS MUNDI 6271 (SEPTEMBER 1, 778—AUGUST 31, 779)

4. 4. 10. 14.

In this year the Arab ruler Mahdi, furious, sent out Hasan with a large force of Black-cloaks, Syrians, and Mesopotamians, who advanced as far as Dorylaion. The Emperor arranged with his generals that they should not meet the Arabs in the field, but secure the fortresses and bring in men to guard them. He also sent high-ranking officers to each fortress, who were to take about 3,000 select soldiers to dog the Arabs' heels so their raiding party would not break up. Even before this, they were to burn whatever fodder was to be found for the Arabs' horses.

After the Arabs had been in Dorylaion for fifteen days, they ran out of supplies and their animals went begging; there were heavy losses among them. They retreated and besieged Amorion for one day, but when they realized it was strong and well-garrisoned, they withdrew without accomplishing anything.

ANNUS MUNDI 6272 (SEPTEMBER 1, 779—AUGUST 31, 780)

Bishop of Constantinople Paul: 5 years
5. 5. 11. 1.

In this year the Arab ruler Mahdi went to Dabekon with a large force and armament. He sent his son Hasan against Romania, while he himself returned to the holy city. He also sent out Moukhesias, known as the Zealot, with the authority to devastate the holy churches and to make the Christians' slaves apostasize. Moukhesias went as far as Emesa, and reported that he could not make them apostasize (except for those who had been from peoples outside the faith) until he knew who the Hebrews and Christians were. Thereupon he godlessly began to torture them more than even Lysias and Agrikolaos[260] had ever done, putting many to death. But, by the grace of Christ our Lord, women overcame his madness. They were fine ladies: the daughter of the archdeacon of Emesa and the daughter of Hesaios' son. They were tortured over a long period, but did not yield to impiety. They took

453   as many as a thousand strokes from a leather lash, and were tested by many other punishments, but gained the crown of victory from Christ. Disregarding the guarantees the Arabs had given the Christians, Moukhesias went all the way to Damascus while laying waste their churches.

On February 7 (the Sunday of cheese-eating) of the third indiction died the Slavic eunuch Niketas, the patriarch of Constantinople. Although he tried to beg off, on the second Sunday of Lent the honored Paul was chosen patriarch of Constantinople; he was under strong duress because of the dominant heresy. A Cypriot in origin, he was a reader brilliant in speech and action.

In the middle week of Lent, Jacob the protospatharios, Papias, Strategios, and Theophanes the cubicularii and parakoimomenoi,[261] and Leo and Thomas (also cubicularii) were arrested with other pious men, because they had given reverence to the august, holy icons. Then Leo the son of the persecutor revealed his concealed wickedness: he mercilessly cudgeled them, tonsured them and, once he had made them parade through the Mese, imprisoned them in the Praitorion. Theophanes died there, becoming a confessor and acquiring the crown of martyrdom. After Leo's death, all the rest were shown to be excellent monks.

Harun invaded the Armeniac theme and besieged the fortress of Semalouos all summer long; in September he took it on terms. He sent 50,000 men to Asia under Thumama. Michael Lakhanodrakon encountered and attacked a small raiding party, killing Thumama's brother.

On September 8 of the fourth indiction Constantine's son Leo died in this way: he was mad about precious stones, and was in love

---

260. Lysias was a Seleucid general who fought against the Maccabees when they rebelled in the 160s B.C. No Agrikolaos appears in Pauly-Wissowa-Kroll's *Real-Encyclopädie der klassischen Altertumswissenschaft.*

261. These officials performed functions virtually identical to those of the cubicularii, and like them were almost always eunuchs.

with the great church's crown. Coals came out from it onto his head and caused a severe fever. He died after ruling five years, less six days.

454 **ANNUS MUNDI 6273 (SEPTEMBER 1, 780—AUGUST 31, 781)**

A.D. 773
Roman Emperor Constantine (with his mother): 10 years: year 1
Arab ruler Mahdi: 9 years: year 6
Bishop of Rome Hadrian: 27 years: year 12
Bishop of Constantinople Paul: 5 years: year 2

In this year—the fourth indiction—on September 8 God unexpectedly entrusted the rule to the most pious Irene and her son Constantine, so He could work a miracle through a widow-woman and an orphan child. By this means He intended to destroy the boundless impiety against Him and His helpers, as well as His enemy Constantine's tyranny over all the churches, as long ago He had cured the sailors and illiterates from the illness of the devil.

After Irene had ruled for forty days, some of the men in power formed a cabal. Because Irene's son was only ten years old, they wanted to summon the Caesar Nikephoros and make him Emperor. When this plot was revealed, Gregory the logothete of the drome, Bardas (who was then general of the Armeniacs), Constantine (spatharios of the vicarius and domesticus of the excubitores), Theophylaktos Rhangabe (the drungarius of the Dodekanese), and many others were arrested. Irene beat and tonsured them, then exiled them to various places. She tonsured her in-laws the Caesars and nobilissimi and made them priests, then made them minister to the people at the festival of Christ's birth. At that time she also regally went out in public with her son and presented to the church the crown her husband had stolen away, which she had ornamented further with pearls.

As he had previously commanded the men there, she appointed the patrician Elpidios general of Sicily, and sent him off in February. But in April Elpidios was denounced on the grounds that he was of the Caesars' party. Irene immediately dispatched the spatharios Theophilos with orders to arrest and bring back Elpidios. But when Theophilos got there, the Sicilians would not give up Elpidios. Irene beat

455 and tonsured Elpidios' wife and sent her and his sons to the Praitorion under guard.

In June she sent all the opposite shore's[262] thematic armies to guard the passes and be on the lookout for the Arabs' military expedi-

262. That is, those thematic armies from the themes of Asia Minor, where iconoclastic sentiment was strongest.

tion. At their head she put the sakellarios John, a eunuch who was an intimate of hers. Mahdi dispatched a large force under Abd al-Kabir, and they met each other at a place called Melon. When battle was joined the Arabs were defeated and many of them were killed; they retreated in disgrace.

The pious began to speak freely, the word of God began to wax, those who wished to be saved began to be appointed without hindrance, the monasteries began to be delivered, and everything good began to become manifest. At this time a man digging in Thrace found a coffin. He cleaned it and, looking inside, found a man lying in it. There were also letters inlaid on the coffin, whose content was this: "Christ was certainly born of the Virgin Mary, and I believe in Him. Sun, look on me again in the reign of the Emperors Constantine and Irene."

ANNUS MUNDI 6274 (SEPTEMBER 1, 781—AUGUST 31, 782)

2. 7. 13. 3.

In this year Irene sent Konstaes the sakellarios and Mamalos the primikerios[263] to Charles the king of the Franks to betroth his daughter (who was called Erythro[264]) to her son the Emperor Constantine. After they came to an agreement and exchanged oaths with each other, the eunuch scribe Elissaios was left behind to teach Erythro the Greeks'[265] letters and customs and to educate her in the customs of the Roman Empire.

Irene armed a large fleet with select troops from the thematic forces and competent officers. She appointed Theodore, a vigorous man, as its leader and sent him to Sicily against Elpidios. After many great battles, Theodore's men won. Taking fright as he saw this, Elpidios took such money as he had and crossed to Africa with the duke Nikephoros. He went over to the Arabs after receiving a guarantee that he would not be harmed. They received him favorably and let him

456 continue as Roman Emperor, vainly crowning him and clothing him with boots and crown.

While the Roman army was occupied in this area, Mahdi's son Harun sallied forth with an overwhelming force and armament gath-

263. A high palace official.
264. A Greek translation of Rotrude, her true name: both mean "red."
265. τῶν Γραικῶν. Unlike his usual practice, here Theophanes does not call the Byzantines "Romans," nor does he use the classical Greek word for a Greek: Hellene. This had developed a new meaning, as it was usually used to refer to the pagan Greeks when contrasting them to Christians (see above, under *annus mundi* 6241, where Theophanes uses "Hellene" to describe the pagans of Harran).

ered from among the Black-cloaks and from all Syria, Mesopotamia, and the desert. He advanced all the way to Chrysopolis, leaving ibn Yunus behind to besiege Nakoleia and guard his back. He also sent 30,000 men into Asia under Barmak,[266] who attacked Lakhanodrakon at a place called Darenos; of his 30,000 men, Lakhanodrakon killed 15,000. The Empress dispatched the imperial guards under the domesticus Antonius: he took Banes and shut up its inhabitants.

Tatzatios the general of the Bukellarii fled to the Arabs because he hated the patrician and logothete of the drome Staurakios, a eunuch who administered all affairs and was the most important man of his time. After Tatzatios had made a plan for them, the Arabs asked for peace. But when Staurakios, Peter the magistros, and Antonius the domesticus came to negotiate, they did not accurately weight the promise that they would receive as hostages the children of important men, but senselessly advanced, only to be captured and bound by the Arabs.

Both sides were compelled to make peace. The Augusta and Harun gave each other many friendly gifts and arranged to pay tribute at the appropriate time. After the peace the Arabs withdrew, freeing the fortress of Nakoleia. Tatzates [sic] lost his wife and all his property.

ANNUS MUNDI 6275 (SEPTEMBER 1, 782—AUGUST 31, 783)
3. 8. 14. 4.

In this year Irene, because she had made peace with the Arabs, found an opportunity to send a large force under the patrician and logothete of the imperial drome Staurakios against the Sklavinian tribes. He went to Thessalonike and Greece, subjected them all, and made them tributary to the Empire. He also entered the Peloponnese, took many prisoners and much booty, and brought it to the Roman Empire.

ANNUS MUNDI 6276 (SEPTEMBER 1, 783—AUGUST 31, 784)
4. 9. 15. 5.

In this year—the seventh indiction—in January Staurakios returned from the Sklavinias and held a triumphal procession to the hippodrome.

In May of the seventh indiction the Empress Irene went to Thrace

266. The Barmakids were the hereditary wazirs (prime ministers) of the early Abbasid caliphs, and grew fabulously wealthy. They retained their prominent position until 803, when Harun executed Jafar Barmaki and confiscated the family's property.

with her son and a large force; they were carrying tools and musical instruments. She went as far as Beroia and, ordering it rebuilt, renamed it Irenopolis. She rebuilt Ankhialos and went all the way to Philippopolis without any harm whatever, then withdrew in peace.

In the same year the Arabs' ruler Mahdi (also known as Muhammad) died, and his son Musa took power.

On August 31 of the seventh indiction Paul, the devout and holy patriarch, abandoned his throne because of illness. He went to the monastery of Florus and received monastic garb without the Empress' knowledge. When she learned of this she went to him with her son and, distressed, cried out, "Why have you done this?"

With deep mourning he told her, "You should be used to the fact that I did not willingly sit on the throne of holiness, as the church has been ruled tyranically. It is in schism from the remaining catholic thrones and has been anathematized by them." Irene summoned the patricians and picked men from the senate and sent them to hear what he was saying. He told them, "If there is no ecumenical council, and if the error in our midst is not corrected, you will not be saved."

They asked him, "At the time when you were appointed, why did you subscribe to giving no reverence to icons?"

He said, "I am in mourning because of that. I have taken refuge in repentance, and I beg God not to punish me, for I am a priest who kept silent until now and did not proclaim the truth from fear of your anger." In this way he died in peace, leaving behind deep mourning in the Empire and in the pious men of the state. For he was a worshipful man, more than usually compassionate, and deserved total respect. The state and the Empress had had a great deal of faith in him. From this time on everyone began to talk about the issue of the holy, revered icons, which was addressed in open discussion.

458

ANNUS MUNDI 6277 (SEPTEMBER 1, 784—AUGUST 31, 785)

Arab ruler Musa: 1 year
Bishop of Constantinople Tarasios: 21 years
5. 1. 16. 1.

In this year the Empress Irene assembled all the people at Magnaura and said to them, "You know, brothers, what Paul the patriarch has done. And had he lived, we would not have accepted his abandonment of the throne of holiness, even if he did assume monastic garb. But since, as was best to God, he has departed from life, let us think of a man who can be our shepherd and can make the church of God lean on his instructive words." They unanimously agreed that this could be no-one else but the asekretes Tarasios. She told them, "We also chose the same man, but he will not obey. He should state why he does not accept the choice of the Empress and all the people."

He defended himself to the people, saying, "Our faithful rulers are the guardians of the blameless faith of us Christians, and are eager that everything should be done for the glory of God. In order to please Him, they are doing for us all that which is expedient in their thoughts. Most of all, they are now carefully concerned with ecclesiastical affairs and are thinking about them in order to appoint a chief prelate in their imperial city. In their pious minds they have considered me, and have openly ordered me to explain what they have devised for me. But I am a man who has declared himself unworthy for this purpose. I have not acquiesced, because I am unable to lift the yoke of this burden or bear up under it. They have ordered me to come before you in person, because you agree with their plan. And now, gentlemen who fear God and hold Him in your hearts, you who are called by the name of our true God Christ (I mean, Christians), listen to a brief defense statement on my shoddiness and unworthiness. If I defended myself to our rulers, who are pious and absoutely orthodox, I also further defend myself in your sight, and I am very much afraid to agree to this choice.

459

"I am wary of, as it were, thoughtlessly running from God's face in this way, lest I fall under a fearful judgment. For if the holy apostle Paul (who had heard divine, ineffable voices, had heaven as a school, and exalted the name of God before peoples and kings) said when he wrote to the Corinthians, 'Whether or not I have preached to others, I myself am reprobate,' how can I, who have been involved with the world, have always been a layman, and have campaigned in the imperial service, leap into so great a holiness without consideration or examination? The effort is fearful because I am so small, and the matter is risky: this why I am afraid and beg off.

"I see and observe that His church, founded on the rock of Christ our God, is now divided and in schism. We say now one thing, now another, and the eastern Christians (who are of the same faith as ourselves) disagree. Those of the west agree with them. We are estranged from them all and anathematized by them individually. Anathema is a terrible thing. It hurls one far from God and drives one from His kingdom into the outer darkness. The church's rule and law have not known strife and contention. Just as they know they should agree on one baptism and one faith, in that way there should also be agreement on every ecclesiastical matter. For is it not virtuous and acceptable in God's eyes for us to unite and become one catholic church, brothers, just as we crave and confess in the symbol of our true faith? I think even you are brothers, since I know you fear God.

460

"Our pious and orthodox rulers should convene an ecumenical council so the followers of one God might become one, the followers of the Trinity might be united, like of soul, and equal of honor, the followers of Christ our Head might come into harmony and travel together as one body, the followers of the Spirit might be with and not against each other, the followers of the truth might believe and say the same things, and there might be no strife or dissension among us. In this way God's peace, which prevails over every mind, might watch over us all. If our rulers, the champions of orthodoxy, order my request agreed to, I will acquiesce and eagerly follow your choice. But if not, I find it impossible to do so, lest I be put under anathema and find myself condemned by our Lord the Judge of justice on the day when neither Emperor nor priest nor officers nor host of men could deliver me. If any part of my defense—or rather, my request—seems worthy to you, brothers, give me an answer."

Everyone who heard what he had said readily agreed there should be a council. Tarasios once more spoke to the people. He said, "The Emperor Leo overthrew the icons, and the synod,[267] when it took place, found them already overthrown. Because they were overturned by the imperial hand, our council should hold another inquiry since, as seemed good to them, they dared do away with ancient customs handed down in the church. But, speaking apostolically, God's truth cannot be fettered."

On December 25 of the eighth indiction our holy father Tarasios was chosen patriarch of Constantinople. He sent his synodic letters to Rome, and his statement of faith was accepted by pope Hadrian. The Empress also sent a message to that pope, asking him to send letters and men to join in the council. Hadrian sent Peter the administrator of his church and Peter the abbot of the monastery of St. Saba, honorable men adorned with every virtue. The Empress and the patriarch also sent men to Antioch and Alexandria, for the peace with the Arabs had not yet been broken. From Antioch they brought John, who shared the holiness of the patriarch of Antioch and was his synkellos; he was great and famous in speech and action. From Alexandria they brought back Thomas, a zealous, pious man who later became famous as the archbishop of the great Illyrian city of Thessalonike.

461

ANNUS MUNDI 6278 (SEPTEMBER 1, 785—AUGUST 31, 786)

Arab ruler Harun: 23 years
6. 1. 17. 2.

In this year the Arabs' ruler Musa died, and his brother Harun took over the rule. He too showed the Christians many evils.

In the same year the rulers sent messages summoning all the

267. Constantine V's council, which he deemed ecumenical, held at Hiereia in 754.

bishops under their dominion. With their arrival (and that of the men and letters sent from Rome by pope Hadrian, as we said before) came that of the men from Antioch and Alexandria. On August 27 of the ninth indiction they sat in state in the church of the Holy Apostles in the imperial city. By way of preface, they began to read from the holy scriptures and hold discussions with each other while the rulers watched from their special area.

But the troops of the scholarii, the excubitores, and the rest of the imperial guards bared their blades to attack the bishops, threatening the patriarch and the orthodox bishops and abbots with death. Their officers had whispered to them, and they also clung to the precepts of their wicked teacher.[268] When the Empress tried to repulse the troops through some close associates standing by her, the men would not obey, but instead dishonored the prelates even more. The patriarch grew agitated and ascended to the altar with the orthodox bishops and monks, while the bishops who were of the same wicked spirit as the troops went out to them, crying, "We have conquered!" By the grace of God, these mad, inhuman men mistreated no-one, but after the synod was disrupted in this way, each of them went back to his own barracks.

462

ANNUS MUNDI 6279 (SEPTEMBER 1, 786—AUGUST 31, 787)

7. 2. 18. 3.

In this year—at the beginning of the tenth indiction—in September the Empress sent the patrician and logothete Staurakios to the thematic forces from the opposite shore which were then in Thrace. Staurakios persuaded them to cooperate with her and oust from the city the impious army which the accursed Constantine had levied and trained. Irene was pretending to campaign in the east, using the excuse that the Arabs were moving out. The entire imperial retinue and the court advanced to Malagina; meanwhile, the troops from the outer themes entered and took the city. Irene sent the palace guards a message: "Give me your weapons, for I have no service for you." Since God had made them foolish, they gave them up. Then she loaded their families into ships and exiled them from the city, ordering each of them to return to his own native village.

Once she had officers loyal to her and her own army, in May she again sent messages everywhere, summoning bishops to the Bithynian city of Nikaia for a synod there. Everyone assembled at Nikaia all through the summer; nor had Irene sent the men from Rome and the

268. That is, Constantine V.

146

easterners away from the court, but rather had kept them by her.

On Sunday, September 9 of the eleventh indiction, there was a great solar eclipse at the fifth hour of the day, while the divine liturgy was being celebrated.[269]

ANNUS MUNDI 6280 (SEPTEMBER 1, 787—AUGUST 31, 788)

8. 3. 19. 4.

In this year Tarasios, the holy archbishop of Constantinople, went to Nikaia to convene the seventh holy ecumenical council of three hundred fifty bishops. The catholic church regained its ancient form: the council did not establish anything new, but preserved the tranquil doctrines of the holy, blessed fathers. Renouncing the new heresy, it anathematized the three men falsely known as patriarchs (I mean, Anastasios, Constantine, and Niketas) and all their partisans. The first meeting and session of the bishops took place in the church of St. Sophia of Nikaia on October 11 of the eleventh indiction.

In November everyone entered the imperial city. The rulers sat in state with the bishops at Magnaura. As a preface, a tome was read, and the Emperor and his mother signed it, affirming the holy fathers' piety and ancient doctrines. They honored the priests, then dismissed them. The church of God made peace, even if His enemy did not stop sowing his weeds among his own workers. But whenever it is attacked, God's church conquers.

463

ANNUS MUNDI 6281 (SEPTEMBER 1, 788—AUGUST 31, 789)

9. 4. 20. 5.

In this year an Arab raiding party sallied forth against Romania in September. It invaded the Anatolic theme at a place called Kopidnadon. The Romans' generals assembled to attack it, but were defeated. Many died, not a few of them from among the exiled scholarii. Diogenes, the able turmarch of the Anatolic troops, also fell, as did officers from the theme of the Opsikion.

The Empress Irene broke off her reconciliation with the Franks. She dispatched Theophanes the protospatharios to bring back a maiden, by name Maria of Amnia, from the Armeniac theme. Irene married her to her son the Emperor Constantine, although he was quite distressed and unwilling because he was being parted from the daughter of the Frankish king Charles, to whom he had already been

269. This is actually the eclipse of September 16, 787: Newton, op. cit., 544–545.

147

engaged. They celebrated his marriage in November of the twelfth indiction.

464 Philetos, the general of Thrace, made camp at the Strymon River without adequate guard. When the Bulgars fell on him, he and many others were killed.

Irene sent the sakellarios and minister of military affairs John to the land of the Lombards with Theodotos (who had once been king of great Lombardy) to hold off Charles—if they could—and to detach some men from him; with them was Theodore the patrician and general of Sicily. But when battle was joined, John was defeated by the Franks and horribly killed.

ANNUS MUNDI 6282 (SEPTEMBER 1, 789—AUGUST 31, 790)

10. 5. 21. 6.

In this year, out of envy of the rulers' piety, the devil incited wicked men to engage the mother against her son and the son against his mother. As if from foreknowledge, they persuaded her, "It is not ordained that your son should rule the state if you do not, as God gave it to you," and were fully believed. Since Irene was a woman (and was also power-hungry) she was deceived, and felt assured this was so. She did not reckon that they had used it as a pretext because they wanted to manage affairs themselves.

The Emperor was twenty years old, strong and competent, but saw he had no power. He was dismayed when he saw the patrician and logothete Staurakios occupied with everything. Everyone went to Staurakios, and no-one dared visit the Emperor. Constantine plotted with his own few intimates and with the magistros Peter and the patricians Theodore Kamoulianos and Damianos; they decided to seize Staurakios and exile him to Sicily. Constantine himself would hold power with his mother.

On February 9 of the thirteenth indiction there was a terrifying earthquake, so that some people did not dare sleep indoors, but passed their time in orchards and open-air tents.

465 The Empress and her son went to St. Mamas. When Staurakios learned what was afoot, he set the Augusta in motion against her son. She arrested the Emperor's men; after she had cudgeled and tonsured them all (as well as his tutor the protospatharios John, who was known as Pikridios), she exiled them to the southern lands: as far as Sicily. She dishonored and put under house-arrest the magistros Peter, and treated the patrician Theodore Kamoulianos in the same way. She beat and tonsured the patrician Damianos, then exiled him to the fortress of Apollonias. She also beat and reviled her son, and did not let him

go out for a number of days. She even began to make the army swear, "As long as you live, we will not agree to your son's ruling." Everyone swore in this fashion, since no-one dared oppose the whole body on the question.

An Arab fleet had gone to Cyprus; as the Empress had foreknowledge of this, she assembled all the Roman naval forces and sent them against the Arabs. When they reached Myra, both Roman admirals doubled the cape of Khelidonion and entered the bay of Attaleia. The Arabs moved out from Cyprus and, since they had fair weather, turned about on the sea. When they reappeared, the Roman admirals saw them from land; mustering their forces, they made ready to attack. But Theophilos the general of the Kibyrhaiotai, a competent, powerful man, was overbold, and went out to engage them ahead of anyone else. They defeated him and brought him to Harun, who, after observing him, urged him to become a traitor and acquire temporary gifts. Since he would not agree, he was tortured for a long time, yet still did not yield. He submitted to the sword, and was revealed as a noble martyr.

ANNUS MUNDI 6283 (SEPTEMBER 1, 790—AUGUST 31, 791)

A.D. **783**
Roman Emperor Constantine: 7 years: year 1
Arab ruler Harun: 23 years: year 6
Bishop of Rome Hadrian: 27 years: year 22
Bishop of Constantinople Tarasios: 21 years: year 7

466
In this year—the fourteenth indiction—Irene's sworn men arrived in the Armeniac theme. Its troops, however, would not agree to swear, "We will not be ruled by your son in your lifetime," nor would they put Irene's name before Constantine's, but Constantine's and then Irene's,[270] as they inherited it from the beginning. Irene then dispatched the spatharios and drungarius of the watch Alexios (surnamed Mousoulem) to put pressure on them. But they overpowered him, choosing their general—Nikephoros the patrician—to lead them. While staying on guard, they acclaimed Constantine sole Emperor. When the troops of the remaining themes learned this, they drove away their generals and also proclaimed Constantine sole Emperor.

Oh, the trickery of the wicked devil! How eager is he to destroy mankind by many wily devices! For, fifteen years before, these men had sworn a fearful oath, made written agreements, and put them away in the holy altar. Then they swore again to Irene that they would not be

270. Putting Irene's name before Constantine's would have implied that she had greater authority than did her son.

ruled by her son in her lifetime, but they forgot this and acclaimed Constantine autokrator. The wretches did not consider that it is not proper to make a contradictory oath, for on the heels of a contradictory oath will come a false oath, and a false oath is a denial of God.

In October of the fourteenth indiction the troops of the thematic armies gathered at Atroa; their common desire was that Constantine should become Emperor (he was in his twentieth year). Irene, fearing the onset of the army, tried to dismiss it. But it confirmed Constantine as autokrator and renounced his mother. The Emperor immediately dispatched Michael Lakhanodrakon and the protospatharios John (his tutor), who made the Armeniac troops swear they would not accept his mother Irene as Emperor. Constantine confirmed Alexios as their general.

Returning to the city in December, the Emperor beat and tonsured Staurakios, then exiled him to the Armeniac theme, thus fully assuring its troops. He also exiled the eunuch Aetios (Irene's protospatharios and bosom friend) and all the eunuchs who were her intimates. With a guarantee that she would not be harmed, he settled her in the palace of Eleutherios, which she had built—and in which she had hidden away a large sum of money.

467

There was a conflagration in the same month. The patriarchal residence's reception hall, known as the Thomaites, burned, as did the quaestor's residence and many other buildings all the way to the Milion.

In April Constantine campaigned against the Bulgars and entered the fortress known as Probaton[271] at the St. George River. When he met Kardamos the lord of Bulgaria, there was a small battle around sunset. The Romans lost their courage because of nightfall; they ingloriously ran away in retreat. The Bulgars, also fearful, retreated.

ANNUS MUNDI 6284 (SEPTEMBER 1, 791—AUGUST 31, 792)

2. 7. 23. 8.

In this year the Emperor campaigned against the Arabs in September. Setting out from Amorion, he advanced to Kilikian Tarsos. But when in October of the fifteenth indiction he came to the waterless towers, he at once turned about again, empty-handed.

On January 15 the Emperor was summoned by his mother and many of the men in power. He proclaimed her once more, and she was acclaimed with him as it had been in the beginning: Constantine and Irene. Everyone obeyed except for the theme of the Armeniacs.

271. "Sheep."

Its men resisted this and rebelled, asking for Alexios, who had been their general a short time before. At this time the Emperor had summoned him with a safe-conduct, honored him with patrician's rank, and kept him with himself. But because of their request—and because of some things said about Alexios (that he intended to become Emperor)—Constantine thrashed and tonsured him and held him in the Praitorion.

In July Constantine campaigned against the Bulgars and built a fortress at Markellai. On July 20 Kardamos the lord of Bulgaria sallied forth with all his forces, whom he stationed in his strong points. False prophets persuaded the eager Emperor that victory would be his. He joined battle without calculation or order and was severely defeated.

468 He fled back to the city after losing many men, not only common soldiers, but also powerful men, among whom were the magistros Michael Lakhanodrakon, the patrician Bardas, the protospatharios Stephen Kameas, Niketas and Theognostos (who were both generals), and Pankratios the false prophet and astronomer, who had predicted Constantine would win. The Bulgars captured the baggage-train, money, horses, the court, and the entire imperial retinue.

The imperial guards assembled in the city and decided to bring out the Caesar Nikephoros and make him Emperor. When Constantine learned this, he dispatched men who brought all his grandfather Constantine's sons to St. Mamas. He blinded Nikephoros and cut out the tongues of Christopher, Niketas, Anthimos, and Eudokimos, and at the same time also blinded the patrician Alexios. The warnings of his mother and the patrician Staurakios had persuaded him that if he did not blind Alexios, the troops would choose him Emperor. The punishment took place on a Saturday in August of the fifteenth indiction, but not for long did God's avenging justice permit this unjust act. For, five years later, Constantine was blinded by his own mother on a Saturday of the same month.

ANNUS MUNDI 6285 (SEPTEMBER 1, 792—AUGUST 31, 793)

3. 8. 24. 9.

In this year the troops of the Armeniac theme heard Alexios the patrician had been blinded, and imprisoned their general, the patrician Theodore Kamoulianos. When the Emperor learned this, he dispatched the protospatharios Constantine Ardaser and Chrysokheres the general of the Bukellarii to overpower them with an army from the rest of the themes. But in November of the first indiction the rebels

469 attacked them, captured them both, and blinded them. Many men from both sides were slaughtered.

At the second hour of the night on December 25 there was thunder and lightning, which ignited part of the imperial embroidery workshop by the goldsmiths'.

After holy Easter the Emperor campaigned against the Armeniac troops with all the remaining thematic forces. On May 26 of the first indiction (the Sunday of Pentecost), he attacked them and won, thanks to the double-crossing Armenians with them. Once he had captured them, he killed their turmarch Andronikos the spatharios, the turmarch Theophilos, and Gregory the bishop of Sinope; he subjected the rest to fines and confiscations. He bound a thousand men from their fortress, then brought them into the city through the gate of Blakhernai at the second hour of June 24. He tattooed "Armeniac traitor" on their faces with black ink and scattered them to Sicily and other islands. But their betrayers the Armenians, who were not honored at all by the Emperor, then betrayed the fortress of Kamakhon to the Arabs.

ANNUS MUNDI 6286 (SEPTEMBER 1, 793—AUGUST 31, 794)
4. 9. 25. 10.

In this year—the second indiction—the Arabs took the fortress of Thebasa in October on terms. Because of that, they freed its officers to be conveyed back to their own country.

ANNUS MUNDI 6287 (SEPTEMBER 1, 794—AUGUST 31, 795)
5. 10. 26. 11.

In this year the Emperor forced his wife Maria to become a nun; once he had made her obey, he tonsured her in January of the third indiction. He hated her because of the insinuations of his mother, who was aiming at the rule: Irene did this to make everyone accuse him.

In April he campaigned against the Arabs. On May 8 he engaged one of their raiding-parties at a place called Anousan; he defeated and routed them and drove them all the way to the river. He went to Ephesos and offered to the Theologian[272] the revenue of its trade-fair, which was a hundred pounds of gold. He felt his burden lightened by the aid of the holy apostle and evangelist John.

In August the Emperor crowned the cubicularia Theodote Augusta and illegally became engaged to her.

470

272. St. John, the patron saint of Ephesos.

ANNUS MUNDI 6288 (SEPTEMBER 1, 795—AUGUST 31, 796)

6. 11. 27. 12.

In this year—the fourth indiction—the Emperor celebrated for forty days his marriage to Theodote at the palace of St. Mamas.

On a Saturday in April of the same fourth indiction there was a terrifying earthquake on the island of Crete during the night. There was also a frightful one at Constantinople on May 4.

Kardamos the lord of Bulgaria told the Emperor, "Either pay me tribute or I will advance up to the Golden Gate and devastate Thrace." But the Emperor put horse-turds into a towel and sent him this message: "I have sent you such tribute as is appropriate for you. You are an old man, and I do not want you to grow weary until it gets to you. But I will come to Markellai, and come you out. If there is any issue, God shall be the judge." The Emperor sent messages to the thematic forces of the opposite shore, assembled his forces, and advanced to Bersinikia. Kardamos came as far as the woods of Abroleba; then, because he grew fearful, he stayed in the woods. The Emperor encouraged his army and advanced to the unwooded parts of Abroleba. He summoned Kardamos for seventeen days, but the Bulgar did not endure; he fled back to his own country.

In the same year the Arabs advanced all the way to Amorion. They withdrew without accomplishing anything, although they did take prisoners in the villages surrounding it.

In the same year Plato the abbot of Sakkoudion broke from communion with the patriarch Tarasios because Tarasios accepted the Emperor in communion[273] and had ordered his catechist to tonsure Constantine's wife Maria, and also had urged the abbot Joseph (abbot of the Purified monks) to crown the Emperor and Theodote. When the Emperor learned this, he dispatched the patrician Bardanios (the domesticus of the scholae) and John (the count of the Opsikion), who brought Plato into the city and imprisoned him in a cell in the churches in the palace's arkhistrategos.[274] Constantine beat the rest of the monks and Plato's nephew, then exiled them to Thessalonike. The Emperor's mother had been their shield, as they opposed her son and brought him disgrace.

471

273. He did so even though Constantine VI had put aside his wife to marry his mistress Theodote.

274. A church dedicated to the archangel Michael or Gabriel, each of whom was a marshal (*arkhistrategos*) of the heavenly host.

ANNUS MUNDI 6289 (SEPTEMBER 1, 796—AUGUST 31, 797)

Bishop of Rome Leo: 8 years[275]
7. 12. 1. 13.

In this year in September the Emperor went to the hot baths at Prusa with his mother. On October 7 of the fifth indiction a son was born to Constantine, who named him Leo. When the Emperor learned of the birth, he left his mother behind at the baths with all the imperial regiments and their officers and hurried back to the city. His mother took this opportunity to talk with the guards' officers; she piled up gifts and promises so she could oust her son and rule alone herself. She flattered some officers personally, others through her men, and she drew everyone over to herself, then waited to find the right day.

After pope Hadrian died in Rome, Leo, a highly honored man and one famous in every respect, was chosen.

In March the Emperor sallied forth against the Arabs; with him were the patrician Staurakios, the rest of his mother's friends, and a select body of 20,000 light-armed soldiers from all the themes. Staurakios' men saw the fine morale of the army and the Emperor; they became afraid lest perchance he should join battle, win, and so throw their plot into confusion. They bribed the sentries and convinced them to say untruthfully the Saracens had fled. The Emperor, greatly disappointed, reentered the city without having done anything.

On May 1 his son Leo died; Constantine mourned him deeply.

On Friday July 17 of the fifth indiction, while the Emperor was going from the horse-races to St. Mamas, the aforementioned members of the palace guards moved to seize him. When he learned this he boarded one of his warships and crossed to Pylai, intending to flee to the Anatolic theme. With him were his mother's friends, although they were not recognized as such by him. His wife also went up to Triton. His mother's friends with him took counsel among themselves and said to themselves, "If he musters an army, he will no longer be mastered; we shall not escape him, and he will destroy us."

At Eleutherios his mother assembled the imperial guards to whom she had already spoken, then entered the palace. But when she learned the army was cooperating with Constantine, she became terrified, and intended to send bishops to him to gain a safe-conduct so she could go into seclusion. She also secretly wrote to her friends with him, "If you do not devise some way to betray him, I promise I will reveal to him your discussions with me." They became afraid and overpowered

272

275. Thus the manuscripts, but Leo III was pope much longer than eight years (795–816). In *annus mundi* 6304 the length of his reign is given as sixteen years, and in *annus mundi* 6305 (812/813) he is given a seventeenth.

Constantine at prayer at dawn. On Saturday they put him into his warship, which reached the city on August 15.

They shut him up in the Purple Chamber,[276] where he had been born. By the will of his mother and her advisors, at around the ninth hour he was terribly and incurably blinded with the intention of killing him. For seventeen days the sun grew dark, making ships wander and go astray. Everyone agreed the sun stored up its rays because the Emperor had been blinded. In this way his mother Irene took power.

In the same year some Roman relatives of the blessed pope Hadrian incited the people to rebel against pope Leo. They overcame and blinded him, but were not able to quench his light forever, as the men who blinded him were charitable and had mercy. Leo fled to Charles the king of the Franks, who took bitter vengeance on his enemies and once more restored him to his own throne. Rome has been under the power of the Franks ever since.[277] In order to repay Charles, Leo crowned him Emperor of the Romans in the church of the holy apostle Peter, anointing him with olive oil from head to foot and clothing him in the imperial regalia and crown. This was on December 25 of the ninth indiction.

473

ANNUS MUNDI 6290 (SEPTEMBER 1, 797—AUGUST 31, 798)

Roman Empress Irene: 5 years
1. 13. 2. 14.

In this year, as soon as she had taken power, Irene immediately sent Dorotheos the abbot of Chrysopolis and Constantine the chartophylax of the great church to Abu Malik, who was devastating Kappadokia and Galatia. She sent them out to negotiate for peace, but it did not come to pass.

276. The lying-in chamber of the palace, covered with tiles of imperial purple: thus many Emperors were literally "born to the purple" *(porphyrogenitus)*. Indeed, this is the title by which Constantine VII is often known.
277. As Theophanes states, Charles' rescue of pope Leo was a motivating factor in Leo's coronation of the Frankish king as Emperor. Others were Charles' great conquests, which had united much of western Europe under his rule and given him a domain imperial in scope, and the fact that in A.D. 800 the Byzantine throne was occupied by a woman, something westerners did not find constitutionally valid. The Byzantines deemed Charles' coronation as Emperor a usurpation of a title rightfully theirs alone, and refused to recognize him as Emperor until their own weakness after Nikephoros I's death at the hands of the Bulgars in 811 compelled them to do so. Having recognized Charlemagne as "Emperor" in 812, the Byzantine Emperors thereafter increasingly styled themselves "Emperor of the Romans" to distinguish their title from his. The later weakness and division of Charlemagne's successors allowed the Byzantines virtually to forget they had recognized his legitimacy as Emperor; few of his successors were so recognized.

In October some rebels went to the imprisoned sons of God's enemy Constantine at the monastery of Therapeia. These men persuaded them to flee to the great church and ask for a firm promise that they would not be harmed. Using this as a pretext, the rebels would then acclaim one of them Emperor. When many people had assembled in the church, the eunuch patrician Aetios came in to lead them out for their pledge (which no-one furnished them), but then exiled them to Athens.

The two patricians Staurakios and Aetios, who were intimates of the Empress, became enemies and openly revealed their hatred. Each of them had plans to procure the Empire for his own relatives after Irene's death.

ANNUS MUNDI 6291 (SEPTEMBER 1, 798—AUGUST 31, 799)

2. 14. 3. 15.

In this year Abu Malik attacked Romania; he sent out a raiding party of light-armed troops, who advanced as far as Malagina. When he reached Staurakios' stables, he took the patrician's horses and the imperial equipage, then withdrew unharmed. The rest of his men advanced all the way to Lydia, taking many prisoners. Another one of their raiding-parties on a sally descended on the patrician Paul the count of the Opsikion, his entire thematic army, and the optimatoi; it caused them many casualties, and even took their baggage-train before withdrawing.

474 In March of the seventh indiction Akameros (the ruler of the Sklavinoi of Belzetia), spurred on by the troops of the theme of Hellas, wanted to bring forth the sons of Constantine and choose one of them Emperor. When the Empress Irene learned this, she sent to the patrician Constantine Serantopekhos his son the spatharios Theophylaktos, who was also her nephew. She blinded all her opponents and broke up the plot against her.

On the second day of holy Easter the Empress left the church of the Holy Apostles borne on a golden chariot drawn by four white horses and controlled by four patricians: I mean, Bardanes the general of the Thrakesian theme, Sisinnios general of Thrace, Niketas the domesticus of the scholae, and Constantine Boïlas. She distributed abundant consular largess.

In May the Empress believed she was near death. The eunuchs' strife increased. Aetios took as a partner the patrician Niketas the domesticus of the scholae; the two of them attacked Staurakios, persuading the Empress that he was aiming at the rule. Incensed at him, she attacked him in the palace of Hiereion, saying he was planning riots and insurrections, and that he was the means of his own swiftest destruction. He defended himself to her and gained his safety, but waxed furious at the patricians Aetios and Niketas.

ANNUS MUNDI 6292 (SEPTEMBER 1, 799—AUGUST 31, 800)
3. 15. 4. 16.

In this year—the eighth indiction—in February Staurakios devised a revolt and insurrection in the imperial city. He had pledged money and gifts for the scholarii and excubitores there, as well as for their officers. The pious Irene convened a silentium in the triklinos of Justinian and kept all the military units from approaching Staurakios. His heart failed; he brought up through his mouth foaming blood from his chest and lungs. Observing this, his doctors declared it a mortal sign. But until the very day of his death, which was June 3 of the eighth indiction, the rest of his hangers-on and fools convinced him with oaths that he would yet live and rule. With them he devised and drove home a rising in Kappadokia against Aetios, but was not deemed worthy to hear about it while living, for the news of it arrived two days after his death. The rebels were quelled and subjected to exile and punishment.

ANNUS MUNDI 6293 (SEPTEMBER 1, 800—AUGUST 31, 801)
4. 16. 5. 17.

In this year—the ninth indiction—on December 25 Charles the king of the Franks was crowned by pope Leo. He wished to marshal an expedition against Sicily, but desisted, wanting instead to marry Irene. In the following year—the tenth indiction—he dispatched ambassadors to gain that end.

In March of the ninth indiction the pious Irene forgave the Byzantines the city taxes, and lightened the "commercia"[278] at Abydos and Hieron. These and many other benefactions earned her great thanks.

ANNUS MUNDI 6294 (SEPTMBER 1, 801—AUGUST 31, 802)
5. 17. 6. 18.

In this year the patrician Aetios, free of Staurakios, planned to gain power, eager to transfer it to his brother, whom he appointed chief general in both Thrace and Macedonia. He himself controlled the thematic armies of the other shore: the troops from the Anatolic theme

278. Customs duties on imports and exports.

and that of the Opsikion. Full of excitement, he paid little attention to the important officers, taking none of them into account. But they were extremely disturbed about *him,* and planned and carried out a revolt against the Empress.

The legates sent to the most pious Irene by Charles and pope Leo arrived, asking her to join Charles in marriage and unite East and West. Had Aetios not put a stop to this by his frequent speeches, she would have done so; he, as co-ruler, was accumulating power for his brother.

476   **ANNUS MUNDI 6295 (SEPTEMBER 1, 802—AUGUST 31, 803)**

Roman Emperor Nikephoros: 9 years
1. 18. 7. 19.

In this year—the eleventh indiction—on October 31 at the fourth hour of the night, while Monday was drawing toward dawn, Nikephoros the patrician and minister of public finances rebelled against the pious Irene. By His ineffable judgment, God acquiesced in this because of the multitude of our sins. The treacherous, oathbreaking Triphyllioi—the patrician and domesticus of the scholae Niketas and his brother the patrician Sisinnios—worked with Nikephoros. Also with them were the patrician Leo Serantopekhos, the patrician Gregory son of Mousoulakios, Theoktistos the patrician and quaestor, and the patrician Peter; they also beguiled some of the officers of the imperial guards.

When they came to the Bronze Gate, all at once they tricked the guards, whom they falsely convinced that Irene had sent them to proclaim Nikephoros Emperor because Aetios was going to force her to name his brother Leo Emperor. The guards swallowed this huge lie, and acclaimed the tyrant as Emperor. This is how these patricians went to the great palace and got inside. From there they sent obscure men and slaves all through the city to make the acclamation. They also surrounded with guards the monastery of Eleutherios, where Irene happened to be.

At dawn they summoned Irene and imprisoned her in the great palace. Then they went on to the great church to crown the sinner. All the city masses went with them but, because of what had been done, everyone was upset and unable to stand the crowner, the man who was crowned, or those who rejoiced with them. Those who had spent their lives in piety and reason marveled at the divine judgment: that He had allowed her (who had struggled for the true faith in martyr's fashion) to be ousted by a swineherd because her friends joined him out of love
477   of money (I mean the eunuch patrician Leo the sakellarios of Sinope,

the God-detested Triphyllioi, and the patricians mentioned above).
She had enriched them with huge gifts and often had eaten with them.
By flattery and oaths they had persuaded her to believe their good will
towards her was more compelling than all the world's terrible affairs.

As if beside themselves, others could not grasp the reality of what
had happened, and thought they were dreaming. Still others, knowing
full well what was toward, blessed the good days which had passed and
mourned the misfortune which, because of the tyrant, would come in
the future. This was especially true of members of his wicked party,
who had formerly favored everything he did. A common, unsum-
moned gloom and depression settled on everyone, so that I would be
tedious were I to prolong the story, and will not write bit by bit the
graceless account of this pitiful day. The weather was quite unnaturally
sullen, dark, and persistently chilly during autumn, which clearly fore-
shadowed Nikephoros' future intractability and impatience, especially
to those who had chosen him.

On the next day he went with some patricians to the imprisoned
Empress. As he usually did, he falsely played the role of an honest man,
by which means he had tricked the masses. His justification of himself
to her was that he had been elevated to the rule against his will and
had no appetite for it, but had been raised by men who had advanced
him and betrayed her, just as the betrayer Judas had treated the Lord
after the Last Supper. He bore witness that they imitated Judas in every
respect.

He secretly showed her that, contrary to imperial custom, he was
wearing black sandals,[279] and maintained that he was pleased to do so.
With oaths he treacherously encouraged her to enjoy the total tranquility an Empress, as opposed to a slave, needed, and to believe there
would be no disaster because she had been ousted.

He advised her not to hide the imperial treasures from him, and
condemned the disease of avarice although he could not bear to control it. For this terribly afflicted the devourer of everything, who placed
all his hopes in gold. The wise and God-loving Irene, although liable
to be affected by her sudden change of status (as she was a woman),
spoke with noble and intelligent purpose to the man who was yesterday
an oathbreaking slave, but today a villainous revolutionary and reck-
less tyrant: "I, sirrah, believe in God, Who, though formerly I was an
orphan, raised and elevated me to the throne, although I am unworthy.
I blame my destruction on my sins. I have always urged in every way
the acclamation of the name of the Lord, the only Emperor of Emperors and Lord of Lords. Since I believe nothing comes to pass without
Him, I yield to the Lord the means of your advancement. You are not

478

279. See above, note 54.

ignorant of the reports against you which were brought to me. They concerned the office you now possess, and were true, as the outcome of this affair reveals. If I had gone along with them, these reports would have had you executed without hindrance. But I was convinced by your oaths; I had mercy on you, and misled many men who meant me well. To God, through Whom Emperors reign and dynasts rule the world, I give back what was once mine. Now I give you reverence as Emperor, as you are pious and have been chosen by Him. I implore you to have mercy on my weakness and suffer me to keep the monastery of Eleutherios (which I built) to guide my soul from its incomparable misfortune."

He said, "If this is what you want for yourself, swear to me on the divine power that you will not hide any of the Empire's treasures, and I will fulfill your request and furnish you with all aid and tranquility."

On the precious and lifegiving wood she swore to him, "I will not hide anything from you, not even an obol."[280] This she carried out. But once he had gained what he longed for, he immediately exiled her to the nunnery she had built on the Prince's Island.

Charles' legates were still in the city; they saw what was happening.

Once he had seized power, this devourer of everything could not even briefly conceal by hypocrisy his innate evil and avarice. Rather, he established his own wicked, unjust court at Magnaura, on the pretext of removing injustice. But, as events showed, the tyrant's aim was not to give the poor justice, but through his court to dishonor and capture all the men in power and transfer to himself control of all affairs.

He saw that everyone was dismayed at him, and grew fearful lest they should perchance recall the pious Irene's benefactions and summon her to rule once more. In November, after winter was firmly entrenched, the heartless man, taking no pity on her, exiled her to Lesbos. He ordered her securely imprisoned and, in general, seen by no-one.

On April 30 Niketas Triphyllios died, killed (as they say) by Nikephoros' poison.

On Thursday, May 4, Nikephoros went to the suburb of Chalcedon. Though he was mounted on a well-trained, gentle horse, by divine providence it threw him, crushing his right foot.

At the first hour of Wednesday, July 18, Bardanes (surnamed Tourkos), the patrician and general of the theme of the Anatolics, was proclaimed Emperor by the thematic troops of the opposite shore. But

479

---

280. A small coin of ancient Greece, worth a sixth of a drachma. Irene is saying she will keep nothing whatever from Nikephoros.

although he harangued them at some length, he could not make them cross. He went to Chrysopolis and besieged it for eight days; when the city did not accept him, he withdrew to Malagina. He feared God and did not think he should be responsible for the slaughter of Christians, so he sent a message to Nikephoros and received a written guarantee from the Emperor's own hand that he and all his men would not be harmed or liable to any penalty. The holy patriarch Tarasios and all the patricians also subscribed to it.

At midnight on September 8 Bardanes secretly ran away to the monastery of Herakleios in Bithynian Kios. He found one of the Emperor's warships which had been left behind, was tonsured, and assumed monastic garb. He boarded the ship and traveled to the island called Prote (on which was a monastery he had built), thinking Nikephoros would respect the fearful pledge he had given him, and would not harm him. But Nikephoros first divested him of his property, then found an excuse to arrest all the officers and property-owners of the themes, as well as some from the imperial city. He let the whole army go unpaid. What tale could one tell worthy of the deeds he did at that time? They opposed God, but were permitted because of our sins.

On August 9 of the eleventh indiction the Empress Irene died in her exile at Lesbos. Her body was moved to the nunnery she had built on the Prince's Island.

480

ANNUS MUNDI 6296 (SEPTEMBER 1, 803—AUGUST 31, 804)

2. 19. 8. 20.

In this year—the twelfth indiction—in December Nikephoros crowned his son Staurakios Emperor at the pulpit of the great church through the holy patriarch Tarasios. Staurakios made an Emperor impossible in all respects: in appearance, power, and will.

Nikephoros, who never kept his word at all, sent some Lykaonians (or lycanthropes) of his will and spirit to Prote. While pretending ignorance, he ordered them to land there at night, blind Bardanes and, after that action, to flee to the church. After this was done, the patriarch, the senate, and everyone who feared God was terribly distressed. The Emperor Nikephoros, that supreme lawbreaker who always did everything for show and nothing for God, demanded on oath that the officials slay the Lykaonians but, as it seems, only pretended to punish them.

This sort of remarkable personality, through which he had deceived many before his reign, he shared with other lawbreakers. However, his practice was quite laughable to those who were well acquainted with it, as his disgusting face always had to blush despite his shamelessness. He was unable to leave the imperial bedchamber for seven days because he kept on weeping; he was naturally given to effeminate tears. This gave rise to many bad and delusively good things, but did not escape the notice of the many.

481

In August he sallied forth against the Arabs; when he met them at Krasos in Phrygia, he attacked but was defeated. He lost many men and was himself almost captured; he would have been if some of his more courageous officers had not barely been able to rescue him from his distress.

ANNUS MUNDI 6297 (SEPTEMBER 1, 804—AUGUST 31, 805)

3. 20. 9. 21.

In this year there was a rebellion in Persia; the Arabs' caliph went off to make peace with the Persians.

Nikephoros found an opportunity to rebuild Galatian Ankyra, Thebasa, and Andrasos. He also sent a raiding-party into Syria, but they withdrew without having accomplished anything; rather just the opposite—they lost many.

ANNUS MUNDI 6298 (SEPTEMBER 1, 805—AUGUST 31, 806)

Bishop of Constantinople Nikephoros: 9 years
4. 21. 10. 1.

In this year—the fourteenth indiction—Tarasios the holy patriarch of Constantinople abandoned his notable life on February 18. His remains were carried out to the Bosporos, and on Wednesday of the first week of Lent were buried in the monastery he had built. On April 12, the great Sunday of Easter, the holy patriarch Nikephoros was chosen by vote of all the people and priests, and also of the Emperors.

However, Plato and Theodore, the abbots of the monastery of Stoudion, were not in sympathy with the appointment of Nikephoros; instead, they were strongly enough opposed to plan a schism. They had a fair reason: it was not proper for him to rise quickly and suddenly from lay status to a bishopric. The Emperor Nikephoros was upset and wanted to drive them from the city, although some men advised him that the choice of the patriarch was not a good one because of the abbots' opposition and because of the prospective dissolution of such a great monastery (Theodore had mustered perhaps seven hundred monks). The patriarch Nikephoros' sudden rise had not formerly been thought strange in the church; indeed, many others from the ranks of the laity had been consecrated to God and become bishops worthy of their station.[281]

482   In the same year Harun, the Arabs' ruler, attacked Romania in the midst of a heavily armed force of 300,000 Black-cloaks, Syrians, Palestinians, and Libyans. When he came to Tyana, he built a home for his blasphemous faith. He besieged and took the very strong fortress of Heraklis, Thebasa, Sideropalos, and Andrasos. He sent out a raiding-party of 60,000 men which advanced all the way to Ankyra, but withdrew after examining it.

The Emperor Nikephoros was terrified but impotent, and in despair sallied forth—which shows the intensity of his distress. After building many monuments to celebrate the enemy's defeat, he sent to Harun the metropolitan of Synnada, Peter the abbot of Goulaion, and Gregory the administrator of Amastris to ask for peace. They negotiated for a long while and arranged a peace whose terms were that Harun would be paid at a rate of 30,000 nomismata per year—as well as three nomismata head-tax for the Emperor himself and three for his son.[282] Harun was more pleased and celebrated more over receiving these nomismata than he would have over 10,000 talents, as they were a token that he had subjected the Roman Empire. The negotiators also arranged that the fortresses the Arabs had taken would not be rebuilt. But after the Arabs retired, Nikephoros immediately rebuilt and fortified these fortresses. When Harun learned this, he sent out a force which took Thebasa. He also sent a fleet to Cyprus, tore down its churches, and resettled the Cypriots. He broke the peace and did a great deal of damage.

ANNUS MUNDI 6299 (SEPTEMBER 1, 806—AUGUST 31, 807)

5. 22. 11. 2.

In this year Nikephoros campaigned against the Bulgars. On reaching Adrianople, he sensed there was a rebellion brewing against him in the imperial retinue and the guard regiments. He returned without success and without having accomplished anything; not only

281. In fact, the patriarch Nikephoros' immediate predecessor Tarasios (patriarch 784–806) was himself a layman before his elevation. Half a century later the scholar Photios would be rushed through the ecclesiastical hierarchy in mere days to assume the patriarchate. His selection, however, would cause profound division within the Byzantine church and between it and Rome.

282. This was a tax paid by Christian subjects of the caliph for the privilege of enjoying their faith in peace. Nikephoros' payment of it to Harun ar-Rashid implied that he admitted he was Harun's vassal, a humiliating concession for a Byzantine Emperor to make.

did he punish the men of his party with beatings and exile, he also subjected many to confiscation.

He sent out the spatharios Bardanios (surnamed Anemas), who crossed into Thrace and captured every traveler and sojourner. Nikephoros thought he could acquire no small amount of gold from them as a yearly payment. He acted in this way because he loved gold, not God.[283]

ANNUS MUNDI 6300 (SEPTEMBER 1, 807—AUGUST 31, 808)

6. 23. 12. 3.

In this year—the first indiction—the Arabs' ruler Harun sent a fleet under Khoumeid against Rhodes in September. However, the garrison on it survived without being overrun. On Khoumeid's return it is plain he was overthrown by the miracle-working St. Nicholas. When Khoumeid came to Myra, he tried to break up the saint's holy coffin, but instead broke another one lying nearby. At once a great tumult of wind, wave, thunder, and lightning overran his expedition and shivered a large number of ships to atoms. When the opponent of God, Khoumeid himself, acknowledged the power of the saint, he escaped from his danger, contrary to expectation.

After a great deal of selection from the maidens from all the land under his dominion, on December 20 Nikephoros chose Theophano the Athenian, a relative of the blessed Irene, to marry his son Staurakios. She had been engaged to a man and had often slept with him, but Nikephoros separated her from him to marry her to the wretched Staurakios. He shamelessly broke the law in all matters—in this one as well. With Theophano he also chose two other girls more beautiful than she, then openly debauched them on the very wedding days; everyone laughed at the dirty man.

In February many of the men in power, contemplating a rebellion against Nikephoros, chose Arsaber the patrician and quaestor, a pious, eloquent man. When the wily Nikephoros learned this, he beat and tonsured Arsaber and made him a monk, then exiled him to Bithynia. He subject the others to beatings, exile, and also confiscation: not only those who were leaders in wordly life, but also holy bishops, monks, and officials of the great church—the synkellos, the sakellarios, and the chartophylax. They were famous men who deserved respect.

283. This is a slight mistranslation to preserve Theophanes' wordplay. The literal rendering is "he loved gold, not Christ," which is a play on words in the Greek.

ANNUS MUNDI 6301 (SEPTEMBER 1, 808—AUGUST 31, 809)

Arab ruler Muhammad: 4 years
7. 1. 13. 4.

In this year—the second indiction—in March the Arabs' ruler Harun died in inner Persia, which is known as Khorasan. His son Muhammad, who was altogether incompetent, succeeded to the rule. With his father's forces his brother Abd Allah rebelled against him from Khorasan: this led to a civil war among their people. Thereupon the inhabitants of Syria, Egypt, and Libya divided up into different states and upset public affairs and each other. They were ruined by murders, robberies, and every kind of misdeed toward both themselves and the Christians under them. It was then that the churches in the holy city of Christ our God were laid waste, as were the monasteries of the two great groups of eremitic monks[284] (Khariton and Kyriakos), that of St. Saba, and the remaining coenobitic communities of Sts. Euthymios and Theodosios. This slaughter, directed against each other and us, continued through five years of anarchy.

Theodore the abbot of the monks of Stoudion, his brother Joseph the archbishop of Thessalonike, Plato the solitary monk, and their monks had broken from communion with the holy patriarch Tarasios because of his administrator Joseph, on the grounds that Joseph had illegally crowned Constantine and Theodote. The Emperor Nikephoros seized the initiative, assembled many bishops and abbots, and ordered a synod convened against them. Through it they were expelled from their monastery and from the city; they were sent into exile in January of the second indiction.

In the same year the Bulgars fell on an army at the Strymon while it was being paid. They took away 1,100 pounds of gold and killed a great number of soldiers, including the army's general and officers. Not a few regimental officers from the other themes were also present, and every one of them who was there was lost.

Before the festival of Easter in the same year, the Bulgars' ruler Krum marshalled his forces against Sardica and by treachery took it on terms. He slaughtered a Roman army of 6,000—not to mention a host of private citizens. On the third day of the week of our Savior's passion, Nikephoros moved out against him, but accomplished nothing worth mentioning. When the officers who had survived the massacre asked him to guarantee they would be granted safety,[285] he deemed this

---

284. Eremitic monks, as opposed to their coenobitic brothers (see above, note 250) live as hermits and, though they may meet for meals and some prayers, do not form a true community; each monk goes his own way on most occasions.

285. That is, that they would not be held responsible for Krum's massacre.

unworthy of himself, which forced them to flee to the enemy. Among them was the spatharios Eumathios, who had experience with engines. On top of his not having gathered much glory, Nikephoros was eager to convince the city with sacred oaths that he had celebrated the festival of Easter in Krum's court.

He wanted to rebuild the sacked Sardica but, afraid that his troops opposed this,[286] suggested to his generals and officers that they persuade the mob to ask the Emperor to rebuild the town. But the troops understood this action had been suggested at his evil instigation, and for six hours rebelled against him and their own officers. They attacked them and ripped up their tents, and came all the way to the imperial tent, where they showered Nikephoros with insults and curses, swearing they could no longer tolerate his boundless avarice or his wicked, scheming mind.

He was disheartened by the sudden insurrection, but clambered up onto a table. First of all, he tried to lull the army with oaths and persuasive speeches given by the patricians Nikephoros and Peter. The thrice-wretched soldiers, forgetting the matter at hand, went over to a hill and cried out, "Lord, have mercy!" as in an earthquake or drought. Nikephoros was ready for any evil action, and during the night he beguiled many of the officers with secret gifts. On the next day he went into the midst of the mob to talk with them. He assured them with frightful oaths that he was confident of success and that he loved them like his children. Then he went straight to the imperial city, letting the patrician and promoskrinios[287] Theodosios (surnamed Salibaras) examine the rebels through each other. At the host's return, he pretended he would pay them, but near St. Mamas took vengeance on most of them with beatings, shearings, and exile. He transported the rest to Chrysopolis, trampling on his great fearful oaths. Because of this disaster they termed the Perama River a pyre.

486

ANNUS MUNDI 6302 (SEPTEMBER 1, 809—AUGUST 31, 810)

8. 2. 14. 5.

In this year, after his disgusting withdrawal, Nikephoros aimed at humbling the army in every way. He removed Christians of every theme from their homes, compelling them to sell their property and come to the Sklavinias. This deed was nothing less than a taking of prisoners, and many blasphemers and evildoers senselessly asked for directions to the Sklavinias. Others mourned around their ancestral graves and blessed the dead. There were even those who hanged

286. The army would have to do the work of reconstruction.
287. Comptroller-general.

themselves to deliver themselves from their dire straits, for, seeing destroyed the property which had been acquired by their ancestors' labor, they could not bear the additional harsh move. All sorts of hardships befell everyone: the poor in these ways and those mentioned next, while those who had an abundance suffered with them but could not help, as they were awaiting worse misfortunes. These measures were initiated in September and completed around holy Easter.

Nikephoros ordered a second evil with this one: the poor were to be levied as soldiers and armed by the fellow citizens of their villages by means of paying a tax of 18½ nomismata. Each was responsible for the others' taxes.[288]

Nikephoros' third evil notion was that everyone should have their property resurveyed and their taxes increased; they had to pay two keratia[289] in clerks' fees.

Fourth, in addition to this he ordered all remissions restored.[290]

Fifth, he demanded hearth-taxes dating back to the first year of his tyranny paid by the peasant tenants of the pious houses, orphanages, hostels, and imperial monasteries. The greater part of their wealth was carried off to the imperial treasury. Moreover, the taxes on this were added to those due from the remaining property and peasant tenants of the pious houses, so that many had their taxes doubled. Their dwellings and lands were reduced.

487

Sixth, men who suddenly acquired wealth were examined by the generals,[291] and money was demanded of them as if they had discovered treasure.

Seventh, those who found wine-jars or vessels dating from twenty years before up to that time were taxed.

Eighth, the poor who had divided up an inheritance from their grandparents or parents in that same twenty-year period had to make a payment to the fisc.

Nikephoros also ordered those who bought household slaves outside of Abydos[292] (and especially those doing so around the Dodekanese) to pay a two-nomisma tax.

Ninth, shipmasters who lived near the sea (especially those of Asia Minor), men who had never lived by farming, were compelled, unwill-

288. This extends the thematic system of military recruitment (see above, note 39) down to those peasants too poor for each to provide all his own equipment.

289. Per nomisma, or 8 1/3 percent.

290. See above, under *annus mundi* 6293. Irene's tax remissions had badly damaged the finances of the state.

291. Of the themes (see above, note 39).

292. A chief customs center of the Empire (see above, note 278).

ing or no, to buy the lands he had seized so he could tax them.[293]

Tenth, he assembled the principal shipmasters in Constantinople and loaned them twelve pounds of gold at an interest rate of four keratia per nomisma;[294] they also had to pay the usual commercia.

I have recorded these small matters in a chapter from among many, as it were, in order to make plain his nature, which constantly schemed after every sort of profit. The terrible things done to the important, the middle-class, and those of few means in the imperial city are beyond recording. He tracked down some to make them live at home, and bore down on their evil slaves so he could bring charges against their masters. In the beginning he was hesitant about their testimony but, once he had made certain of their calumnies, he used people of no account in the same way against the notables. He honored and esteemed those who did a good job of slandering. He hurled many building-owners headlong from the first to the third class, in the hope that they might soon pass away so he could inherit.

The following is worth mentioning by way of seasoning or example: at the Forum there was a candle-maker who lacked for nothing, thanks to his own labors. Summoning him, the devourer of everything said, "Would you put your hand on my head and swear to me how much gold you have?" For a little while the man begged off with the excuse that he was unworthy, but Nikephoros forced him to do this. He said he had a hundred pounds of gold. Nikephoros ordered it brought in to him within the hour, saying, "What need do you have for distraction? Have breakfast with me, take away a hundred nomismata,[295] and go away well-pleased."

ANNUS MUNDI 6303 (SEPTEMBER 1, 810—AUGUST 31, 811)
9. 3. 15. 6.

In this year Nikephoros stepped up his machinations against the Christians. There was godless supervision of the sale of every sort of horse, kine, and grain, and there were unjust confiscations and penalties against important people, as well as usury on shipping. The Emperor promulgated a law forbidding anyone to practice usury,[296] and had tens of thousands of other evil devices. Relating them one by one

293. Nikephoros is establishing these sailors as thematic troops, on the model of the thematic soldiery.

294. A rate of 16 2/3 percent.

295. Or one seventy-second of what the Emperor had taken from him.

296. Unlike the case in the medieval west, where any lending at interest was forbidden to Christians, the Byzantines sensibly defined usury as lending money at an excessive rate of interest. Nikephoros is merely setting up money-lending as a state monopoly, so he can gain all the profit from it.

is tedious for those who seek to learn about such matters, so they have been abridged.

On Thursday, October 1, some nobody carrying a sword under monastic garb ran into the palace, seeking to kill Nikephoros. When two bystanders ran up and attacked him, he badly wounded them. He was arrested and severely punished, but used madness as a defense—he made no false accusations. Even while suffering, he swore on the cross that he was mad. Many thought this was a sign of great evil for both the rulers and those under their hand, just as it had been in the time of the impious Nestorios.

Nikephoros was a fiery friend of the Manichaeans (now called Paulicians) and his near neighbors the Athinganoi[297] in Phrygia and Lykaonia. He took pleasure in their oracles and rites. Among such occasions was the time when the patrician Bardanios [sic] rebelled against him: Nikephoros summoned the Athinganoi and subjected Bardanios to their sorcery. In a pit he bound to an iron stake a bull with its head bent back to the ground, and had it killed while it was bellowing and writhing in this way. He put Bardanios' clothing backwards through a mill, winning his victory by the use of enchantments, since God conceded it because of the multitude of our sins. During his reign the heretics received land and carried on their business without fear; many of the more foolish folk were lost to their illegal doctrines.

In Hexakonion there was a false hermit, Nicholas by name—he and his men blasphemed against the true faith and the revered icons, which Nikephoros also opposed.[298] Nikephoros dismayed the chief prelate and everyone who lived in a godly way, for he was often angry at them and made accusations against them. He was greatly pleased when they opposed each other and, since he was an upsetter of the divine commandments, jeered at every Christian who loved his neighbor.

Because of his ambition, he transferred trials (fair and unfair) for every Christian to the house of correction at Magnaura, so that no-one could cause a delay against his impiety. He ordered his soldiers to use the bishops and clergy like slaves; his men actually entered bishops' residences and monasteries to consume their substance. He found fault with the gold and silver utensils which for ages had been stored up for God, and declared that the churches' holy utensils were good enough to be shared—as Judas had with his Master's sweet oil.

He reproached all the previous Emperors on the grounds that they had lacked guidance, and in general he confuted their fore-

489

297. A heretical Phrygian sect.
298. This is untrue; Nikephoros, although certainly not a fanatical iconophile, did not ban the use of images.

thought and said there was no-one more powerful than the ruler, if the ruler wanted to rule skillfully. But he, who was killed by God, was deluded in his assessment of affairs.

In February of the same fourth indiction (on the first Saturday of Lent), Leo the general of the Armeniacs met the Saracens at Eukhaita. They captured Eukhaita, as well as the thematic army's wages and a large number of soldiers. But not even by this was Nikephoros shamed into halting his greed. The modern Ahab, more insatiable than Phalaris or Midas,[299] did not learn from such signs.

With his son Staurakios he drew up his men in battle array against the Bulgars, and on [date lost] of May left the imperial city.

He ordered the patrician and public finance minister Niketas to increase public taxes on the churches and monasteries. Niketas was also to demand eight years of back taxes on the homes of Nikephoros' officers. There was deep mourning. One of his intimate aides (I mean the patrician Theodosios Salibaras) objected, "Everyone is crying out against us, my lord, and at the time of trial everyone will exult in our fall."

Nikephoros said to him, "If God, Who hardens, has hardened my heart like Pharaoh's, what good will come to the people under my hand? Theodosios, do not expect anything from Nikephoros save what you see." Lord knows that I myself, he who is writing, heard that from Theodosios in his living voice.

Nikephoros collected troops not only from Thrace, but also from the themes of the opposite shore; then he marched against the Bulgars. With the soldiers there were many poor men, armed with their own hunting-slings and clubs, as well as many blasphemers. Krum feared their numbers, and when they came to Markellai he asked for peace. But his own lack of good sense and the counsel of his advisors, who were of his opinion, prevented Nikephoros from making it. After much hesitation, the brave coward recklessly invaded Bulgaria through difficult passes on July 20: it was the time of the destructive rise of the Dog.[300] He was continually saying, "Who will go forth and trick Ahab?" and answering, "Whether it is God or His Opponent, He will drag him away unwilling."

Before the invasion, his intimate body-servant Byzantios fled to Krum from Markellai after stealing the imperial regalia and a hundred pounds of gold. Many thought his flight augured ill for Nikephoros.

490

299. Phalaris, in legend, built a hollow bronze bull, in which he roasted his opponents alive. Midas, granted a wish, asked that everything he touch turn to gold, a wish that, when granted, had predictably unfortunate results.

300. The time when Sirius, the Dog Star, could be seen rising in the east at sunrise (see above, note 147).

For three days after the first engagements, Nikephoros wrote that he successfully gained his glory not because of God (Who made the victory a success), but instead acclaimed only the good fortune and good advice of Staurakios. He threatened the officers who had hindered the invasion. He ordered horses still living (foals and beasts of all ages) mercilessly slain and let the dead bodies of his own men remain unburied, planning only to collect his spoils. He sealed and barred Krum's treasures, making sure they would be his own thereafter. He cut off the ears and other members of Christians who were plundering, and burned down the court of Krum.

Greatly humbled, Krum told him, "Very well, you have conquered. If anything pleases you, take it, and go in peace." But peace's enemy thought this unfitting. Thereupon Krum grew angry and took security precautions, sending messages to seal off the entrances and exits to his land with wooden fortifications.

When Nikephoros learned this, all at once it was as if he was thunderstruck; he turned this way and that, at a loss as to what to do. He spoke of doom to the men with him: "Even if we grew wings, no-one could hope to escape ruin." He had two more days for these contrivances: Thursday and Friday. Saturday night the tumult of armed men surrounded Nikephoros and his forces; when the Bulgar formations were heard, they unhinged everyone. Before day the barbarians attacked the tents of Nikephoros and his magnates and pitifully slew them.

Among the magnates were the patrician Aetios, the patrician Peter, the patrician Sisinnios Triphylles [sic], the patrician Theodosios Salibaras (who had distressed and maltreated the blessed Irene), the patrician prefect, the patrician Romanos (general of the Anatolic theme), many other protospatharioi and spatharioi, and the officers of the palace guards: the domesticus of the excubitores, the drungarius of the imperial watch, the general of Thrace, many officers of the thematic forces, and countless men. All the flower of the Christians was destroyed, as were all their arms and the imperial gear. God forbid even yet that Christians should know the charmless reports of that day, as it surpassed all mourning. These events took place on July 26 of the fourth indiction.

Krum cut off Nikephoros' head and hung it on a pole for a number of days, as a display for the tribes coming to him and for our disgrace. Then he took it, bared the bone, coated it with silver on the outside and, while boasting over himself, made the Sklavinians' leaders drink from it.

Many widows and orphans were made in a single day, and there was unquenchable mourning, but the slaying of Nikephoros was a relief to many. Not one of the survivors gave exact details of his murder, for some say even the Christians were encouraged when he fell. His menials (the effeminate men with whom he had lain) died with him, some by fire at the palisade, others by the sword. Christians had never been more grievously unfortunate than during his reign. In his greed, his licentiousness, and his barbaric cruelty he outdid everyone

492 who had ruled before him. It would be hard to believe and irksome for us fully to discuss his deeds one by one. However, as the saying goes, a robe is revealed in advance by its border.[301]

Nikephoros' son Staurakios had been wounded in a vital spot: the right part of his back. He barely emerged from the battle alive, and reached Adrianople critically wounded. The patrician and domesticus of the scholae Stephen (and Theoktistos, who was there with him) proclaimed Staurakios Emperor. He spoke out against his own father to the surviving troops, who were very pleased. Michael the curopalates had survived unharmed, and was strongly urged by his friends to let himself be proclaimed Emperor, but would not agree because of his oaths to Nikephoros and Staurakios. The domesticus Stephen spoke against him from hope for Staurakios' life, but the magistros Theoktistos agreed Michael should rule.

Staurakios was bleeding violently and excessively in his urine, and the blood was dried on his thighs and legs when he came to Byzantium by litter. The patriarch Nikephoros, who was devoted to him, advised him to propitiate God and make amends for the greedy deeds his father had done. But he, the true heir to his father's mind, told the patriarch he was unable to restore more than three talents. This was a small fraction of Nikephoros' wrongdoing. Moreover, as he was anxiously seeing whether he would live, Staurakios even hesitated about this.

As he had his father's implacable will in a still greater form, he heaped dishonor on Theoktistos the magistros, Stephen, the domesticus, and Michael the curopalates. He also absolutely rejected his sister Prokopia, since she had plotted against him at the suggestion of Theophano the Augusta. That wretch, although she was childless, hoped presently to rule the Empire in imitation of the blessed Irene. When Staurakios saw he could not recover, he wanted the Empire made over to his wife, lest mob-rule agitate the Christians on top of the evils they had already received. Nikephoros the patriarch, Theoktistos the magistros, Stephen the domesticus, and Michael the curopalates were dismayed at this, and from their great enmity became friendly with one another around the end of September of the fifth indiction.

301. An interesting contrast to the English proverb, "You can't tell a book by its cover."

493   On the evening of October 1 Staurakios summoned Stephen the domesticus to ask how he could bring his brother-in-law Michael from his house to blind him. Stephen said this was impossible at that time because of the force around Michael and his house's secure location. Staurakios demanded that Stephen tell no-one what had been said. With plausible words, Stephen convinced him not to worry.

Through the whole night Stephen assembled the surviving soldiers of the imperial guards and friendly officers in the covered hippodrome to proclaim Michael Emperor. At daybreak the whole senate went into the palace to proclaim Michael Emperor, as will be made clear next. The patriarch Nikephoros demanded of Michael a statement of the true faith written in his own hand, and that he keep his hands unstained with the blood of Christians, and also that he not beat holy men, monks, or any member of the whole ecclesiastical hierarchy.

ANNUS MUNDI 6304 (SEPTEMBER 1, 811—AUGUST 31, 812)

A.D. 804
Roman Emperor Michael: 2 years: year 1
Arab ruler Muhammad: 4 years: year 4
Bishop of Rome Leo: 16 years: year 16[302]
Bishop of Constantinople Nikephoros: 9 years: year 7

In this year—the fifth indiction—at the first hour of Friday, October 1, the pious curopalates Michael was proclaimed Roman Emperor in the hippodrome by all the senate and the guard regiments. On hearing of Michael's acclamation, Staurakios immediately tonsured himself and, through his relative the monk Symeon, put on a monastic cloak. He repeatedly called out for the patriarch, who came to the palace with the Emperor Michael and Staurakios' sister. The patriarch urged him not to be distressed at what had happened, for it had not occurred due to a plot, but from despair for his life. Staurakios, however, did not believe him. Raging with his inherited wickedness, he told the patriarch, "You will not find him a better friend than myself."

At the fourth hour of the day Michael was crowned by the patriarch Nikephoros at the pulpit of the great church, at which time there was general rejoicing. Michael gave fifty pounds of gold to the patriarch and twenty-five to the clergy. As he had a great soul and was not avaricious, he abated all the injustices caused by the Emperor Nikephoros' greed and gave gifts to the senate and army. On the twelfth

494 of the same month Prokopia was crowned Augusta in the triklinos of the Augusteion, and was delighted to honor the senate with many gifts.

302. See above, note 275.

Michael gave five talents to the wives of the thematic soldiers killed in Bulgaria. He enriched Staurakios' wife Theophano (who had become a nun) and her relatives, who had lived pitifully during the reign of Nikephoros. Among the riches provided her was a fine home known as the Hebraika, for use as a monastery. Staurakios was buried there. Michael enriched all the patricians, senators, prelates, priests, monks, soldiers, and poor people, as well as the inhabitants of the imperial city and the themes. Thus Nikephoros' boundless avarice, because of which he had been foully destroyed, was obliterated in a few days.

In addition to his many other fine habits, Michael was pious and orthodox. He was disturbed by those who had separated from the holy church on whatever pretext, reasonable or unreasonable. He continually called on the most holy patriarch and the others to cooperate in a common peace. Among these men were Theodore the abbot of Stoudion, Plato, and Theodore's brother Joseph, the archbishop of Thessalonike, who with the leaders of their monastery had been held in bitter imprisonment. Michael was eager to unite them, and did so.

Through his son Theophylaktos, he also sent messages to Charles the Emperor of the Franks concerning peace and reconciliation.[303] The holy patriarch Nikephoros sent synodic letters to Leo the holy pope of Rome; before this he had been prevented from doing so by the Emperor Nikephoros. On Friday, December 25 of the fifth indiction, the gentle Michael crowned his son Theophylaktos Emperor at the pulpit of the great church through Nikephoros the patriarch. Michael brought rich ornaments for the holy altar: stuffs of gold encrusted with precious stones, with ancient worked covers woven from gold and purple and adorned with marvelous holy icons. He also gave twenty-five pounds of gold to the patriarch and a hundred to the pious clergy; this made brilliant the holy festival and the proclamation of his son.

495   Out of great zeal for God the most pious Emperor moved against the Manichaeans (now known as Paulicians) and Athinganoi in Phrygia and Lykaonia. At the behest of the holy patriarch Nikephoros and other pious men, he decreed them liable to capital punishment. However, thanks to other, malignant, advisors he let the pretext of repentance mitigate this—those captured by this heresy cannot repent. These men ignorantly declared that their opinion was that the priests were not allowed to use capital punishment in their opposition to the impious. In this matter they opposed the holy scriptures in every respect. For if Peter the prince of the apostles killed Ananias and Sappheira solely for lying, and the great Paul said with a shout, "Those who do

303. The weakened state of the Byzantine Empire made this imperative (see above, note 277).

such things deserve death" (which he said about bodily sin alone), how would not those who release from the sword men who are absolutely impure in spirit and body and who worship demons be enemies of theirs? But the pious Emperor Michael cut down not a few of these heretics.

Staurakios was so terribly injured by the wound in his lower back that no-one could approach him because of the great stench. He died on January 11 of the fifth indiction, having reigned (as it were) two months and six days.

On Saturday, May 14, there was a great solar eclipse for three and one half hours: from the eighth to the eleventh.[304]

On June 7 Michael moved out against the Bulgars; Prokopia accompanied him as far as Tzouroulon. Krum the ruler of the Bulgars had taken Debeltos by siege and resettled its people (who went over to him) and their bishop. Because the Emperor's evil counselors were massively ill-advised, the troops—especially those of the Thrakesian theme and that of the Opsikion—turned to plots and insults. Michael appeased them, silencing them by gifts and speeches. But when the Bulgars learned of the soldiers' rebellion, that they feared battle, and that their garrisons were in disorder, the barbarians subjected more of Thrace and Macedonia.

496

Then, though no-one pursued them, the Christians fled, giving up Ankhialos, Beroia, Nikaia, the fortress of Probaton, and some other strongholds; they did the same at Philippopolis and Philippi. The settlers who lived by the Strymon seized the excuse to flee back to their own lands. This was the wrath of God condemning Nikephoros' madness; because of it, what appeared to be his successes (over which he had boasted) rapidly crumbled.

People stopped censuring the wicked doctrines of the presumptuous heresies which opposed God: the many Paulicians, Athinganoi, Iconoclasts, Tetraditoi,[305] and the rest of the lawbreakers (I am omitting reference to their adultery and whoredom, their licentiousness and greed). They wagged their tongues against the revered divine icons and against monastic garb.

They blessed Constantine [V], abominable to God and thrice-wretched, because he had done very well against the Bulgars. Because of this, these wretches impiously said he was pious. Some of them in the imperial city prepared to overturn the orthodox faith after its ecumenical council. These men, maimed in spirit, wished the blind to rule: they wanted secretly to release by night the sons of God's enemy

---

304. This is precisely correct: Newton, op. cit., 546.
305. Those who celebrated Easter on the fourteenth day of the paschal month, regardless of the day of the week.

Constantine (who were imprisoned on the island of Panormos) and take them to the army. But the Lord put them to shame and roused Michael to avenge the truth. He discussed with the army the reasonable policy on the faith and, wisely taking into account the revolutionaries' small numbers, terrified them with a few blows. He also exiled Constantine's blind sons to Aphousia.

He cut out the tongue of one false hermit out of those who were going around: one of Nicholas Hexakionites' fellow wizards, who had scraped at and dishonored an icon of the wholly holy Mother of God. This man was dead both in spirit and body. Michael triumphed when 497 the man's partisan Nicholas was reported to have totally repented and fully confessed his evils. Michael committed him to a monastery so he would not remain his own master. The Emperor spoke to the troops in an audience at Magnaura, clarifying his pious mind's thoughts on God.

Through Leo the general of the theme of the Anatolics he confiscated the property of the Athinganoi and exiled them.

In August of the fifth indiction Thabit campaigned against the Christians. Leo the general of the Anatolics won glory by engaging him; he killed 2,000 men and captured horses and weapons.

Harun's first son Muhammad, who was ruling his people, attacked his brother Abd Allah in the Persian interior but was defeated. He took refuge in Baghdad and ruled there. A different rebel held Damascus, and two divided up Egypt and Africa; yet another piratically plundered Palestine.

ANNUS MUNDI 6305 (SEPTEMBER 1, 812—AUGUST 31, 813)

6305. 805. 2. 17. 8.[306]

In this year the Bulgars' ruler Krum sent a peace-embassy to the Emperor Michael in the person of Dargameros. He asked about the terms that had been arranged with Kormesios, lord of Bulgaria during the reign of Theodosios the Adramytinian and the patriarch Germanos. The contents of these were that the border marched from Thracian Meleonai, and the payment of clothing and scarlet-dyed skins worth a hundred pounds of gold. In addition to this, fugitives from each side were to be returned to it, even if they had conspired against the state. Those doing business in each of the two lands were regulated by seals and signets; the property of the seal-holders was not to be confiscated or registered in the public ac-

306. The Arabs' ruler disappears from the chronological scheme, presumably thanks to the Abbasids' civil war (in one manuscript, Muhammad [Al-Amin] is given a fifth regnal year).

counts. Krum also threatened the Emperor: "Should you not be se-
rious about peace, it will be by your decision that I marshal my
forces against Mesembria."

When the Emperor received this communication, it was at the
urging of his evil advisors that he did not accept peace. For with false
498 piety (and, even more, out of stupidity and lack of care for public
affairs) the evil advisors declared it was improper to return fugitives.
They cited as witness the biblical statement of the Lord: "I should not
cast out him who comes to Me."

In mid-October Krum marshalled his forces against Mesembria.
He had siege-engines and helepoleis, of which he had learned thanks
to the folly of Nikephoros the destroyer of Christians. For Nikephoros
had enlisted an Arab who had come to him for baptism, and who was
very experienced with engines. Nikephoros settled him at Adrianople,
but gave him not a single benefaction or means of support to match
his rank. Nay worse, he docked the Arab's wages and beat him when
he grumbled. Because of this the Arab grew desperate, fled to the
Bulgars, and taught them all the requisite skills for siege-engines.
Under these circumstances, Krum besieged Mesembria for a whole
month and took it, as no-one opposed him.

On November 1 the Emperor summoned the patriarch; he had
come round and now accepted advice favoring peace. Also present
were the metropolitans of Nikaia and Kyzikos, as well as the evil advisers and Theodore of Stoudion. The patriarch and the metropolitans
espoused peace along with the Emperor, but the evil advisors upset it,
declaring, "It is improper to choose peace, because it would overturn
the divine commandment. For the Lord declared, "I should not cast
out him who comes to Me.' " They neither knew what they were saying
nor what they were making affirmations over. First of all, since no-one
had fled from the Bulgars to us, we had abandoned our men within
their court; we would have been able to save them by keeping the
peace. Second, even if some very few men did flee, it would be more
fitting to exert ourselves to save the many (who were also our fellows)
than to gain profit by uncertain and obscure means. For it is more
pleasing to God to save many rather than fewer. The punishment was
very heavy over a small, foolish advantage.[307]

Because of his lack of foresight, Michael inclined toward his intimates and denied the faith according to Paul; he was adjudged worse
499 than a man of no faith. How could these men say, "I kept the peace
with men who hate it," unless they were wiser than Paul and David?
Who now is wiser than the thrice-blessed Germanos, except these evil

307. It is interesting to note Theophanes here arguing from the point
of expediency, rather than from Biblical precepts.

advisers, these men who have prevented peace, who are in wicked in the conceit which will destroy their souls?

As has been said, this took place on November 1. On the fourth of the same month a comet was seen shining in the shape of two little moons. They joined and once more separated, taking a different shape —the likeness of a headless man. On the next day the pitiful news of Mesembria's destruction reached us, terrifying everyone because of our expectation of greater evils. The enemy had found it full of settlers and merchants.

The Bulgars took Mesembria and Debeltos as well, in which places they found thirty-six bronze siphons and not a little of the liquid fire shot through them, and also a great quantity of gold and silver.

In the same year many Christian monks from Palestine and all Syria reached Cyprus, fleeing the boundless evil of the Arabs. For general anarchy had seized Syria, Egypt, Africa, and their entire empire: in villages and cities their people, cursed by God, murdered, robbed, committed adultery and acts of licentiousness, and did all sorts of things hateful to God. The revered sites of the holy resurrection, the skull,[308] and others in the vicinity of the holy city were profaned. In the same way, the famous eremitic monasteries of Sts. Khariton and Saba in the desert, as well as other churches and monasteries, were devastated. Some men became martyrs; others got to Cyprus, and from it to Byzantium. The Emperor Michael and the holy patriarch Nikephoros kindly entertained them. Michael helped them in every way. He gave the men who entered the city a famous monastery, and sent a talent of gold to the monks and laymen still on Cyprus.

500   Michael was totally honest and fair, but unfit to administer affairs; he was a slave to the magistros Theoktistos and the rest of the officers.

When two Christians fled from Bulgaria in February, they informed the Emperor that Krum wanted to lay a sudden ambush against the troops in Thrace. On the fifteenth of the month the Emperor left the city; by divine providence Krum withdrew without success after losing not a few men. The Emperor reached Adrianople, set its affairs aright, and joyfully returned. He went to the holy Tarasios' monastery and, with the Augusta Prokopia, celebrated his memorial rites. He clothed Tarasios' grave with ninety-five pounds of silver.

After the destruction of Mesembria the Emperor had refused Krum's peace-overtures. He levied troops from all the themes and ordered them to cross into Thrace before spring, with the result that they were all unhappy, especially the Kappadokians and the Armeniac troops. When the Emperor sallied forth with the imperial guards in May, the Augusta Prokopia once more accompanied him to Akedouk-

308. Golgotha.

ton, which is near Herakleia. Displeased at this, the army insulted and swore at Michael.

On May 4 the sun was eclipsed while rising;[309] according to the horoscope, it was in the twelfth degree of Taurus. The masses became panic-stricken.

The Emperor wandered about in Thrace with his generals and troops. He did not move on Mesembria, nor did he do any of the things necessary to destroy his enemies. Rather, he only obeyed the empty words of his counselors, who were inexperienced at war. They declared his enemy did not dare advance against him while he was encamped in his own territory.

The mob of our fellow citizens was harder to bear than a barbaric onslaught, as they lacked necessary supplies and were maltreating, robbing, and attacking the locals. Around the beginning of June, Krum the ruler of the Bulgars came forth with his armies, although he suspected the Christians' numbers were very large. Leo the patrician and general of the Anatolics and John Aplakes the patrician and general of Macedonia camped about thirty miles from the imperial frontier. They were eager to attack Krum's men, but the Emperor, thanks to his evil advisors, stopped them.

501

While the city was praying with its chief prelate in the church of the Holy Apostles, some impious followers of the heresy of Constantine [V] (who was abominable to God) pried open the door to the imperial tombs.[310] While no-one was paying any attention to them because of the crowd's anguish, they suddenly opened the door with a crash, as if by a divine miracle. Rushing inside, they fell at the feet of the heretic's remains and called on him, not on God, saying, "Arise and help the state, which is being destroyed." They put it about that Constantine, who dwells in Tartaros with the demons, rose up on horseback and went off to attack the Bulgars.

The city prefect arrested them; at first they falsely stated the doors had been opened of their own accord by God. But while they were still standing before the prefect's tribunal, before they had been tortured at all, they told of how they had pried them open. The prefect properly removed them and sent them round in a public parade, while they cried out the reason for their punishment.

The diabolical inventor of evil had so thoroughly indoctrinated his soldiers that they did not accuse themselves of sin, but rather the orthodox faith (which has been handed down from the Fathers) and the monks' holy garb (the training ground for God's philosophy). Many of those who blasphemed like this were Christians only in ap-

309. This is also precisely correct: Newton, op. cit., 547.
310. Most Emperors were interred in the church of the Holy Apostles.

pearance, but Paulicians in fact. They were not able openly to display their loathsome doctrines, but contaminated the unlearned with this pretext: they blessed the Jewish-minded[311] Constantine as a prophet and conqueror, and blessed his evil doctrine too. This was so they could overturn the incarnate dispensation of our Lord Jesus Christ.

On June 22 Christians and Bulgars mustered not far from Adrianople. In the battle the Christians failed badly, terribly. The enemy was so overwhelmingly victorious that most of the Christians did not even see their first assault, but incontinently fled. Krum, amazed, thought this happened in order to set an ambush, and checked his men in their pursuit after a short distance. But when he saw the Romans definitely had fled, he pursued and killed a great many. His men also overran the Romans' baggage-train and took it away as booty.

502

The Emperor fled back to the city cursing his host; nay more, he was swearing he would abdicate. Among the men to whom he communicated this was the patrician Leo the general of the Anatolics, since he was pious,[312] brave, and had totally supported Michael's ruling the Empire. Although Michael did not altogether abdicate, he did allow Leo to command the thematic forces. Michael himself returned to the imperial city on June 24. He wanted to put aside his power and choose someone else; however, his wife and those who had great influence on him did not permit this. But the holy patriarch consented to it, as long as Michael and his children would be kept safe if someone else were appointed.

When the soldiers and troops learned the Emperor had fled to the city they refused to be ruled by him any more. They took counsel among themselves and entreated the patrician Leo the general of the

311. Jews, of course, were forbidden graven images. The prohibitions of Deuteronomy had had a heavy influence on Leo III's opposition to the use of icons in Christian worship. The iconoclasm of Constantine V was much more theologically sophisticated, and closely related to earlier debates over the relationship of Christ's humanity and divinity. Constantine's argument was that any representation of Christ was either Nestorian in its separation of His humanity from His divinity, or monophysite in attempting to depict what was in fact a wholly transcendant and unrepresentable Godhead. The iconophile answer to this attack was to remark that Christ was in fact both human and divine, and that to say His humanity was incapable of being shown was to deny the reality of the incarnation. Further, to the iconophiles, contemplation of the images of Christ and the saints would lead worshipers to emulation of the prototypes' virtues.

312. Leo the general of the Anatolics, who became Emperor as Leo V (813–820), restored iconoclasm in 815. Theophanes must have first composed this passage before that restoration (see above, note 208, and introduction, pp. xi–xii).

Anatolics to help the state by laying claim to government over the Christians. For a certain length of time he tried hard to delay them, looking for the proper moment because the irresistible barbarian attacks boded ill. He also kept faith with and did not plot against the rulers. But when he saw the army putting heavy pressure on the city, he wrote to the patriarch Nikephoros, strongly reassuring the patriarch of his orthodoxy and asking to take power with Nikephoros' prayers and assent.

When with his generals and soldiers he reached the tribunal in front of the city, he was shown to be a legal Roman Emperor. He entered Constantinople through the Charisian gate and came to the palace. On hearing of Leo's acclamation, Michael ran to the church of Pharos with Prokopia and their children. They were tonsured and assumed monastic garb on Monday, July 11 of the sixth indiction. On the next day the patriarch Nikephoros crowned Leo at the pulpit of the great church.

503   He ordered the area round the city fortified, and went about the walls night and day, urging everyone on and encouraging them to be of good cheer, as God would soon accomplish the unexpected at the intercession of his wholly immaculate Mother and all the saints, and would not allow us to be entirely disgraced by our numerous misfortunes. Krum the new Sennacherib[313] had grown confident at his victory. He left his brother behind to besiege Adrianople with his own forces; six days after Leo had become autokrator, Krum attacked the imperial city in the midst of his forces and horses.

He paraded before the walls from Blakhernai to the Golden Gate, and made plain his might. He celebrated bloody, demonic sacrifices in the small stream that flowed from the Golden Gate to the sea, and demanded that the Emperor fix his spear on the Golden Gate.[314] Since Leo would not agree to this, Krum returned to his own tent. He was marveling at the city's walls and the Emperor's well-ordered battle-lines, and when he despaired of the siege for which he had had hopes, he made a truce and began peace talks.

The Emperor took the opportunity to try to ambush him. But because of our numerous sins he could not bring it off, as his servants were not suitable for erecting such a monument to their enemy's defeat. They wounded Krum, but could not deliver a mortal thrust. The accursed wretch was furious at the attempted ambush; he sent a

313. Sennacherib (king of Assyria 704–681 B.C.) attacked the kingdom of Judah, and was only prevented from capturing Jerusalem by the payment of exorbitant tribute. He then marched south to attack Egypt, but a plague which fell on his army forced him to withdraw.

314. As a sign of the Bulgar lord's triumph.

raiding-party to St. Mamas and burnt down the palace there. He loaded the bronze lion from its hippodrome, the bear, the water-spouting dragon, and selected marbles into wagons, then withdrew.

He took Adrianople, which had been under siege.

REFERENCES

THE TEXT

Theophanes, *Theophanis chronographia,* ed. Carolus de Boor, 2 volumes (Leipzig, 1883, 1885; reprint, Hildesheim, 1963).

Lexica

Du Cange, *Glossarium ad scriptores mediae et infimae graecitatis* (Paris, 1688).

Liddell, Henry George and Scott, Robert, *A Greek-English Lexicon,* ninth edition (Oxford, 1940).

Sophocles, E.A., *Greek Lexicon of the Roman and Byzantine Periods (From B.C. 146 to A.D. 1100),* 2 volumes (Cambridge, Mass., 1887).

Secondary Literature

Alexander, Paul J., *The Patriarch Nicephorus of Constantinople: Ecclesiastical Policy and Image Worship in the Byzantine Empire* (Oxford, 1958).

Anastos, Milton V., "Iconoclasm and Imperial Rule 717–842," chapter III of the revised edition of the *Cambridge Medieval History,* IV, 1 (Cambridge, England, 1966): pp. 61–104.

———, "Leo III's Edict Against the Images in the Year 726–27 and Italo-Byzantine Relations Between 726 and 730," *Polychordia: Festschrift Franz Dölger zum 75. Geburtstag* (Amsterdam, 1968) III: pp. 5–41.

———, "The Transfer of Illyricum, Calabria and Sicily to the Jurisdiction of the Patriarchate of Constantinople in 732–33," *Silloge bizantina in onore di Silvio Giuseppe Mercati* (Rome, 1957): 14–31.

Brockelmann, Carl, *History of the Islamic Peoples* (New York, 1960).

Bury, J. B., *A History of the Eastern Roman Empire from the Fall of Irene to the Accession of Basil I (802–867)* (London, 1912).

———, *A History of the Later Roman Empire from Arcadius to Irene (395–800)*, 2 volumes (London, 1889).

———, *A History of the Later Roman Empire from the Death of Theodosius I. to the Death of Justinian (395–565)*, 2 volumes (London, 1923).

Cameron, Alan, *Circus Factions: Blues and Greens at Rome and Byzantium* (Oxford, 1976).

Christensen, Arthur, *L'Iran sous les Sassanides*, second edition (Copenhagen, 1944).

de Camp, L. Sprague, *The Ancient Engineers* (Ballantine reprint, New York, 1974).

Dunlop, D. M., *The History of the Jewish Khazars* (Princeton, 1954).

Frye, Richard N., *The Heritage of Persia* (Mentor reprint, New York, 1966).

Gallatin, Harlie Kay, "A Study in Civil Government and Imperial Defense in the Seventh Century Byzantine State under Emperor Constans II, 641–668" (Dissertation, Urbana, 1972).

Gibbon, Edward, *The History of the Decline and Fall of the Roman Empire*, edited by J. B. Bury, 7 volumes (London, 1923).

Grumel, Vénance, "L'année du monde dans la Chronographie de Théophane," *Echos d'Orient*, 37 (1934): 396–408.

———, "L'annexion de l'Illyricum, de la Sicile et de la Calabre au patriarcat de Constantinople," *Recherches de science religieuse*, 40 (1952): 191–200.

———, *La chronologie*, volume I in the series *Traité d'études byzantines*, pp. 95–97 (Paris, 1958).

Head, Constance, *Justinian II of Byzantium* (Madison, Wisconsin, 1972).

Hitti, Philip K., *History of the Arabs from the Earliest Times to the Present*, tenth edition (New York, 1970).

Janin, R., *Constantinople byzantine: développement urbain et répertoire topographique: deuxième édition* (Paris, 1964).

Jenkins, Romilly J. H., *Byzantium: The Imperial Centuries, A.D. 610–1071* (New York, London, 1966).

Jones, A. H. M., *The Later Roman Empire 284–602: A Social Economic and Administrative Survey*, 3 volumes (Oxford, 1964).

Kelly, J. N. D., *Early Christian Doctrines*, second edition (New York, 1960).

Krumbacher, Karl, *Geschichte der byzantinischen Literatur von Justinian bis zum Ende des oströmischen Reiches,* second edition, 2 volumes (Munich, 1897).

Lilie, Ralf-Johannes, *Die byzantinische Reaktion auf die Ausbreitung der Araber: Studien zur Strukturwandlung des byzantinischen Staates im 7. und 8. Jhd.* (Munich, 1976).

Mango, Cyril, *Byzantium: The Empire of New Rome* (New York, 1980).

————, "Who Wrote the Chronicle of Theophanes?" *Zbornik radova Vizantološkog instituta,* 18 (1978): 9–17.

Moravcsik, Gyula, *Byzantinoturcica,* second edition, 2 volumes (Berlin, 1958).

Newton, Robert R., *Medieval Chronicles and the Rotation of the Earth* (Baltimore, 1972).

Ostrogorsky, George, "Die Chronologie des Theophanes im 7. und 8. Jahrhundert," *Byzantinisch-neugriechische Jahrbücher,* 7 (1928/1929): 1–56.

————, "Les débuts de la querelle des images," *Mélanges Charles Diehl* I, pp. 235–255 (Paris, 1930).

————, *History of the Byzantine State,* revised edition translated by Joan Hussey (New Brunswick, New Jersey, 1969).

————, "Theophanes," *Paulys Real-Encyclopädie der classischen Altertumswissenschaft,* Reihe 2, Band 5, cols. 2127–2132 (Stuttgart, 1934).

Pelikan, Jaroslav, *The Christian Tradition, A History of the Development of Doctrine: Volume I: The Emergence of the Catholic Tradition (100–600)* (Chicago, 1971).

————, *The Christian Tradition, A History of the Development of Doctrine: Volume II: The Spirit of Eastern Christendom (600–1700)* (Chicago, 1974).

Pertusi, A., "La formation des thèmes byzantins," *Berichte zum XI. Internationalen Byzantinisten-Kongress* I (Munich, 1958): 1–40.

Proudfoot, Ann S., "The Sources of Theophanes for the Heraclian Dynasty," *Byzantion,* 44 (1974): 367–439.

Runciman, Steven, *The Eastern Schism: A Study of the Papacy and the Eastern Churches During the XIth and XIIth Centuries* (Oxford, 1955).

Sharf, Andrew, *Byzantine Jewry from Justinian to the First Crusade* (New York, 1971).

Speck, Paul, *Kaiser Konstantin VI.: Die Legitimation einer fremden und der Versuch einer eigenem Quellenkritische Darstellung von 25 Jahren byzantinischer Geschichte nach dem ersten Ikonoklasmus. I: Untersuchung. II: Anmerkungen und Register* (Munich, 1978).

Stratos, A. N., Τὸ Βυζάντιον στὸν Ζ΄ αἰῶνα, 5 volumes (Athens, 1965, 1966, 1969, 1974, 1974). Volumes I and II have been translated into English by Marc Ogilvie-Grant as *Byzantium in the Seventh Century* (Amsterdam, 1968, 1972).

Toynbee, Arnold, *Constantine Prophyrogenitus and his World* (Oxford, 1973).

Vasiliev, A. A., *History of the Byzantine Empire,* 2 volumes (Madison, Wisconsin, 1952).

Vryonis, Speros Jr., *The Decline of Medieval Hellenism in Asia Minor and the Process of Islamization from the Eleventh through the Fifteenth Century* (Berkeley, 1971).

Whitting, P. D., *Byzantine Coins* (New York, 1973).

INDEX

NOTE: Names of persons are indexed wherever they occur, whether in the text or in the chronological lists accompanying many *anni mundi*. Names of peoples and cities (e.g., Arab, Constantinople) are only indexed in the text proper, not in the chronological lists, as their appearance in the latter entries has no independent historical significance. Persons possessing surnames are indexed by surnames (e.g., Michael Lakhanodrakon is indexed as Lakhanodrakon, Michael).